TASTE
MAKERS

TASTE
MAKERS

Seven Immigrant Women
Who Revolutionized Food in America

Mayukh Sen

W. W. NORTON & COMPANY
Independent Publishers Since 1923

For information about permission to reproduce selections from this book, write to Permissions, W. W. Norton & Company, Inc., 500 Fifth Avenue, New York, NY 10110

For information about special discounts for bulk purchases, please contact W. W. Norton Special Sales at specialsales@wwnorton.com or 800-233-4830

Manufacturing by Lake Book Manufacturing
Book design by Lisa Buckley Design
Production manager: Lauren Abbate

Library of Congress Cataloging-in-Publication Data

Names: Sen, Mayukh, author.
Title: Taste makers : seven immigrant women who revolutionized food in America / Mayukh Sen.
Description: First edition. | New York, NY : W. W. Norton & Company, independent publishers since 1923, [2022] | Includes bibliographical references and index.
Identifiers: LCCN 2021029600 | ISBN 9781324004516 (hardcover) | ISBN 9781324004523 (epub)
Subjects: LCSH: Women cooks—United States—Biography. | Women immigrants—United States—Biography.
Classification: LCC TX649.A1 S46 2022 | DDC 641.5092/2 [B]—dc23
LC record available at https://lccn.loc.gov/2021029600

W. W. Norton & Company, Inc., 500 Fifth Avenue, New York, N.Y. 10110
www.wwnorton.com

W. W. Norton & Company Ltd., 15 Carlisle Street, London W1D 3BS

1 2 3 4 5 6 7 8 9 0

For Sakti Sengupta (1951–2017), my father,
and Lê Lan Anh (1993–2020), my friend.
I hope I'll see you again someday.

As an immigrant, I understand how the soul gets lonely for its origins.

—MADELEINE KAMMAN

Contents

The Taste of Papaya
Norma Shirley 139

Introduction

ONE DAY in the 1880s, Elizabeth Black Kander spotted a boy selling matchboxes. The sight disturbed her.

The boy, a recent arrival from Russia, must have been 12 years old. His face was caked in dirt. Everyone in that store in Milwaukee, Wisconsin, that day could hear him practically shouting as he offered to sell the owner matches for cheap.

Kander confronted the boy outside. Why wasn't he in school, she wondered aloud. He responded sincerely, telling her he needed to work to support his family.

The boy's admission saddened Kander, but she also felt a flush of shame—for the kid, for herself. Kander's parents, Jewish immigrants from Germany, had come to the United States in the 1840s. They had done a remarkable job of blending in by the time Kander was born in 1858, mastering American English, American ways of dressing, the American art of making money. But in the 1880s, a new wave of Jewish immigrants from Russia like this boy made Kander worry. She found them so uncouth. Kander feared their behavior would reflect poorly on previous Jewish immigrants like her parents who had gone to great lengths to acclimate to America. Maybe these immigrants would inspire a new rush of anti-Semitism.

Kander's concern kindled a lifelong crusade as a social worker who pushed for immigrants to assimilate to America. "It is a selfish motive that spurs us on," she would say of her mission, "it is to protect ourselves, our own reputation in the community that we must work with tact, with heart and soul to better the home conditions of our people." As part of her project, she began working at the Settlement House, a social service agency in Milwaukee. She spent her evenings teaching immigrant Jewish women, many of them fresh from Poland and Russia, how to cook American dishes.

In 1901, Kander had the idea to compile a charity cookbook. *The Settlement Cook Book: The Way to a Man's Heart* (1901) was a bricolage of German, Jewish, Eastern European, and American recipes. In its 174 pages, the book presented more than five hundred recipes for a variety of dishes. Some were unmistakably American, like pot roasts, creamed cod, and Boston-browned potatoes, while others came from Jewish and German traditions, like kugel, gefilte fish, and pfeffernüsse.

The Settlement Cook Book would go on to become one of America's most enduring cookbooks, selling over two million copies across more than forty editions, many of which Kander herself revised. Subsequent editions would contain tips for housekeeping and cleaning. This wasn't just a cookbook; it was a manual on how to be an American woman. The preeminent food authority James Beard considered it one of his favorite cookbooks. The cookbook and its countless permutations meant a great deal, in particular, to Jewish American communities, passed along like talismans from one generation to the next.

Kander may have been working with sincere intentions. She wanted safety for her people and, in particular, for women. But scholars today acknowledge that Kander's aims were also somewhat patronizing, born of what some would refer to as an "Americanizing impulse." She wanted these women to mute any differences that revealed they were born outside of America.

Whatever the case, it's hard to deny that Kander's book shifted the publishing landscape in America, creating a future in which immigrant women could write cookbooks on their own terms. Kander would keep revising editions of *The Settlement Cook Book* until her death at 82 in 1940. The same decade she died, World War II would end, and more opportunities would open up in the American market for immigrant women to author cookbooks. By the 1960s, once-stiff American immigration laws would loosen, nudging America further away from ethnic homogeneity. The era that came immediately after saw an influx of talented immigrant female chefs and food writers from all around the globe. Upon arriving in America, some of these figures would find ways beyond writing cookbooks to showcase their food: They'd teach cooking classes, or operate their own restaurants.

In this book, you will meet seven immigrant women who used food to construct an identity outside their home country. Quite a few plainly rejected any Americanizing impulse through their work, refusing to compromise their visions to satisfy a white American audience. Others wanted to have their food reflect the multicultural bent of their adoptive home. All of these women used their food to tell the world where they came from and what remained of it in America. They did so with no shame, only pride.

❧

AT ITS CORE, this book is an attempt to trouble the canon of culinary brilliance, so often homogeneously male. I want to celebrate the lives of seven women who made an especially deep impression on the way America cooks and eats. Thanks to these women, "stir-fry" is no longer a puzzling pair of words, just as most Americans now know there is more to Italian cooking than pasta in a puddle of red sauce. The women in this book have all left their mark, but

America honors some of them more than others. With this book, I seek to understand why.

When I first had the idea for this book in the summer of 2017, I wanted to tell the story of immigration in America through the prism of food. That's not quite what this book ended up being. As I wrote, I found myself interrogating the very notion of what success looks like for immigrants under American capitalism, using food as my lens of narrative inquiry. Why focus on women, you may wonder? History is often sheepish in assigning authorship to women in any cultural sphere, including food. It follows, then, that immigrant women—many of whom are doubly marginalized (at the very least)—are especially vulnerable to such cultural deletion.

Capitalism can encourage artists, including chefs and cookbook authors, to suppress parts of themselves to cater to the market's desires. I started to see this book as a critique of capitalism: how it devalues labor to the point where it makes people into products, longevity in American memory contingent on your ability to sell yourself. These seven women, their food, and what they represent could fall out of fashion due to the ebbs and flows of the market, through no fault of their own.

But it's awfully patronizing to frame any of these women as "forgotten" or "overlooked" victims of cultural amnesia. Such a narrative orientation renders them passive figures in their own stories. I've tried to define these women in terms of what they accomplished, not in terms of what happened to them. In putting these women side by side, I hope to push against the individualistic notion of creative genius. Grouping these women together allows readers to see the shaping of food in America as the endpoint of collective labor, not the work of any one extraordinary mind.

FROM THE EARLY STAGES of my research, I cast a wide net, if only to see what my scavenging might yield. I prioritized racial and class diversity. I paid attention to immigrant women who'd been reduced to an offhand mention in a story about a well-known figure. I also turned to highly visible immigrant women in the food industry and asked myself if there were sides of them that were underdiscussed.

Even then, I knew that one of the chief missions of this book would be to present women in their own voices. I found myself drifting toward women who had a surfeit of extant material to draw upon: cookbooks, memoirs, interviews. This book tries to reconcile how these women saw themselves and what the American public saw of them in their work.

I encountered roadblocks. Historically, the American food media and publishing landscape have shunned women without material privileges, and they have done a poor job of giving Black women opportunities. With these constraints in mind, I eventually settled on seven women from seven very different countries: China's Chao Yang Buwei, Mexico's Elena Zelayeta, France's Madeleine Kamman, Italy's Marcella Hazan, India's Julie Sahni, Iran's Najmieh Batmanglij, and Jamaica's Norma Shirley.

But it wasn't enough for me to write only about the lives of these women, I soon realized. If I were to make a truly radical statement about how immigrant women have revolutionized food in America, I would have to set their stories alongside a figure who'd found irrefutable success—a figure who wasn't an immigrant woman. The exercise would be clarifying, I thought. Perhaps setting such a story within the narrative would guide me toward a more striking conclusion. I decided to devote an interlude to one American-born woman whose influence over this country's tastes is indisputable: Julia Child. Though the story of her remarkable life is now familiar to many Americans, there are aspects of her stardom that popular narratives have neglected, and thus deserve more sustained consideration.

The subject of my first chapter, Chao Yang Buwei, wrote *How to Cook and Eat in Chinese* (1945), arguably America's first genuinely comprehensive and ambitious Chinese cookbook. But there's something unresolved at the core of her legacy: Her command of English was shaky, so her husband, the linguist Chao Yuenren, and the couple's eldest daughter, Chao Rulan, interfered in the writing of this cookbook, suppressing her voice. The cookbook was a success, while a subsequent memoir truer to her spirit, *Autobiography of a Chinese Woman* (1947), didn't fare as well. In Buwei, you will meet a woman who refused to make herself too easily legible to a white American audience.

Elena Zelayeta, the subject of my second chapter, fit the parameters for immigrant success in post–World War II America, with an inspirational story to boot. Elena lost her sight in adulthood due to a mature cataract and a detached retina, but she taught herself to cook through her blindness. She even hosted her own cooking show on television, broadcast throughout California. Her cooking was not just Mexican; she had a fondness for the flavors of her adoptive home in California. Some may deride her cooking as accommodationist today, but she made no apologies about her desire to live and cook as an American woman, an outlook I sought to understand rather than to judge. For a time, she was a star.

Nobody embodied stardom in the purest sense more than Julia Child, the subject of the interlude that follows. Julia had the reverse trajectory of the other women in this book. She was born in California in 1912 and eventually traveled to France, the country that turned her into a cook. Once she returned to America, she established herself with *Mastering the Art of French Cooking* (1961), co-authored with the Frenchwomen Louisette Bertholle and Simone Beck, and a startlingly successful run on American public television beginning with *The French Chef* (1963–1973). Though Julia faced numerous sexist obstructions in her career, she possessed privileges that allowed her to rise to fame in America: She was white, and she was American. Her homegrown advantages meant that she never posed the threat of the outsider to American audiences.

If Julia Child cast a long shadow, the subject of my third chapter, Madeleine Kamman, spent much of her career fighting her way out of that darkness. Madeleine made her distaste for Julia well known in the American media, wondering why an American woman like Julia would become the emissary for French cooking when others, like Madeleine herself, may have been more qualified. Historically, the American food media has framed Madeleine in opposition to Julia. It's a hobby of the patriarchy— pitting two accomplished women against one another—and a shame, for Madeleine's progressive message about food, and how the surrounding culture rarely celebrates women for cooking, became muffled as a result. This chapter, I hope, will cause you to ask who has a right to be angry, and at what cost.

Marcella Hazan, the subject of my fourth chapter, continues to command reverence as an authority on Italian cooking, even after her death in 2013. When Marcella first began writing in the early 1970s, America hadn't yet found an interlocutor as skilled as she for Italian cooking. She also had the support of her husband, Victor, who often assisted her in writing thanks to his confident control over English. Marcella endures because of her talent, yes, and also because the zeitgeist leaned so heavily in her favor.

The subject of my fifth chapter, Julie Sahni, is a woman of many gifts—an accomplished cookbook author, cooking teacher, and restaurant chef. In the 1980s, she reportedly became the first Indian woman to serve as an executive chef of a fine dining restaurant in New York. She is utterly unconcerned with the demands that the food industry places upon people to maintain their celebrity. The work comes first.

Najmieh Batmanglij has been living in exile in America as a result of the Iranian Revolution of 1979. She settled in Washington, DC, in 1983, a time when Americans harbored great prejudice toward her native country, so much that she couldn't sell her cookbook to a major publisher. That book turned into the self-published *Food of Life: A Book of Ancient Persian and Modern Iranian Cooking and Ceremonies* (1986), which established her as an authority on Iranian cooking. Najmieh has written eight cookbooks since, all of them self-published. What has motivated her throughout is the desire to preserve what she would term the "soul" of her home country, even if the Iranian state tried to suppress that spirit. Living and writing in exile limits your audience. Recognition from the food establishment hasn't equaled her reach, though she wasn't writing for them.

The subject of my seventh and final chapter, Norma Shirley, is an outlier: She never wrote a cookbook or memoir. In fact, she spent the majority of her life back in Jamaica after working as a restaurant chef and food stylist in Massachusetts and New York during the 1970s and 1980s. Upon returning to Jamaica in 1986, Norma established a number of restaurants that led to a food revolution in the country. The work she did back home marshaled Jamaican cuisine to a place of respect in America, even though this was not her intention. She maintained a fierce devotion to her mission to cook for Jamaicans and, in particular, Black audiences—not tourists, not Americans.

As you read, you may ask where I've gathered some of the details about the women's lives in this book, as many of them are no longer with us. In retracing the lives of these women, I worked from the memoirs and cookbooks they wrote, along with interviews they gave to the press; these materials helped me glean how they presented themselves to the world. (When it came to Julie and Najmieh, the two of my subjects who are alive at writing, I spent countless hours speaking to them.) But to round out these portraits, I also spoke to family members, friends, and other figures who were in the professional orbit of these women. I conducted archival research, too, engaging with and interpreting articles on these women, while always reminding myself to read these documents skeptically, knowing that the way the press renders a subject does not always comply with the way that she wanted the public to see her. In assembling these stories, I sought to cede the stage to these women, keeping their interior lives in the narrative foreground while also setting these stories in a historical context. Because of this goal, I made a decision that may strike some readers as peculiar: I did not quote sources I spoke to directly, a journalistic gesture that I feared would impose distance between the reader and the subject. In spending so much time with these women and their words, I felt a sense of intimacy with their voices; I wanted to preserve that feeling for you. I hope you will inhabit these women's lives while understanding the social, political, and cultural pressures they were up against. A more detailed, chapter-by-chapter note on my process follows the Afterword at the end of this book, on page 167.

You may spot some similar narrative beats in these stories. A number of these women never intended to devote their lives to cooking, for one. They became figures of profound importance through a confluence of talent, hard work, and luck. Some began cooking in the face of troubled marriages, while others found support from their husbands. Each of these women had to combat the perception that cooking is "women's work" by nature, belittled as performance of duty rather than an avenue for artistic expression.

This book is partially a recovery project, capturing these women's legacies in all their fullness. But as you read, I also urge you to question which immigrant stories our American culture values versus those it tosses aside—and why. Reading this book may warm your heart, but it should unsettle you at certain points, too. It should make you squirm.

⁓

IN EACH BIOGRAPHICAL SKETCH, you will see me frequently deploy two terms: the "food establishment" and the "food media." It's necessary to explain what each exactly constitutes, though I should note that the line between them is often quite porous.

You may rightly believe that the job of the journalist is to keep power in check. My observations lead me to believe it's a bit more distorted in food journalism. Too often, the people sitting at the top of mastheads of food publications have doubled as the food industry's most powerful figures. They still have the sway to dictate American tastes.

To better understand how this happened, I turn to the late writer Nora Ephron. Her 1968 dissection of what she called the Food Establishment (capitalization hers) in *New York* magazine vividly captures how food moved to the center of American culture in the postwar era. The Food Establishment "consists of those people who write about food of restaurants on a regular basis, either in books, magazines, or certain newspapers, and thus have the power to start trends and, in some cases, begin and end careers," Ephron wrote. You'll notice that for each of the women in this book, her success was contingent upon her ability to ingratiate herself with this establishment, which could often be difficult to permeate. Becoming a culinary star so often depended not just on a woman's talent but, too, on her ability to play by the establishment's rules.

In those postwar years, the establishment quickly coalesced around three key figures, whom the late food writer Molly O'Neill called the "gastronomic trinity" in an essay for the *Columbia Journalism Review* in 2003. They were the aforementioned Julia Child and the buoyant food personality James Beard, along with Craig Claiborne, who assumed the post of food editor at the *New York Times* in 1957 after the trailblazing Jane Nickerson. All of them were white.

Perhaps the most influential food publication of the period was the *New York Times* food section. Armed with degrees in both journalism and the culinary arts, Claiborne initially set out to treat food with journalistic rigor rather than as some piffle of a genre. Tough luck. In his post, Claiborne would soon learn that American readers would take a fawning chef profile over a gloomy story about famine any day.

In O'Neill's eyes, food journalism slowly morphed into a form of fluffy advocacy in the late twentieth century. As Ephron intimated, writers and editors at the top of mastheads had tremendous influence over American taste. For this reason, Claiborne makes an appearance in a number of my chapters. He was the kind of man whose endorsements could open doors for women who previously lacked access to capital or fame, and that's precisely what he did for a number of the women in this book.

Power was concentrated in the paper of record until the 1980s, the same decade that Claiborne would step away from the *Times*.

Influence then began to drift to such magazines as *Bon Appétit*, *Gourmet*, and *Food & Wine*, colloquially referred to as the "Big Three" food glossies. This shift, too, meant that power was no longer confined to the East Coast, as *Bon Appétit* was then headquartered in Los Angeles. Another key development came in 1990 with the establishment of the James Beard Awards, which honored chefs and food writers, becoming a reflection of the establishment's approval.

Some of these conditions have altered today—*Gourmet*, for example, folded in 2009, while digital-native publications now have power to shape public opinion. Many of these conditions are in flux as of this writing. But the underlying structure remains: The food establishment and food media are still close companions.

⁓

ONE QUESTION may hang over you as you read this book: Why is a man writing this?

It's a justified question. I am aware that I present as a cis male to the public, and I prefer to use the privileges afforded to me because of that to amplify the voices of women, whom our cultural attention skews away from. I am sensitive to the limits of this very hand, which is why I feel it is crucial to decenter myself in the process of writing rather than interject or cast judgment on my subjects.

The more elaborate response I have to such a concern is that I, like many queer-identifying people, have had a complex, evolving relationship to gender expression throughout my entire life. I realize that my appearance might bely this tension. This project is intensely personal, forged by my own sense of isolation in this field as a queer person of color. I began writing about food professionally in 2016, when I was 24. Even then, I could sense that I was writing from a center of gravity that differed from those of my peers as a queer child of Bengali immigrants to America.

Early in my career, perhaps these feelings directed my narrative gaze toward story subjects who, like me, once felt that they did not belong. These figures tended to be people of color, queer people, women, or immigrants; often they were even part of more than one of those groups. Their trajectories invigorated me: They floated on the margins of the food world when they first landed in it, only to push their way to the center by sheer force. These subjects had something to say. They were persuasive enough to get powerful people to listen.

With time, I would come to understand what it's like to have people reduce me to my identity. The very aspects of myself that once seemed like liabilities—my queerness, my color—also started to make me, in a word, marketable. Actual engagement with the substance of my work was suddenly secondary to those superficial factors.

No matter the case, the acute sense of alienation I entered this industry with does not fade easily. There will always be a sliver of me that feels as though I am on the margins—the margins of the food world, the margins of this country's dominant social structures. Maybe the answer to why I gravitate toward the stories of these women lies somewhere in my identity, how lonely I often feel because of it and what I create from that solitude.

Around the time I wrote this book, I also weathered two particularly difficult losses: I lost my father to cancer in 2017, and I lost a best friend to mental illness in 2020. These deaths weighed on me. I found myself forgetting so much about these people who'd been such vital presences in my own life: their voices, their mannerisms. I understood the fragility of memory, how easily the essence of a person can disappear once they're no longer around.

Writing is one way of ensuring someone's story doesn't die along with them.

The seven women in this book have been my teachers. Through spending time with their stories, I have come to question and ultimately better understand my own place in America. I hope these women will inspire a similar journey for you.

A Note on Names

FOR THE PURPOSES of this book, I have opted to use the given (as in, first) names of my chapter subjects: I will refer to Elena Zelayeta as "Elena," to Madeleine Kamman as "Madeleine," and so forth. This goes against the rule in more traditional forms of journalism, where it is customary to refer to story subjects by their surnames. In writing this book, I wanted to assemble rich accounts of how these women experienced life at every turn. Doing so, I hoped, would retain the kinship I felt with them as I pored over their words in the archival materials I found. In referring to these figures by their given names, I hope to foster that intimacy between reader and subject, rather than to tell their stories from a dispassionate remove, as I wrote in the Introduction.

When it comes to my first chapter on Chao Yang Buwei, I have chosen to follow the Chinese order of her name, with her family name coming before her given name. She would make the distinction between the American and Chinese sequencing of her name clear in her memoir: "When I sign my name in English, it is Buwei Yang Chao, but in China, I am Chao Yang Buwei," she wrote. My chapter on Chao Yang Buwei reckons with the peril of translation, and how the essence of a person may get lost in the course of migration and the subsequent pressure to assimilate in an adoptive home. My decision to order her name as Chao Yang Buwei honors her fealty to her Chinese heritage. It is in keeping with the way she saw herself in the world. Other Chinese-born chefs, such as Florence Lin and Cecilia Chiang, appear in the chapter. Because the chapter deals with those women's work in a purely American context, rather than discussing their lives in China when they would've been referred to by the Chinese order of their names, I have chosen to stick to the American ordering of their names: their given names, followed by their surnames.

TASTE
MAKERS

Mother Tongue

Chao Yang Buwei

B. NOVEMBER 25, 1889, NANKING, CHINA

D. MARCH 2, 1981, OAKLAND, CALIFORNIA, USA

THE WORDS THAT began Chao Yang Buwei's colossus, *How to Cook and Eat in Chinese* (1945), still provoke and unsettle: "I am ashamed to have written this book."

The cookbook took time away from her work as a doctor, she explained in her author's note. More crucially, though, she clarified that she didn't actually write the book alone. "You know I speak little English and write less," she told the reader. She had come to America from China in 1921. Still wobbling her way to fluency in English as she worked on the book in her mid-fifties, she wrote her recipes for dishes like stirred dandelion and jellied lamb in Chinese. Her eldest daughter Rulan then translated them into English.

Buwei's husband, a Harvard linguist named Chao Yuenren, found his daughter's renderings stilted, bordering on lifeless. He took it upon himself to tinker with the language. These interferences resulted in garbled wording. Even Buwei herself recognized certain turns of phrase as clumsy. Take, for example, the dish that normally might have been called "Shrimps Fried with Mushrooms." Thanks to Yuenren, it became "Mushroom Stir Shrimps," which made no sense to Buwei. Her husband retorted that, well, if Mr. Smith can go to Washington as James Stewart did in the 1939 film, mushrooms can stir shrimp in a dish.

Fine. Yuenren's logic puzzled Buwei, but she deferred to him anyway. The resulting cookbook minimized Buwei's presence. The slim three-page author's note was ostensibly the closest the reader got to Buwei in her own voice. In that passage, she noted the frequent quarrels between mother and daughter that nearly severed their relationship, writing that "all the credit for the good points of the book is mine and all the blame for the bad points is Rulan's."

She reserved the bulk of her ire, though, for Yuenren, whom she chided "for all the negative contributions he has made towards the making of the book. In many places, he has changed Rulan's good English into bad, which he thinks Americans like better."

Buwei's outspoken nature made her a woman ahead of her time. She made the decision to study medicine abroad, in Japan. She opened her own birth control clinic in China, rare for Chinese women of the era. She broke off an engagement to a cousin and then had a love marriage to Yuenren without a formal ceremony. She moved to America with her husband instead of staying in her native country.

Buwei accomplished all of this before embarking upon her culinary odyssey in America, so substantially different from her medical career. But she had no desire to perform docility in this new arena. If her family members wanted to silence her into submission, she would not go down without a fight.

HOW TO COOK AND EAT IN CHINESE was America's first systematically thorough cookbook on Chinese cooking. It arrived in an era when chop suey, a Chinese American innovation, held a tyrannical sway over the American imagination. The cookbook exposed America to the culinary glories of north China and the Jiangnan region below the Yangtze River. It was a runaway success.

The American mind once gleefully cast Chinese cuisine as an object of cryptic fascination, occasionally staining it with accusations of being too unclean for white Americans to consume. This prejudice coincided with wider Sinophobia that flourished in America ever since Chinese migrants arrived during the California Gold Rush of 1849, legitimized in restrictive immigration laws. Some, like the Page Act of 1875, shut out Chinese women specifically, while the more expansive Chinese Exclusion Act of 1882 would keep poorer Chinese laborers out of the country. Buwei disentangled Chinese cooking from the concept of impurity, showing white Americans that it was, like French cooking, a language worthy of study.

Traces of Buwei's work linger in the way Americans still speak about food, even if few may recognize the significance of her work in this regard today. The book ferried phrases like "stir-fry" into the modern American lexicon. That Buwei could accomplish this feat is all the more remarkable considering the circumstances of the cookbook's production: Her silencing occurred on the page.

BUWEI WAS BORN with the name Lansien in 1889, in the city that was then known as Nanking. She was a child of the late Qing era, when change was still far away for China. The first Sino-Japanese

War wouldn't begin for another five years. She lived in a sprawl-
ing house with 128 rooms, big enough to accommodate her 34-
person family and their 27 servants. The house was one of many
on a busy street, a street so narrow that sedan chairs moving in
opposite directions would have to tread carefully to avoid grazing
one another.

Lansien's father already had eight children of his own, while
his younger brother had none, so she became a gift to the childless
couple. When Lansien was a year old, her grandfather arranged
a photograph of the family in its entirety. But she was a fidgety
child, unable to hold still before the camera. Her grandmother
lost patience. "Let us take the photograph without the baby," she
said. "She's only a girl. What difference does a girl more or a girl
less make?"

Her grandmother eventually began calling her Ch'uanti, or
Ch'uan'er, meaning "bring along a little brother." She got used to
such casual denial of her femininity. In fact, she saw it as a blessing. Even in childhood, she knew that girls occupied a second
class. When people mistook her for a young man, she never cared
to correct them.

As she got older, she didn't care much for convention. When
she heard, for example, that the revered philosopher Confucius
refused to eat meat unless it was cut into regular shapes, she
scoffed. "What a wasteful man Confucius was!" she protested
aloud. "If only regular cuts are fit to eat, what's going to be done
with the corners and things?"

Such signs of insurgency rankled her family members. When
she was a child, they betrothed her to one of her cousins, whom
she'd marry once she came of age, but they gradually disabused
themselves of the fantasy that she'd become an obedient housewife. Perhaps, they predicted, she would even cause trouble
beyond the home.

People stopped confusing her for a boy by the time she turned 13. Her defiant nature grew even more ardent. She attended a school for girls in Nanking, where she thrived. Her academic performance was so strong that she even had the opportunity to go to America on a scholarship. Ultimately, she decided against it. Her grandfather said it was purposeless to go to America without knowing the language.

She stayed in China through her teens, slowly establishing her independence. Just before she turned 19, she called off the preordained engagement to her cousin, a decision that bred animosity within the family. Among her few supporters was her grandfather, who stoked her disobedience. He suggested she study medicine, a discipline she could study only in England or Japan. By then, leaving China may have in fact been the best option: The 1911 Revolution, which toppled the Qing Dynasty, gave way to a period of violence in Nanking. Of the two options before her, she found herself more attracted to Japan. For one, her family was close by. Traveling there would certainly be easier than acclimating to England, where the language would be more of an impediment. She couldn't speak Japanese, either, but the language at least had some written characters in common with Chinese that might help her get by.

She even knew someone who'd made the same journey to Japan, which made her decision even easier. Kuanhung, a friend of hers from her school days in Nanking, was a student at the Tokyo Women's Medical School. On a visit back home in China, Kuanhung decided to rename her friend. Sensing the girl's free spirit, Kuanhung insisted on putting the word *wei*, or "great," in her name.

"And you will start making great strides towards greatness now," Kuanhung reminded her. So she would have *bu*, or "stride," in her name, too.

"So you are going to call me Weibu?" she asked.

"Yes, Weibu. No, Buwei—Weibu—Buwei," Kuanhung replied. "Yes, Buwei is better. So from now on you will be Yang Buwei."

❧

BUWEI ARRIVED IN NAGASAKI, Japan, by sea in late 1913. The voyage, which lasted three days and three nights, was excruciating. She couldn't stomach a meal.

Her appetite returned once she set foot on Nagasaki's shores. But the city felt disconcertingly different from Nanking. Its tiny houses barely rose from the ground; its small rooms had tatami, strips of mats that lined the floors. In public, she often felt like a trespasser, especially when she heard natives there refer to Chinese folks like her with the pejorative "Shinajin," or Chinese person.

She held out hope that Tokyo might be more welcoming. It wasn't. Medical school was tougher than she anticipated. And the food made things even worse. She lived alone in a Japanese boarding house where the staff provided her with three daily meals. They were of such poor quality that she hankered for the eggplant cakes and salted duck of her home. Buwei realized that she needed to learn how to cook. It was a simple matter of survival.

So she started by teaching herself how to stir an egg. She would beat the yolk with chopsticks and cook the egg in animal fat until it resembled a cross between a scramble and an omelet. After she perfected this formula, Buwei cooked by trial and error, guided solely by her intuition of how a dish should taste. Necessity drove her to invent many odd dishes in this period, but she became an assured cook through the process. She would occasionally stumble upon a dish that didn't taste so strange.

She would not be able to savor true Chinese cooking again until after World War I, in May 1919, when her adoptive father died. She headed to her family in the city that was then known as Peiping, now Beijing, by train. On one of the last legs of the journey home, Buwei ate a breakfast of spiced roasted chicken, large prawns stewed in a pot, and hot biscuits strewn with sesame. These tastes reminded her where she came from.

Once she reached her family in Peiping, Buwei volunteered to cook a vegetarian meal for a mourning feast, feeling confident enough in her abilities. Her family laughed at her proposition.

"That's right, Ch'uanti," her aunt sneered, calling her by her childhood name. "Your cooking will be only fit for dead people to eat."

Buwei wanted to prove her aunt wrong. She struck a deal with her family's hired cooks: They could help her wash and cut the ingredients, but she would do all the cooking. Buwei followed her impulses, making a simulacrum of roast duck from pea starch. Expecting a disaster, Buwei's family was stunned by what they saw on the sacrificial table. She surprised herself, too. Mourning ceremonies usually involved ritualized crying, but Buwei's food dazzled her family. They forgot to cry.

∽

IT WAS SEPTEMBER 1920 when she met Yuenren, the nephew of a former classmate of hers in Tokyo. Buwei had settled in Peiping by then. She and a friend from her days in Japan had opened Senjen Hospital, among the first medical practices in China begun by nonmissionary women. Work kept Buwei so busy that she initially saw Yuenren's presence in her life as an interruption.

In truth, he both mystified and attracted Buwei. He wore

unpressed clothes, a slovenly appearance that betrayed his pedigree. An only child, Yuenren came from a well-off family in Changchow, born a few years after Buwei in 1892. Both of his parents died when he was 11. He worked hard in school, traveling to America on the same scholarship that Buwei herself had once declined as a student back in Nanking. Yuenren studied math at Cornell University and obtained a doctorate in philosophy from Harvard. A chance to teach math at Tsing Hua College in Peiping lured him back to China, though he had a secret passion for linguistics. He once translated Lewis Carroll's *Alice's Adventures in Wonderland* (1865) into Chinese for pleasure.

Like Buwei, Yuenren had a habit of resisting tradition. Yuenren, too, was engaged to a relative before birth; he, too, decided his independence was more important than following family rules, so he broke off the marriage via letter from America.

Steadily, Yuenren's rebellious qualities wooed Buwei. Buwei noticed that he also took an interest in her mind. He would visit Buwei in the hospital, where she found herself speaking with him for hours into the night. With time, Buwei no longer saw him as a nuisance. They were more alike than she'd initially realized.

They married in June of the following year. The pair agreed to forgo a proper ceremony, instead inviting two of Yuenren's classmates to witness them procure a marriage certificate. "New-Style Wedding of New-Style People," read a headline in a local paper the next day.

Buwei and Yuenren didn't have a honeymoon, either; they didn't really have time for one. Harvard offered Yuenren a chance to teach philosophy, meaning they'd have to move within a month. Buwei would have to give up her hospital job, the first of her marital sacrifices.

The ride across the Pacific by ship was hell. Buwei became wildly ill. Psychological uncertainty gripped her, too: She was going to a new country without a job, without any promise of being able to continue her medical career. It was also an English-speaking country, exactly what she'd avoided earlier in life when deciding where to go to school. She still barely spoke the language. Medical work was likely out of the question. What if she had to become a housewife?

⌒

AMERICA'S COMPLICATED INFATUATION with Chinese food began decades before Buwei's arrival in America. The country's first Chinese restaurants started sprouting following the 1849 California Gold Rush, which saw an influx of laborers from China's Guangdong Province flocking to the American West. The Chinese population in California ballooned from roughly four thousand to fifty-two thousand between 1850 and 1852. A handful of these immigrants opened inexpensive restaurants in San Francisco and other large cities, establishing enclaves known as Chinatowns.

But the 1882 Chinese Exclusion Act forced Chinese restaurants into a difficult position. Congress passed the Exclusion Act following years of long-simmering animus toward Chinese laborers in America, especially in the American West. Its proponents believed that Chinese immigrants posed a threat to the sanctity of white labor in America, and that their foreign traits were fundamentally at odds with American values.

"It is a fact of history that wherever the Chinese have gone they have always taken their habits, methods, and civilization with them; and history fails to record a single example in which they have ever lost them," declared one of the act's vocal supporters, California Senator John F. Miller. "They remain Chinese always and everywhere; changeless, fixed and unalterable."

The law prevented Chinese laborers from coming to America for ten years. Subsequent legislation over the next sixty years bolstered the Exclusion Act's basic tenets. In 1892, for example, the Geary Act added a provision that forced Chinese residents in America to secure certificates of residence and present them to authorities upon demand. The following decade, the Chinese Exclusion Act was renewed yet again, indefinitely. It would remain in effect until the 1943 Magnuson Act introduced incremental repeals.

Following the passage of the Chinese Exclusion Act, white Americans began to openly disparage Chinese cuisine as unsanitary, spreading rumors that ingredients mingled with vermin or opium. But one dish was immune to such prejudice: chop suey, a tangle of meat and vegetables stir-fried in a thick sauce. It became so integral to the American diet that the United States War Department incorporated two recipes for it in its *Manual for Army Cooks* (1916). It was, in other words, a very American dish.

The cultural fixation on chop suey, a dish some believed originated at the hands of Chinese cooks in America (who, precisely, is responsible for its creation is still disputed), belied Chinese cooking's diversity. A few writers in the early twentieth century tried to show Americans the plurality of Chinese cuisine. Chicago-based newspaper writer Jessie Louise Nolton wrote *Chinese Cookery in the Home Kitchen* (1911), a book featuring instructions on how to make "chop sooy" and "eggs fo yong." Missing from Nolton's book were words that could adequately capture techniques like stir-frying. The sisters Sara Bossé (née Eaton) and Onoto Watanna (a pen name for Winnifred Eaton), both of partial Chinese parentage, wrote the *Chinese-Japanese Cook Book* (1914). The book muddied the lines between Chinese and Japanese cooking in an unapologetically Orientalizing fashion. In *The Chinese Cook Book* (1917), Shiu Wong Chan made imaginative but imperfect efforts to express what was inexpressible, referring to an eggplant as a "Chinese tomato" and to a wok spatula as a "cooking shovel."

Despite these issues, the very existence of books dedicated to Chinese cooking in America signaled some progress. Other forms of print media, too, suggested positive shifts. In the early twentieth century, recipes for Chinese restaurant dishes filled the pages of lifestyle magazines like *Harper's Bazaar* and newspapers like the *Chicago Tribune*.

But for every *Harper's Bazaar* spread on how to throw a lavish Chinese dinner party, there was a column slandering Chinese food. "China being a country of topsy-turvydom, it is not surprising that the Chinese menu contains many fearsome dishes which would turn the stomach of the average foreigner," opined a 1927 article in *Catholic World*. Chinese food, the periodical groaned, was unfit for even a dog to eat.

~⁓

WHEN BUWEI FIRST ARRIVED on American shores in 1921, she did not understand the way Americans ate. She visited a cafeteria in San Francisco, the city where the ship docked after a brief stopover in Hawaii. Soup, fish, steak, egg salad, watermelon, a soft drink, a glass of iced tea: She piled her tray with all she could fit. She was used to multi-course meals in China, after all. Minutes later, barely halfway through her tray, she was full. The meal was an early lesson in just how confusing life in this new country would feel.

Soon after, Buwei and Yuenren boarded a transcontinental train that crawled across the country to Boston, a journey that typically took days in that era. From there, the couple went to Cambridge, where they settled in a third-floor apartment. Buwei and Yuenren didn't have the money to buy proper furniture, so they spread their bedding on the floor, just as the Japanese did on their tatami mats.

The apartment didn't even have a full kitchen, just a tiny electric stove. But Buwei made do, making cottony boiled rice and soups of mushroom and pork. Yuenren would tell Buwei that her cooking reminded him of what they ate in China. Such compliments, however, did not quiet Buwei's unease. As she feared, she was becoming a housewife. Who was this woman who spent her days knitting and shopping for pots and pans? Buwei couldn't recognize herself.

She soon had more obligations at home: Her first daughter, Rulan, was born in April 1922; another girl, Nova, followed a year later. During her early days of motherhood, Buwei longed for her past life as a doctor. She tried to find ways to keep her mind alive, becoming particularly interested in the topic of women's health. Restless, she carved out time to translate *What Every Girl Should Know* (1916), a book by birth control pioneer Margaret Sanger, from English into Chinese. To aid her efforts, Buwei relied on an English-to-Chinese dictionary. The exercise showed her how often the two languages refused to agree. When referring to the ova in women's bodies, for example, she accidentally used the Chinese word for hen's eggs.

In America, Yuenren's professional needs always came before Buwei's. This changed in the spring of 1924, when he accepted an offer for a research professorship at Tsing Hua University, requiring the family to move back to Peiping. Back in China, Buwei and Yuenren were on equal footing, and Buwei seized the opportunity to resume her medical career. She began teaching anatomy and physiology at the National Peiping University, and then opened a birth control clinic, radical for the era. Buwei had been mulling over launching a birth control clinic in China ever since her days in America. The rich, she noticed, had access to resources about contraception that lower classes did not. Furthermore, poorer people could not shoulder the financial burden of caring for large families. Buwei tried her hardest to equalize access to family planning resources, offering free services to those who couldn't afford a visit while charging more for afflu- ent clients. Few took advantage of perks like this, though. The clinic wasn't a success.

Though Buwei resumed her medical career in China, food called to her. She noticed, for example, that her university served awful meals. Buwei took matters into her own hands. With her own money, she rented a three-room house near campus and began what she called a "community kitchen" meant for stu- dents and faculty. Really, it was a restaurant. She hired chefs from around the city to prepare delicacies like Changchow-style hot biscuits cooked in bean oil and capped with sesame. Yuenren hated the fact that she was opening a restaurant. Food was one domain in which he couldn't exercise control over her.

The restaurant stayed open for two years, its success a sign that food could be in her long-term future. Buwei traveled often in those years back home, exposing herself to the vast diver- sity of Chinese cooking. Cities south of Peiping, like Soochow and Hangchow, introduced her to pudding flavored with lotus starch, rose candies, and drunken shrimp that somersaulted in her mouth. Farther down south in Canton, today known as Guangzhou, she ate shreds of snake meat and chicken crowned with white chrysanthemum petals. Buwei found herself grow- ing curious about food on these visits. During her travels, she would bombard cooks with questions about how they prepared a certain dish and where its ingredients came from.

The succeeding years were hectic. She had two more chil- dren in that period, Lensey and Bella. Yuenren's different jobs throughout the 1930s had them move to various cities in China.

Buwei's medical career fell by the wayside due to this constant motion, so she focused her energies on raising her children. The family lived through World War II, dodging bombs as they went from city to city: Nanking, Hangkow, Changsha, Kunming. On the leg of their route from Changsha to Kunming, they found themselves riding a bus along a border town that brought them to what was then known as Langson in French Indochina (modern-day Vietnam), which they had to pass through in order to reach their destination.

No matter where she went, Buwei ached for the pleasures of good food. After that brief stay in Langson, she came across a vendor at a train station on her way back into China in January 1938. He carried a pole with food on both ends: noodles boiling over a charcoal fire on one, skinny-sliced Yunnan ham on another. When she encountered this food, it was as if the war's tumult came to a halt.

The war was still trudging along in 1939, the year Buwei and her family returned to America for good. Yuenren received a visiting professorship at Yale, bringing them to New Haven for a brief two-year period, but the family moved back to Cambridge in 1941, when Yuenren resumed teaching at Harvard. Buwei was unable to pursue a medical job in America, her English still subpar. With a husband at work and four children in school, she had to keep herself occupied somehow. So she cooked. During the war, Yuenren appointed twenty instructors to teach Chinese to American soldiers. He'd conduct training at the family house, and Buwei made them midnight suppers of shrimp noodles. With practice, Buwei reached a point where she felt she could cook any dish she'd ever eaten, drawing only from memory. Perhaps it would serve her well to record that knowledge, she thought. Maybe she should write a cookbook.

⌒

BOOKS THAT FOCUSED on Chinese cuisine were few and far between in that era just before the war, but at least one major American publisher had confidence in the commercial viability of Chinese cookbooks. The prominent publishing house Macmillan printed the chef Henry Low's *Cook at Home in Chinese* (1938). Low was the chef at Port Arthur, a Chinese restaurant in New York's Chinatown that appealed to white American audiences. With its spacious banquet hall outfitted with fish tanks and hanging lanterns, the restaurant became a frequent site of weddings and parties.

Buwei came to cookbook writing with significant advantages over someone like Low. Though Buwei had experience running a restaurant in China, she was fundamentally a home cook. She thus understood the abilities, needs, and limitations of Americans cooking in kitchens like hers. And while Low certainly had visibility within New York's culinary circles, Buwei had access to a different crowd. She rubbed elbows with well-connected white intellectuals in Cambridge, and they considered her their equal thanks to her academic credentials. One such person was Agnes Hocking, wife of Harvard professor William Ernest Hocking. It was Agnes who encouraged Buwei to write a cookbook.

In 1942, Buwei and her eldest daughter, Rulan, began working on the book. Buwei tested her recipes so often that Yuenren joked that their kitchen resembled a chemistry research department. As the two women worked on the book, he made it clear that he trusted neither Buwei nor Rulan's facility with the English language. Yuenren combed through the text and made changes to Rulan's translations.

The outside world, however, knew little about this tense family dynamic. Writer Lin Yutang, a friend of the couple, was an early champion of the budding manuscript. In the spring of 1944, Yutang and his wife, Lin Tsui-feng, mentioned the cookbook to Pearl S. Buck and Richard J. Walsh, a white couple they knew. Walsh had published Yutang's nonfiction book, *My Country and My People* (1935), at his publishing firm, the John Day Company. One of the publisher's earliest successes was Buck's *East Wind: West Wind* (1930), a novel set in China. Buck was a white American woman raised by two Presbyterian missionaries in China, where she spent most of her adolescence. She followed this book with critical and commercial juggernaut *The Good Earth* (1931), also published by John Day; it received the Pulitzer Prize for Fiction in 1932.

John Day was committed to promoting harmony between China and America, as publishing these two titles demonstrated. Buwei's book would be an ideal fit. Buck and Walsh fell in love with Buwei's manuscript. "Mrs. Chao's cook book is splendid and we must certainly have it," Walsh wrote in a May 1944 letter to his son, Richard Jr., a John Day editor. "Pearl says it is the best Chinese cook book that she has seen."

Not everyone was an immediate fan. The lower-level editor at John Day into whose hands it landed was less effusive, noting the manuscript's demerits: The kinks in language. The discursive asides, mired in family drama. The use of the alien phrase "stir-frying," unheard of back then. Even the title, *How to Cook and Eat in Chinese*, seemed confusing.

But Buck and Walsh overrode these concerns, recognizing the text's inherent value in advancing cross-cultural understanding between China and America. Following their lead, the publishing house treated the book with care, even printing a table of recipe names with Chinese characters, a financial extravagance for the era.

How to Cook and Eat in Chinese, published in 1945, belonged to an encouraging wave of cookbooks that looked beyond America's borders. Among those titles was Mexican-born Elena Zelayeta's *Elena's Famous Mexican and Spanish Recipes* (1944). Americans may have regarded China's food with greater trepidation than Mexico's, though. Mexico was America's southern neighbor, whereas China was on the other side of the planet. Just a decade before, Countess Morphy, author of the cookbook *Recipes of All Nations* (1935), decried the foods of China, India, and Japan as "too remote to be fully understandable," capturing popular sentiment about the seeming difficulty of explaining Chinese cuisine to American home cooks.

Buwei vowed to undo such attitudes. For one, her book's recipes departed from previous literature on Chinese cooking in America, most of which focused on the cuisine of Canton. Buwei made room for specialties from the Jiangnan region, like red-cooked meats with dried lilies or pea starch noodles, large "lion's head" meatballs that were more like meat cakes, and the cold "salt-water" duck of Nanking. She also inserted recipes from the country's north, offering soy jam noodles, the rinsed lamb of Peiping dipped in boiling soup, and mutton-stuffed dumplings.

The book gave Americans a new vocabulary for speaking about cooking, too. Buwei defined the process of stir-frying as "a big-fire-shallow-fat-continual-stirring-quick-frying of cut-up material with wet seasoning." Not all such linguistic quirks stuck, though: The book referred to dumplings as "wraplings" and wontons as "ramblings."

Buwei's introduction was methodical, walking through Chinese meal systems, the nuances in table etiquette between China and America, and cooking methods like clear-simmering, shallow-frying, and pickling. The first recipe didn't appear until more than fifty pages in. She separated the recipes into red-cooked meat (stewed in soy sauce), meat slices, meat shreds, meatballs and cakes, meat specialties, beef, mutton and lamb, chicken, duck, fish, shrimps, seafood, eggs, vegetables, soups, pots, sweet things, rice, noodles, and pastry. Buwei allowed for substitutions, letting readers use peanut butter in lieu of sesame jam, for example. (She later attributed such leniency to the book's success. "All the ingredients in my recipes are American," she would tell a journalist in 1966, after the book's third edition had been published. "Perhaps that is why the book has sold so many copies.") Buwei closed with a guide to composing meals and menus, teaching readers how to *eat* in Chinese as she teased in the title.

The cookbook served as the flagship title for John Day's newly established Asia Press imprint. It couldn't have come out at a more opportune time. The passage of the Magnuson Act in December 1943 repealed swaths of the Chinese Exclusion Act and allowed Chinese immigrants to once again enter the country (albeit capped at a maximum of 105 per year). Though prejudice by no means vanished overnight, the Act was an important step in eliminating institutional discrimination against Chinese people in America. By the time the book appeared, World War II was over, and Buck and Walsh positioned the book for maximum impact in this more forgiving political landscape. An advertisement for Buwei's cookbook in *Asia and the Americas*, a popular magazine owned by John Day, emphasized the "human appetites, human aspirations and all human ways" of the Chinese people. Like Buwei, Buck and Walsh believed that food could tell a broader story about Chinese culture. "I would like to nominate her for the Nobel Peace Prize," Buck wrote of Buwei in the preface for the cookbook. "For what better road to universal peace is there than to gather around the table where new and delicious dishes are set forth, dishes which, though yet untasted by us, we are destined to enjoy and love?" The recommendation held particular power coming from Buck, fresh off a 1938 Nobel Prize in Literature of her own. *How to Cook and Eat in Chinese* was not just a cookbook, in other words. It was a manual of gastronomic diplomacy.

Buwei didn't end up winning a Nobel Peace Prize, but reception to the book was still sterling in the press. Preeminent food personality Ida Bailey Allen, who authored over fifty books on cooking and homemaking, lauded the book on her nationally syndicated radio show, increasing its visibility across the country. Howard Taylor of the *Philadelphia Inquirer* surmised it was "probably the most literary and the most amusing cookbook ever written," filled with turns of phrase that were "reminiscent of James Joyce but easier to understand." *New York Times* writer Margot McConnell, writing under the pen name Jane Holt, praised the book as "something distinctly novel in the way of a cook book" thanks to its "authentic account of the Chinese culinary system." Like many other reviewers, Holt skimmed over the book's tortured genesis. Holt briefly noted that Buwei's daughter translated the text into English before her husband retooled it. Even in the noise of positive publicity, the woman behind the cookbook remained a cipher.

IF BUWEI'S COOKBOOK concealed her voice, perhaps a memoir would let her articulate her inner life more fully. She had been chipping away at an autobiography of sorts since 1913, though she initially pictured it as a novel drawn loosely from her life. Buwei all but abandoned the project as the decades passed, but the cookbook's publication compelled her to resurrect it. Her friend Lin Tsui-feng informed Buwei that she wanted to write a short biography about Buwei's life. When Buwei approached Yuenren with Tsui-feng's proposition, Yuenren surprised her by saying that he'd been working on her biography for nineteen years. He showed her a forty-page story. It was all wrong, Buwei thought, too lengthy to be an article, too truncated to be a substantive biography. She politely offered to edit his biography into an object that felt truer to her spirit, but Yuenren gave her permission to begin anew. Buwei wrote in Chinese, still uncomfortable with communicating in English. Buck and Walsh agreed to print the book under John Day's Asia Press imprint, though they'd have to do so in English. There was only one candidate for translating the manuscript: Yuenren. The book, over three hundred pages long, was published in 1947 and opened with a lengthy disclaimer from Yuenren: "Since my wife has the last word, I shall have the foreword," he wrote. In response, Buwei made her aggravation toward Yuenren clear. Her husband "has not always been a well-behaved translator," she wrote. "While he tries to render my simple Chinese into Basic English, he constantly lapses into his academic style of involved qualifications."

The book soon shifted to Buwei's voice. She was a typical Chinese woman, she explained in the book's opening pages, for she learned to read and write at home. She married; she had four children. Yet she reneged on her stance sentences later when she called herself "a woman with an unusual experience." Here was a woman who had four parents rather than two, who broke her engagement against parental orders, who didn't even have a formal wedding ceremony when she got married. Food itself played a supporting role in this memoir. Buwei wrote little of the legendarily awful meals she ate in Japan, for example. Instead, this book aimed to show readers an aspect of Buwei that the cookbook could not display. "If you want to know what I really am, you should read the story of my life," she wrote.

Autobiography of a Chinese Woman was published in 1947, the year the family moved west for Yuenren's job teaching what was then referred to as "Oriental languages" at the University of California, Berkeley. An advertisement for the book sold it as "the most delightful account of family living since *Life with Father*," referring to the writer Clarence Day's 1935 autobiographical story compilation that became a hit Broadway play in 1939 and a film in 1947, suggesting that its appeal would transcend cultural barriers. That didn't quite happen. *Kirkus Reviews* gave the book a middling review. "Mrs. Chao may term herself a 'typical Chinese woman' but her story does not support the picture," the review opened, disregarding her own acknowledgment of the fact that she was anything but typical. Writing in the *New York Times*, reviewer Harry E. Wedeck was more generous: "She is amazingly *sui generis*," he wrote of Buwei, "mercurial in temperament, endowed with immense gusto in living, plunging into challenging experiences, confronting the immediacies even when they are far from diverting." Still, the book barely caught on with readers. Far more successful was the second edition of Buwei's cookbook, which John Day published in 1949. It contained the addition of a few recipes like Peiping roast duck and stirred crabmeat, corrections of small errors, and a new author's note from Buwei. Preparing a revised edition was a "pleasure," Buwei wrote, because "in the few years since the publication of this book, there has already been a noticeable increase in things Chinese at American markets. (No cause and effect implied!)" She noticed, for example, that fava beans were no longer confined to Italian vegetable stands, that fresh ginger was more widely obtainable than it had been in 1945, that "tender peas eaten with the pod" were now populating general markets.

John Day struggled after Walsh suffered from a debilitating stroke in 1953, but Buwei's cookbook remained a touchstone of Chinese cookbooks in America well into the 1950s. She did not face much competition. Authors like Doreen Yen Hung Feng, who wrote *The Joy of Chinese Cooking* (1950), lacked the ability to break down techniques for the American reader as Buwei did. Chinese cookbooks couldn't convince Americans that they could replicate the seemingly elaborate dishes of Chinese restaurants, which became storied institutions in America as restrictions for Chinese immigrants gradually loosened in the 1950s. The Refugee Relief Act of 1953, for example, allowed Chinese refugees to seek permanent resident status. (Buwei and Yuenren, for their part, both obtained their citizenship in 1954.) Laws like this resulted in major growth for the Chinese population in America, which was 150,005 in 1950; by 1960, that number grew to 237,292.

The new wave of Chinese immigrants to America in the 1960s led to innovations on the part of cookbook authors to make Chinese cooking more legible to American audiences. Grace Zia Chu's *The Pleasures of Chinese Cooking* (1962) was one of the first signs of what a path forward might look like for Chinese cookbooks in America. Madame Chu, as many called her, was a Shanghai-born, Wellesley-educated single mother who worked as a cooking instructor in New York. She had the muscle of a major publisher, Simon & Schuster, behind her. Living in New York gave Chu access to influential supporters like Craig Claiborne, the food editor of the *New York Times*, a privilege Buwei did not enjoy in either Cambridge or Berkeley. Chu's book worked its way from the standard repertoire of Chinese dishes in American restaurants, like egg foo yong and chow mein, to more labored fare: bird's nest soup with the nest of a sea swallow, shark's fin with Chinese cabbage. Chu understood that many American readers might view such delicacies as esoteric, but she took an uncomplicated approach to teaching Chinese cooking to white Americans. She avoided including any Chinese characters in the text. Each recipe had preparation and serving tips. She also gave wiggle room to home cooks, like the option to use a can of creamed corn for chicken velvet corn soup. She even included a chapter for "hors d'oeuvres with an Oriental flavor," like a hoisin sauce cream cheese spread and an oyster sauce sour cream dip. Chu displayed patience for her American readers. Her gifts as a writer prompted Claiborne to declare that her cookbook "may well be the finest, most lucid volume on Chinese cooking ever written." Buwei's book maintained influence, though. In an interview with Claiborne published before *The Pleasures of Chinese Cooking* came out, Chu cited Buwei's cookbook as one of her favorites. (Random House published the third, and final, edition of Buwei's cookbook in 1963, a year after the release of Chu's book.)

In 1965, a major legislative development would change immigration patterns to America for good. The Immigration and Nationality, or Hart-Celler, Act eliminated national quotas entirely. It was only a matter of time for Chinese cooking to enter American homes through a new medium: Starting in 1966, the Boston-based public television station WGBH began airing *Joyce Chen Cooks*. The network hoped to capitalize on the success of *The French Chef* hosted by Julia Child, which the station began airing in 1963. Born in Beijing, Chen was a Cambridge-based restaurateur who self-published the modest *Joyce Chen Cook Book* (1962). *Joyce Chen Cooks* was the first nationally syndicated cooking show hosted by a person of color in America. Chen was a quietly charming host who performed culinary tricks like blowing air into a duck carcass with a bicycle pump. The show lasted for only a single twenty-six-episode season. In spite of the show's short run, the confidence that WGBH had in greenlighting Chen's show at all demonstrated how substantially America's appetite for Chinese cooking had grown. That hunger became fiercer in the 1970s.

In 1972, then-president Richard Nixon paid a visit to China, hoping to ease relations with the country. Upon his televised arrival in Beijing, Nixon ate slices of roast duck with pineapple during a banquet held in his honor. The visit led to impassioned American interest in Chinese cuisine. "Chinese Restaurants Flower Following Diplomatic Thaw," read a July 1972 *New York Times* headline. Nixon's historic trip coincided with a golden age for Chinese cookbooks in America. Just months after Nixon's visit, Craig Claiborne co-authored *The Chinese Cookbook* (1972) with Virginia Lee, a cooking teacher and native of Shanghai living in New York. Then, in 1974, Cecilia Chiang, the woman behind the beloved San Francisco Chinese restaurant the Mandarin, published her first book, *The Mandarin Way*, with writer Allan Carr. It was a hybrid of a cookbook and memoir, recounting Chiang's Beijing childhood. The Ningbo-born, New York–based cooking teacher Florence Lin's debut cookbook, *Florence Lin's Regional Chinese Cookbook* (1975), also appeared that decade, and she would go on to write America's first Chinese vegetarian cookbook, *Florence Lin's Chinese Vegetarian Cookbook* (1976). The most ambitious of the cookbooks to emerge in this decade, however, may have been New York–based restaurateur Irene Kuo's *The Key to Chinese Cooking* (1977), published by Knopf. Kuo, born in Shanghai and educated at Barnard College, penned a volume that *Kirkus Reviews* hailed as a "resplendent book of Chinese cuisine." She possessed boundless charisma, working the talk show circuit as a guest of Mike Douglas and Johnny Carson. Authors like Kuo had an ability to bask in the spotlight, helping Chinese cooking gain even greater respect in the eyes of the dominant white American culture.

﹏

CELEBRITY PASSED BY Buwei in old age. In California, far from the epicenter of the culinary establishment in New York, she continued cooking into her eighties. At age 84, she authored her final book, *How to Order and Eat in Chinese* (1974) with Yuenren and her third daughter, Lensey. A slim paperback, it contained no recipes and instead focused on topics like table manners and the differences between Cantonese and Szechuan cooking. "Since the publication of my *How to Cook and Eat in Chinese*, I have received numerous inquiries, from people who do not cook or have no time to cook, about how to order meals in Chinese restaurants," she opened the book. This condensed, information-rich volume torched stereotypes surrounding Chinese food. She dispelled the pervasive notion that tea is always served at meals; she told readers not to ask for Szechuan food in a Cantonese restaurant.

In spite of its strengths, *How to Order and Eat in Chinese* received little attention from the food media. Buwei died of a stroke seven years after its publication, at the age of 91. Her death generated faint coverage beyond the Bay Area. Yuenren died a year later, at 89. The third edition of *How to Cook and Eat in Chinese* barely outlived Buwei, enduring until the mid-1980s before it fell out of print. New personalities began amplifying Chinese cooking in that decade: The Chinese-born chef Martin Yan's *Yan Can Cook* began airing on American public television in 1982 and remained on the air into the twenty-first century.

The *New York Times*, the newspaper that had fêted Buwei three decades before, reduced her to a line in her husband's 1982 obituary. "His wife, Buwei Yang Chao, died in 1981," read the penultimate sentence. She did not receive an obituary of her own.

That America's paper of record deemed her life insufficient for a proper eulogy speaks to how she had slid from public visibility in the three and a half decades since *How to Cook and Eat in Chinese*'s publication. But Buwei had always refused to compromise her identity for the eyes of the white Americans. She was Chinese by blood: "Patriotism is your mother tongue," she would write in her autobiography. "The reason why I am so thoroughly Chinese is because I speak nothing but the Chinese language." She would try to speak other languages, like English, but doing so was futile, she wrote, for "whatever language I speak comes out Chinese in spirit."

You'd Never Give a Thought to Pity Her

Elena Zelayeta

B. OCTOBER 3, 1897, MEXICO CITY, MEXICO

D. MARCH 31, 1974, SAN FRANCISCO, CALIFORNIA, USA

T HE SUN HADN'T YET SET that afternoon in 1934 when Elena Zelayeta stood in the kitchen of her San Francisco apartment on Market Street, trying to peel a potato. The scene was tranquil. She had emptied the place of everyone but her new-born Billy, who was cooing in his crib. But she could detect nothing in the darkness before her. All Elena wanted to do was cook dinner. Months had passed since she last cooked a meal on her own, though. She needed to make something simple to reacquaint herself with cooking. Though she contemplated broiling lamb chops, Elena couldn't trust herself to jump-start the fire. Mashed potatoes, a salad, and a dessert of packaged pudding would have to do. Cooking had once been second nature to Elena. It was now a source of torment. That's what going blind did to her.

She recalled that now-distant era when she'd shuttle back and forth between her kitchen and dining room, playing both chef and hostess without much trouble. In that past life of hers, she ran her own restaurant, Elena's Mexican Village. She based its menu on

the dishes her mother, Doña Luisa, cooked in the Mexican mining town where Elena spent the first few years of her youth, and
later in her adoptive home of San Francisco. Elena herself didn't
start cooking much until she turned 27, when she married a man
named Lorenzo, whom she called Loren. He turned out to be a
serial cheater, though, and theirs was a troubled marriage. Elena
tried to salvage the relationship through their child, Lawrence,
but Loren's infidelities persisted.

A son could not save a doomed marriage, but maybe food
could help. The Great Depression put Elena out of a job, compel-
ling her to open a restaurant. It began as a bootstrapped effort on
the top floor of the apartment building where they lived, but the
restaurant soon moved to a spacious street-level building. Elena
was the restaurant's beating heart. On nights when she wasn't
overseeing the cooking, she would dance before the crowd as a
string orchestra thrummed behind her. But the couple closed the
restaurant in 1934, just after Elena lost her sight. A mature cataract and a detached retina were to blame. Only 36 years old and
seven months pregnant, Elena tumbled into despair. The birth of
her second son, Billy, did not soften the blow of blindness. Confin-
ing herself to her room, she relied on the help of maids, and then
her mother, to cook meals for her family.

But today would be different. She would depend on the senses
that fate had not compromised: to listen, touch, smell, taste.
She drew her knife to the potato, quaking with fear as the skin
fell to the sink. Fighting the constant temptation to give up, she
repeated the process until she had enough potatoes to submerge
in a pan filled with water. She grabbed a teaspoon and scooped
it with salt. Stray crystals scattered as she tipped the spoon into
the pan.

Elena's hands fumbled for a match. She brushed the wooden
stick against the striker, sensing the faint presence of heat near

her. Elena stopped for a beat to pray before she switched on the gas, fanning the matchstick before it until the stove snapped into a flame. She placed the pan on the stove and heard the potatoes hiss, and then she started on the salad. She held the lettuce under sink water, scrubbing her fingers against the leaves to catch any dirt or vermin.

Elena was anxious when Loren returned home. What if he hated her cooking? Or, worse: What if he lied to her about it and treated her with kid gloves? She was relieved when he marveled at her dinner, in spite of small imperfections—the mashed potatoes, for example, still had some skins poking out. Loren's affirmations gave Elena the confidence that she could become herself again.

~

ELENA'S PARENTS HAD both been born in Spain, Doña Louisa in the city of Valencia and Don Manuel Loshuertos in Zaragoza. A woman with no formal education, Doña Luisa had been a seamstress since she was 8 years old. Work was all she knew. The two met in Barcelona, where Doña Luisa served as a wealthy man's housekeeper. Don Manuel was that man's secretary. The pair fell in love on the job.

Though they wed in Spain, Don Manuel long had his eyes on the New World, believing it would be free of persecution. He wanted to move to the United States, but the language barrier deterred him. Instead, in 1896 the couple moved to Mexico City, where Don Manuel's brother lived. Elena, the couple's first child, was born in October of the following year. When she was just a year and a half old, she suffered from a bout of scarlet fever, which left her with a battle scar in the form of a pale, white veil over her left eye. She called it a *nube*, Spanish for "cloud."

Don Manuel had taken on odd jobs since moving to Mexico, seesawing between secretarial work and carpentry. Elena's birth forced the couple to stabilize themselves. Elena's parents wondered what skills they possessed that they could possibly monetize. They thought of Doña Louisa's cooking. She had matured into an exceptional cook since marriage. The couple opened a restaurant, La Valenciana, in the mining town of El Mineral del Oro. By the time Elena was five, they had expanded the restaurant to include a hotel.

Doña Louisa occasionally permitted Elena to join in on the cooking. Elena spent her days hanging red chiles outside the window to toast in the sun, stirring masa for the tortillas, and bruising cumin seeds in her mother's molcajete, the Mexican analog to a mortar and pestle. Elena didn't just find delight in these activities. She discovered a more practical truth: Cooking could provide a means to survive.

More children followed for Doña Luisa: Joseph, Luisa, Teresa, and Manuel. The family lived in a cocoon of joy, but they soon began to feel like outsiders in Mexico. Even many decades after Mexico declared its independence from Spain in 1821, animus for the Spanish still lingered among natives of the town where Elena's family lived. Every Independence Day, villagers took to the streets, chanting "Down with the Spaniards!" Hearing this chorus terrified young Elena. She wondered if she really belonged in the place she called home.

❧

THE FAMILY DID NOT INTEND to leave Mexico. It happened by accident, when Elena was 11 years old. Her parents had sent her to boarding school in Mexico City for three years, which gave her a loose grasp on the English language. This skill made her the family's de facto English language ambassador on a vacation to San Francisco at the end of 1909. The chance to go to the United States thrilled Don Manuel. The seven of them—Elena, her parents, and her four siblings—ironed their finest holiday clothes, stuffed their suitcases with food, and rode a train to San Francisco, where they planned to stay briefly at the pricey Argonaut Hotel near Fisherman's Wharf. But the family's vacation spilled over into 1910, which marked the start of the Mexican Revolution. The conflict would last a decade. Elena's parents had leased out their inn for the duration of the vacation, but they soon learned that all of their possessions in Mexico were casualties of the political upheaval. If they were to go back to Mexico, they would have nothing to return to.

The state now recognized as California had long been a destination for people coming from what is today Mexico. They had come to the region in two waves, first during the Spanish missions in the late eighteenth and early nineteenth centuries, then again during the Gold Rush in the mid-nineteenth century. Elena's family belonged to what would become a third wave, beginning in 1910. In the ten-year period of the Mexican Revolution, some 890,000 documented Mexican immigrants flocked to America.

Still, Elena's family felt orphaned in America, a country that they felt was not yet theirs. They were practically penniless, for one. To make ends meet, they sold Doña Luisa's jewelry. The family scrambled to secure housing, but they were unfamiliar with the language, relying on Elena's grade-school English skills to navigate the city. Elena kept her eyes alert for "FOR RENT" signs. She was unable to find any. Instead, she was puzzled by the "TO LET" signs she saw. Were these signs advertising toilets? They finally found a place after a kind Spanish-speaking street merchant clarified that these signs were, in fact, for vacant apartments. The

family moved to an apartment on the ground floor of a three-
story building on a treeless block on Twenty-Second Street in
the Mission District, then a predominantly Irish enclave. Their
rent was a mere $18 per month. Elena, Joe, and Luisa attended
the nearby Agassiz School. The kids there ridiculed the way the
siblings spoke, with their nervous starts and stops. Elena and her
siblings' manner of dress also made them objects of scorn, Joe
with his overcoat and cape, Elena and Luisa with their unblem-
ished white dresses.

As Elena struggled to acclimate in America, more sadness
tore through her new life: A new sibling died shortly after child-
birth. The family still didn't have much money in those early days,
either, as Don Manuel had trouble finding work. Searching for a
financial bedrock, the family turned again to Doña Luisa's cooking. She prepared tamales in bulk and asked Elena and her other
children to roam the neighborhood selling them.

Elena followed her mother's trajectory, starting work when
she was young in order to provide for her family. In her early
teens, Elena served as a housekeeper and then took a job at a
men's furnishing store on the weekends. With time, her English
began to improve. She studied at the High School of Commerce
in San Francisco for two years, the minimum for accreditation
in that period, and spent the summer before her senior year
working as a file clerk in an office. She then attended Chicago
Business College, located on Mission Street, to gain skills in
typing. To pay her tuition, she scrubbed classrooms clean in the
morning.

Through her adolescence, Elena wanted nothing more than to
be adored by everyone around her for a nice figure and pretty face.
But by 18, she had become sensitive about her looks—her short
stature, her face framed by thick-rimmed glasses. Still, her diffi-
dence didn't extinguish her romantic desires. She cycled through

suitors: a physician and surgeon from Nicaragua who was ten years her senior, a Mexican man whom she dated for four years beginning when she was 21.

As the years passed, Elena began to grow more worried about the cloud over her eye. What she once dismissed as a cosmetic quirk was becoming a serious impediment to her vision. She struggled to complete tasks at her office jobs, squinting through heavy frames until her head began to ache. A fall 1923 visit to a doctor confirmed that the problem was a mature cataract. An operation could possibly help, he told her, though there was no guarantee. The doctor gave her simple instructions after the surgery that December: Do not cry until your eye is fully healed. But she couldn't help it. Her tears soaked the cotton bandages over her left eye. After she took them off, she waited for her vision to self-correct. It didn't.

ॐ

LORENZO ZELAYETA, whom Elena nicknamed Loren, was from Mexico, too. He hailed from the city of Mazatlán. A strikingly handsome man, he had an alluring demeanor that attracted Elena from the start. In the early months of 1924, Loren courted both Elena and her sister Luisa, taking them on joint dates to watch vaudeville shows at the Orpheum. The two women were unsure of whom he liked better, though Elena guessed it must have been Luisa: Luisa was the family's beauty. But after four dates, Loren pursued Elena more tenaciously. Elena found his persistence charming. He proposed in June 1925, when Elena was 27, and they wed in August of that year at City Hall before a handful of friends and family members. Elena's father was furious that she married a Mexican man; he'd raised his kids to become American. During a celebratory dinner cooked by Doña Luisa, Don Manuel refused to even look at Elena. In the eyes of her father, Elena's marriage had turned her into a ghost. Her mother's cooking anchored Elena that night: a soup of carrots, peas, and string beans paddling in chicken stock; artichokes, scraped of their centers and crammed with crabmeat; potatoes that were baked, mashed, and laced with cream puff batter before being deep-fried.

When Elena returned to her apartment with Loren after the wedding, she eyed the gift from her mother-in-law. It was a common wedding present in Mexico, a metate, or three-legged stone tool meant for grinding corn for tortillas. The present sent a clear message: Elena now had a husband to feed. Loren would be busy with his work as a structural engineer. She needed to learn how to cook. As Elena surrendered herself to the new role of a housewife, she confined herself to her apartment. She labored over recipes for casseroles and pies, but no matter how carefully she followed the instructions, they all tended to turn out wrong.

Elena had no rhythm in the kitchen. Her arms became etched with burn marks that she tried her best to hide from friends she saw at the supermarket. She'd lie and tell them that she just spilled some coffee on herself. Loren, meanwhile, grew increasingly embittered by her father's refusal to accept their marriage. Elena hadn't realized how irascible Loren could be. She suppressed her own forthright nature, though, since her parents had raised her to be her husband's subordinate. Her own mother did a spectacular job of performing marital deference, after all. Doña Luisa was a woman who seldom smiled; in her childhood, Elena would remember her mother just humming Spanish folk songs to herself as her body swayed from one side to the other while she cooked. Maybe Elena would age into a woman like her mother. Following such a script of obedience wasn't easy for Elena, though. She tried her best to silence the questions that sprinted through her mind on weeknights, whenever Loren told her he was going to visit a pal or see a cabaret show. Maybe it was just a coincidence that a friend spotted him at a concert one night with an actress. Or that he'd been seen with a waitress on another night. Or with a night-club singer on yet another. Elena dwelled in her own delusions, but Loren's cheating preyed upon her worst insecurities. She still found herself physically undesirable, thinking she must have been a charity case for a man like Loren. On those nights alone, she sought companionship in recipes, reading over them as she wondered where her husband was.

~

ELENA SPENT THOSE YEARS forming an identity independent of her husband, and she did it by cooking. With repetition, she ironed out the rookie mistakes that had hobbled her in her early days of marriage. Elena invited Don Manuel over for lunch, despite the fact that he was still no fan of Loren. She stunned her father with her crisp salads and warm sopa as sensational as her mother's. Don Manuel grew more sympathetic toward Loren from that point forward. If Elena's food could thaw that frigid relationship, perhaps her cooking was more powerful than she thought.

In May 1926, Elena and Loren had a son named Lawrence, known as Larry. Don Manuel passed away shortly after Larry's birth, following a sudden heart attack that left him bedridden for months. Elena, dissatisfied with being a housewife, returned to a job she once held before marriage at the California Arms Company, and the couple hired a live-in maid named Manuelita. But in 1930, both Elena and Loren lost their jobs due to the economic downturn of the Great Depression. Elena seized upon a wild idea that had been in the back of her mind: She wanted to open a restaurant. She knew this was a bold ambition for a woman of her time, but she had confidence in her own abilities. Though Loren reacted with mild indifference, Elena was determined not to let her husband's apathy dim her passion. She went apartment-hunting and found a seven-room place on Green Street in the north of San Francisco. The family repurposed four of those rooms into dining areas.

Elena enlisted friends to help spread the word about her restaurant. She knew reaching American audiences would be a challenge. In that era, Mexican cuisine occupied a subordinate position in white America's culinary hierarchy, a mere notch above Chinese. Mexico's food was "so 'hot' that only a cast-iron throat and stomach can endure it," Louise Rice declared in her book *Dainty Dishes from Foreign Lands* (1909). Moreover, Elena began cooking at a time when Americans actively questioned whether Mexicans like her even belonged in America. "Get rid of the Mexicans!" became a rallying cry during the Depression. White Americans found themselves jobless, and Mexicans in America became a target of their frustrations. This swing in public sentiment resulted in the United States government's forced "repatriation," as some called the program, of over a million people of Mexican origin to Mexico. Nearly 60 percent of those deported were born in America. Elena tried her best to make sure that her restaurant wouldn't suffer as a result of such prejudice. Her customers tended to be non-Mexicans who took an intense interest in the country's culture. Patrons had to buzz in and trek up the staircase to the top floor of the building. They'd leave their coats in the bedroom and walk through the kitchen to get to the restaurant. Elena's days were punishing. After five hours of sleep, she rose at five in the morning and cooked on her own for nearly a hundred people until midnight. Her meals resembled those her mother once made. She cooked enchiladas; chiles rellenos, green peppers bulging with Monterey Jack cheese; and cream puffs filled with rum. Elena purposefully made offerings affordable, $0.50 for lunch and $0.75 for a seven-course dinner. These price points reflected the democratic ethos of the restaurant. She wanted it to be a gathering place, free of pretension.

Loren didn't help much. His infidelities kept him busy. During his nadir, he didn't return home for three days. As punishment, Elena changed the locks on the apartment and stuffed his belongings into a trunk she sent on an express wagon straight to his mother's house. They spent five months apart, but Elena and Loren got back together on her birthday in 1933. He convinced her that he was aware of his mistakes, and that he would change. He didn't want to lose her, he said. Elena had transformed her life in that time away from Loren. She turned to religion and attended church on Sundays. She began dieting. She fantasized about Loren returning to a wife he couldn't recognize, one he'd finally be faithful to.

In Loren's absence, Elena managed to keep business for the restaurant booming. Customers spilled into the hallway as they waited for tables. Many suggested she should move to a more accommodating space. Maybe they were right. Elena couldn't be the only cook in her kitchen forever. She pictured herself moving into more of a managerial role, presiding over cooks rather than putting on a one-woman show as both chef and hostess. She'd need more space regardless. Just months after Loren returned, she became pregnant again. After some scouring, Elena landed on a spot in the King George Hotel, near Union Square. Its kitchen could handle many cooks, and there were even three rooms upstairs, making it an ideal place for a family to live. Elena hired a painter, Darrell Pischoff, to design a mural on the restaurant's facade. It bore emblems of Mexico as America imagined them:

prickly cacti sprouting from the sidewalk, a parade of donkeys, men snoozing beneath sombreros. She named the restaurant Elena's Mexican Village, intending to make the experience as lively as possible. A string orchestra played on Thursdays and Sundays while Elena danced to the music for the crowd. "Straight from Old Mexico," read a listing for the restaurant in the *San Francisco Chronicle*, alongside Chinese and Italian restaurants.

The restaurant attracted a steady stream of customers, and also brought Elena and Loren together: In a change of character, he was heavily involved in the venture, greeting guests and bidding them farewell at the end of the night. They were finally partners. Elena was happier than she'd ever been.

❧

THE FIRST SIGN something was amiss came when Elena woke up one morning seven months into her second pregnancy and tried staring at herself in her bedroom mirror. The glass looked as if it were caked in a thick blanket of fog. When Elena rubbed her handkerchief against the mirror, though, nothing changed. She could make out only the faint contours of her face, as if viewing herself through a veil. Maybe she should've told Manuelita to clean more diligently, or perhaps the blurry vision was just a consequence of fatigue. Whatever the cause, Elena decided she wouldn't tell a soul about the fact that she couldn't see. But as the days passed, images softened like ink blots on paper. When friends approached her in the restaurant, she couldn't recognize them until they were close enough to smell her breath. Elena couldn't even walk past a mirror without trying to stare at herself. She would wait for the image to adjust until, losing patience, she flattened her face against the glass. Nothing. Loren noticed that Elena had been bumping into objects. He asked her why she needed to grasp chairs to feel her way around a room. She was just clumsy, she responded. He wasn't buying it. Loren made an appointment with an eye doctor the following day. As the doctor filled her eyes with drops and shone bright lights into her pupils, he shook his head in regret. "How awful," he muttered to himself, as if Elena couldn't hear him. "How awful, how terrible, such a young woman, how awful—"

She was losing her sight, he told her, and there was nothing any medical professional could do. Elena couldn't process the news. She felt as if she'd died.

IN THE DAYS after hearing about her blindness, Elena locked herself in her bedroom. She couldn't even bring herself to swallow soup. As she felt her unborn son squirming inside her body, she considered leaping from her bedroom window, tumbling seven stories to her death. She wanted to save her unborn son a life raised by a miserable mother.

She nearly acted on these suicidal ideations one day, but Loren caught her just as her hands gripped the windowsill. Elena protested as he talked her out of her delusion. At Loren's request, Elena remained under strict supervision for the following ten days, overseen by Loren himself, Manuelita, and one of Elena's waitresses. Larry, still a child, balanced her meals in his wiry arms and carried them wobbling up to his mother. He offered her enchiladas, cut so she could ingest them more easily, or sandwiches, which she could eat on her own. Anything to spare herself the degradation of being spoon-fed by her son. Elena hated being away from the restaurant. After a month, she asked Loren to take her down to the restaurant kitchen. At least she could distract herself with the taste of food there. She gave her cooks input on the tartness of the salad dressing, the salt in the soup.

Elena was eating dinner in the restaurant one night in August 1934 when she began feeling sharp labor pains. Upon the birth of William, or Billy as Elena called him, she felt unsettled, overcome with joy and despondency in equal measure. People told her the boy was beautiful. Elena took them at their word. She could not even see what he looked like.

❧

MONTHS AFTER BILLY'S BIRTH, Elena's Mexican Village closed down, sinking beneath a $5,000 mountain of debt. The restaurant had slipped into chaos under Loren's tenuous grip. He didn't know how to manage the cooks, and the quality of the soups, the salads, even the beans deteriorated in Elena's absence. Once-loyal customers stopped coming. No longer able to afford to live in their apartment above the restaurant, the family moved in with Loren's mother.

After many months, Loren pooled enough money for Elena to have cataract surgery, but it was unsuccessful, leaving her crestfallen once again. Elena's anguish was too much for others to bear; it even chased Manuelita away from the family. Doña Luisa took over the daily chores that were once the maid's tasks, while hired nurses took care of Billy. Finally, after months of moping around, Elena realized she couldn't last like this forever. She knew she needed to inch back toward self-sufficiency. Maybe cooking could help her. Though she didn't have the restaurant any longer, at least it had left her with a degree of recognition within the city. People knew Elena's name.

❧

THOUGH ELENA BEGAN COOKING modest meals of mashed pota-toes, blindness eventually reshaped the way she cooked. When she cracked eggs, she cradled her hands to catch the whites before they ran through her fingers. She smelled deep fat heating on the stove and determined its temperature. She let fifteen-minute radio programs serve as her timers for baking. With time, she taught herself to deep-fry chiles rellenos without scalding herself. She caramelized sugar without burning the bottom of the pan. She scrambled eggs until they were light as fleece.

Elena spent the next nine years working her way up to elaborate meals like the ones she once cooked in her restaurant. She could make trays of tiny empanadas stuffed with creamed crabmeat, oysters, and chicken livers. When she closed her eyes at night, she saw her life as she once knew it: her family, her friends. She slowly eased her way back into routine, shopping at department stores and hosting friends for meals. Her reputation as a cook didn't suffer while she was out of the public eye. In 1944, a decade after Elena lost her sight, she began teaching cooking at the San Fran-cisco Center for the Blind. Later that year, Elena found commu-nity with a group of home economists. One of the women there, Lou Richardson, suggested that Elena write a cookbook, thinking it might help her afford to buy a guide dog. It wouldn't be hard, Lou reassured her. She and the other women could help her put the book together and market it.

The prospect energized Elena in the same way the idea of running a restaurant once had. She didn't waste any time. Elena rushed back home to her first-floor apartment and asked Billy for help in placing an ad in the *San Francisco Chronicle* for assistants.

She found two, Cornelia Farrell and Daisy Dennis, who, along with Elena's friend Vesta McWhinney, jotted down a hundred of Elena's recipes as Elena dictated them. These were recipes for some of her bygone restaurant standbys, like artichokes dressed in mustard and vinegar or Brussels sprouts in tomatoes, onions, and bacon bits. The home economists then cross-checked ingredient lists and tested each recipe. They recited the recipes back to Elena, probing her with questions about each step. Elena slid $500 into debt just to pay for the first printing of two thousand copies for *Elena's Famous Mexican and Spanish Recipes*, 127 pages long and $1.25 when it was first published in August 1944.

Prior to the book's publication, there weren't many Mexican cookbooks published in America with national impact. There had been books like Encarnación Pinedo's *El cocinero español*, or *The Spanish Cook* (1898), a Spanish-language text. Because Pinedo's book was in Spanish, the book's audience was inevitably limited. Still, the book was significant in its era because Pinedo documented the recipes of Mexicans living in nineteenth-century California. And although Pinedo was born in California, she was of Mexican parentage, whereas most other nominally Mexican cookbooks were authored by white Americans without an obvious attachment to the country. For example, Harriet S. Loury's *Fifty Choice Recipes for Spanish and Mexican Dishes* (1905) included a recipe for "alligator pear salad" (that is, guacamole). May Southworth, who published a volume of *101 Mexican Dishes* (1906), instructed readers to make tortillas from flour, rather than the corn dough known as masa, and cook them in lard. This recipe wasn't exactly a betrayal of Mexican culinary tradition, considering that many northern Mexicans ate flour tortillas, but the recipe's inclusion was born of pragmatism: Obtaining flour was far more convenient for American cooks than grinding corn in a metate.

The cooking instructor Bertha Haffner-Ginger, founder of the Los Angeles Times' School of Domestic Science, may have been the most prominent of these white authors. Upon coming to Los Angeles from the Midwest in 1911, Haffner-Ginger was struck by the sight of women toiling away in a tortilla factory, thus arousing her love of Mexican cooking. "When made properly, there is great merit in this class of foods," Haffner-Ginger wrote in the introduction to her cookbook, *California Mexican-Spanish Cook Book* (1914), asserting the cuisine's inherent worth. She even had a section on how to prepare corn for tortillas. Mexican cookbooks that followed Haffner-Ginger's, including those written by women of Mexican origin, didn't have as wide a popularity as hers. Fabiola Cabeza de Baca, author of *Historic Cookery* (1931); Erna Fergusson, author of *Mexican Cookbook* (1934); and Cleofas Jaramillo, author of *The Genuine New Mexico Tasty Recipes: Potajes Sabrosos* (1939) were all New Mexico residents and who wrote books that appealed specifically to that state's culinary traditions.

Elena's aims were more far-reaching, close to Haffner-Ginger's spirit. Unlike Haffner-Ginger, though, Elena actually hailed from Mexico. Elena aimed to represent Mexican food as "we like it best here in the United States," she wrote. This language implies that Elena wrote the book for both white Americans and immigrants who, like her, may have aspired toward assimilation. The book was a mash-up of tradition and adaptation, including recipes for rabbit stew, pork chops in peanut butter sauce, and chicken with chestnuts. Many of Elena's recipes were forgiving. If readers couldn't find Mexican chocolate in a nearby grocery store, fine—adding cinnamon to American chocolate would do. And instead of spending two hours making leche quemada, a milk pudding laced with cinnamon and almonds, Elena suggested a way to create a "reasonable facsimile": Cooks could place an unopened can of condensed milk in hot water, simmer it for three hours, and then remove it from the can after the water cooled. Elena and her friends promoted the book with such aggression that it sold through its first printing within a month. Some of these home economists had prior connections to members of the media; mostly, however, they possessed remarkable persistence. They wrote letters to publications in cities across the country urging them to pay attention to Elena's book. They nudged friends with radio shows and newspaper columns to endorse it. They held parties throughout California in her honor. Within months, Elena made enough money to pay off the debts from her restaurant, and she was able to get a guide dog named Chulita.

This public relations crusade also established Elena as an expert on Mexican cooking. By October 1944, the *Los Angeles Times* was billing Elena as a "famed authority on the culinary art from south of the border." Her blindness was a crucial part of her story, too. "My friend Elena is blind," wrote one of her fiercest champions, Prudence Penny of the *San Francisco Examiner*, "but you'd never give a thought to pity her."

&

LOREN'S BODY WAS already at the morgue by the time Elena learned of the crash. It was six in the evening on a Saturday in November 1945. He should've been home from work an hour earlier. Rattled, Elena called the wife of Loren's colleague. She told Elena that the two men had been in a car accident, and that Loren's colleague was being treated at the South San Francisco Emergency Hospital. Frantic with worry, Elena called the hospital asking for her husband. He wasn't there. The woman on the other end of the line suggested Elena call the California Highway

Patrol. She did, but they had no information for her either. Elena finally discovered the details of her husband's death on a radio report. Loren had been in a crash with a bus that flipped the car belly-up, fastening him beneath the rubble. The crash had charred his face beyond recognition. It would be a closed-casket funeral. Grief burrowed its way into the marrow of Elena's being. Loren would visit Elena in her dreams, startling her awake at night. She could not grasp her new reality.

⟳

STILL, SHE COOKED. In April 1946, an opportunity presented itself to teach practical living—that is, cooking and the household arts—to a group of thirty blind students in Montana. Elena took Billy, then 11, and Chulita to a cabin perched high in the mountains. She spent four weeks teaching students how to peel potatoes, how to shell peas, and how to fry slices of ham on wood-and-coal stoves. Her students reminded Elena of how she'd once been just after blindness. One young woman, who lost her sight just before she turned 20, didn't think she'd ever be able to cook, whereas another student approached cooking with the giddy enthusiasm of a child. Once Elena was back home, her friends urged her to turn her teaching experiences into a self-help book as a way to help make a living after Loren's death. Positioned as a "spiritual companion" to her cookbook, *Elena's Lessons in Living* (1947) was a manual on how to persevere against adversity. "While this is not a cook book, it was, in a way, born in the kitchen," Elena wrote in the introduction. Cooking, she wrote, had given her a more optimistic outlook on her life. Food was at the book's center, even though Elena included only a few recipes—for her mother's arroz con pollo, a zucchini torte, and chiles rellenos.

The book cemented Elena's status as a celebrity beyond the realm of cooking. It drew scores of admirers to her apartment, as if she'd become San Francisco's public therapist. These strangers requested her advice on various problems afflicting them.

By 1950, Elena's star had risen to such heights that television producer Richard Dinsmore asked her to host a fifteen-minute cooking show on local television once a week. Every Monday evening, Elena headed to the studios of KGO-TV, a local station in the Bay Area. A makeup artist traced her eyebrows with a pencil while a hairdresser hid her silver strands of hair. The crew attached strings to her ankles, tugging on them as they toggled between cameras so she knew where to direct her gaze. Elena carried herself with assurance on screen. In an episode in which Elena prepared pickled tuna fish, her now tall teenage son Billy returned home from a solo fishing trip with a hulking basket in his hands. "Oh, darling! Let me see," Elena said, pretending to sift through its contents. The show began airing in April 1950 every Friday in Los Angeles; it would air in the Bay Area two years later. It wasn't much of a success, but the mere fact that producers would take a gamble on a blind cook to host a television show at all underscored the scope of Elena's fame.

Elena wrote a cascade of cookbooks after *Elena's Lessons in Living*. Her name in the title of each was like a branding statement. "This book is not a Mexican cookbook," wrote Elena's close friend Helen Evans Brown, a cookbook author and authority on California cuisine, in the foreword to *Elena's Fiesta Recipes* (1952). "It is *Elena's* book." The cooking in *Elena's Fiesta Recipes* straddled categories: A recipe for Spanish-style turkey with chestnuts sat next to one for Mexican turkey meatballs. She also retooled a number of her recipes to appeal to American tastes. The Christmas Eve fruit salads she knew in Mexico were slathered with sugar, but for Americans, Elena served that salad with mayonnaise that had been thinned with cream and fruit juices instead. In a similar bid, she made her featherweight chiles rellenos with thicker batter than what cooks normally used in Mexico.

Around the same time as the book's publication, Elena repurposed some of the book's recipes for a frozen food business, Elena's Food Specialties. She began the business with her son Larry's help. Larry took control of the business, leasing a two-story plant on South Van Ness Avenue in San Francisco and hiring a team of workers. Elena's products predated the TV dinner frenzy by a year, just before the country would begin an obsession with waffles and fish sticks you could stow in your freezer. Elena was finding new ways for her food to reach people across the country. Her influence soon began inching its way toward the East Coast: In a 1953 article, Jane Nickerson, food editor of the *New York Times*, referred to Elena as an authority on dining on the West Coast—not Mexican cooking, notably. But Elena's third cookbook dealt almost exclusively with Mexican cuisine. *Elena's Secrets of Mexican Cooking* (1958) was an exhaustive effort. Elena wanted to dispel the misperception that Mexican food was "always searingly hot, exotically and overly spiced, and heavy," as she wrote in the preface. Elena went on to explain that the precolonial foods of the Aztecs formed Mexico's culinary backbone, rich with corn, beans, and peppers. Waves of Spanish invasion introduced rice, olive oil, and wine into the country's diet. She bemoaned the tendency of Americans to reduce Mexican food to tamales and enchiladas. Elena showed them a different path: Her three hundred recipes were for dishes like lamb brain tacos, sardine tostadas, and pressed quince paste. Elena was writing about Mexico from a distance, and for an American audience. As the cookbook author Charlotte Turgeon observed in the *New York Times*, Elena knew "the likes and dislikes of most Americans." To engage reluctant readers, Elena made her turkey in green mole sauce purposefully mild; she said "good old American hot dogs" worked just fine in lentil soup if cooks couldn't find the Spanish longaniza sausage that was beloved in Mexican cooking. Occasional accommodations aside, though, Elena largely resisted the temptation to simplify Mexican dishes. She did not, for example, think cornmeal was an acceptable substitution for masa.

The book landed Elena on the culinary cognoscenti's radar with a 1958 *New York Times* profile by Craig Claiborne, who took over the post of food editor after Nickerson in 1957. Claiborne surmised that *Elena's Secrets of Mexican Cooking* "may well be the definitive volume on the subject."

Claiborne focused on her food, but the headline "Blindness No Handicap to Author of New Book" emphasized Elena's disability. The perceived novelty of a cook with a disability, one whose journey to the kitchen was arduous, made her an inspiring subject to many American readers. Soon, Elena spun her tale of survival into a memoir. The jacket for *Elena* (1960) advertised a story of a woman who was "unable to see with her eyes" but "learned to see with her heart." She spread this narrative over 246 pages, fleshing out anecdotes she'd written about in her self-help book. But after reading the memoir, some critics felt Elena was punching above her weight class. A November 1960 review in *Kirkus Reviews* dismissed the book as "artlessly written," though noting that "the vivid Spanish nature of Elena is as interesting here as is the account of triumph over blindness." A month later, the *Oakland Tribune* wasn't much kinder. "One cannot help but wish that Elena's personality could have come across without the clumsy treatment of someone trying to be literary," the paper's reviewer grumbled.

These critical misgivings had little effect on Elena's position in the culinary world. In 1960, she was asked to serve as a consultant for the New York restaurant La Fonda del Sol. Set to open that year, La Fonda del Sol was a high-end pan-Latin restaurant, with influences stretching from Mexico all the way down to Argentina. Elena took on the consulting gig at the behest of the culinary giant James Beard. The two had a mutual friend in Helen Evans Brown, the woman who had written the foreword to Elena's second cookbook. Beard, like Claiborne, was an enormously powerful figure in the food establishment. Through his many cookbooks, he taught Americans how to be epicures. Claiborne, for his part, used the occasion of Elena's visit to New York as another opportunity to profile her in the *New York Times*. He wrote of Elena as glowingly as he had two years earlier. When it came to cooking, Claiborne wrote, "There is no facet of the art beyond her grasp."

⌒

"I HAVE ALWAYS FELT that Elena learns more about a person through her fingers than most people do with their full senses," Beard would write in the introduction to Elena's final cookbook, *Elena's Favorite Foods California Style* (1967), published when she was 70 years old. Elena had been busy in the seven years since the publication of her memoir. She was overseeing the factory for her frozen food company while also consulting for both La Fonda del Sol and Lawry's Foods, a restaurant chain and seasoning company. *Elena's Favorite Foods California Style* gave her an opportunity to write about the cuisine of California, which had been her home for nearly six decades. The way Elena saw it, the state's food had been forged by the immigrants who lived there: people from China, Japan, various parts of Europe, and, yes, Mexico. Next to burritos and enchiladas in this cookbook were teriyaki lamb chops and arancini, or fried rice balls stuffed with Parmesan cheese. "It takes adventuresome people to uproot themselves and move to a new spot, and this spirit shows in the California approach to food," Elena wrote.

Around the time of the book's publication, new Mexican cookbooks were on the horizon. Entries included *The Art of Mexican Cooking* (1965), by Americans Jan Aaron and Georgine Sachs Salom, and *Mexican Cook Book* (1969), by the editors of *Sunset* magazine. These cookbooks were different from Elena's prior efforts in one crucial way: Their writers, often outsiders to Mexico, traveled to the country to document its foodways. The book from this emerging crop that captured the food media's attention the most, though, was Elisabeth Lambert Ortiz's *The Complete Book of Mexican Cooking* (1967). The *Los Angeles Times* praised the book for its "unique understanding of American kitchens to authentic recipes actually little known outside Mexico." Ortiz, a native of the United Kingdom, didn't know much about Mexican cooking until her husband, a Mexican diplomat, took a post at the United Nations Information Centre in Mexico City. But in the 1970s, another Brit would assume Elena's post of America's Mexican cooking authority: Diana Southwood, whom the world would come to know as Diana Kennedy. Like Ortiz, Kennedy was a native of Britain who took a meticulous approach to writing about the foods of Mexico. She'd met her husband, *New York Times* foreign correspondent Paul Kennedy, in Haiti in 1957 and moved with him to Mexico City. She was charmed by the mazes of Mexico City's marketplaces, brimming with "exotic chiles, herbs, and fruits of vibrant colors and aromas," as she would later write. When Craig Claiborne, then still at the *Times*, visited her in Mexico City, he urged her to write a Mexican cookbook. She may have been a stranger to Mexico, and a white one at that, but she worked with compensatory care. Her debut cookbook, *The Cuisines of Mexico* (1972), delivered on the promise in its title. There were divergent *cuisines*, plural, contained in this single country. Kennedy had recipes for duck in a green mole of pumpkin seeds, fish in caper sauce, and guava stuffed with coconut. She also had a low tolerance for compromise, insisting that making tortillas from scratch would be easy even for novices. This could have put off many American home cooks, but the food establishment enthusiastically welcomed Kennedy's contributions. Kennedy wrote with curiosity, not from a personal place as Elena did. She made few appeals to sentiment, instead striking a high-minded tone. This appearance of neutrality and rigor made Kennedy an easy figure for the establishment to trust. In his foreword to Kennedy's first book, Claiborne predicted that Kennedy's book "will probably rank as the definitive book in English on that most edible art." Just years before, he had called Elena's third book "the definitive volume on the subject" of Mexican cooking.

Elena died in March 1974, at age 76, succumbing to a stroke that left her in a convalescent home for months. At the time of her death, Elena's Food Specialties was serving all of northern California. Her first cookbook, published three decades earlier, had sold half a million copies.

More figures in Mexican cooking would follow Elena after her death. Some, like Barbara Hansen of *Mexican Cookery* (1980) and celebrity chef Rick Bayless, were white outsiders to Mexico like Kennedy. Others, like the chefs Zarela Martinez and Pati Jinich, were born in Mexico but immigrated to the United States as Elena once had. Hansen, in a tribute to Elena published in the *Los Angeles Times* the summer following her death, asserted that Elena's "recipes and happy philosophy live on in her four cookbooks and other writings." But this did not exactly happen: All fell out of print following her death.

In Elena, postwar America had found a homegrown ambassador for Mexican cooking at a time when it needed one, with a backstory that endeared her to the public. She provided a cheery face for a cuisine that Americans had once misunderstood. Granted, her popularity wasn't always about her food. The fixation on Elena's disability was evident in every headline: "Blind Cook to Feature Enchiladas," "Blind Cook to Display Her Skill," "Blind Cook Tells Happiness Recipes," read *Los Angeles Times* stories over three decades. And Elena was no cultural anthropologist; she, a Mexican woman, wrote in America and for Americans. Her comfort with assimilating into America may be one reason why her work hasn't had the stamina to outlive her, no matter how suited it was to her era. Many purists may now disregard her approach as accommodationist, but Elena was content to identify as American, and to have her food reflect that impulse. "What a wonderful place to be stranded," she recalled in one of the final interviews of her life, looking back on her unexpected childhood entry into San Francisco. "I love being an American."

INTERLUDE
JULIA CHILD, AMERICAN WOMAN

B. AUGUST 15, 1912, PASADENA, CALIFORNIA, USA
D. AUGUST 13, 2004, MONTECITO, CALIFORNIA, USA

JULIA CAROLYN McWILLIAMS heard many stories about France as a kid growing up in California. They were lies. Her father, an imperious conservative she called "Big John," liked to tarnish all Europeans as "dark" and "dirty." Never mind that he hadn't even been to the continent he spoke ill of. He made these judgments from the comfort of his home in Pasadena, California, the city where Julia was born in 1912. But Big John reserved an illogical portion of his ire for France. He abhorred the intellectualism that French people seemed to embody. Every encounter Julia had with French culture in America seemed to confirm that conditioning. The only people she knew from France were uptight spinsters. Thumbing through the pages of *Vogue* gave her the impression that French women were prickly things with tightly wound tempers. The movies of the American actor Adolphe Menjou, meanwhile, taught her to believe that French men existed only to treat women terribly or to outsmart unenlightened Americans. Julia feared that she'd stick out if she were ever to travel to France—her six-foot-two frame announced her difference immediately. Meanwhile, her boisterous personality had no hint of the French coyness she saw in movies.

Julia would go on to travel the world thanks to her work with the Office of Strategic Services during World War II, living in what was then Ceylon (now Sri Lanka) and China. Throughout this period, though, France remained little more than "a misty abstraction," she would later write, "a land I had long imagined but had no real sense of." Circumstance pulled Julia to France anyway. While abroad, she met a man named Paul Child, ten years her senior. He was a cosmopolitan man who'd worked in France during the 1920s, mastering the language and developing an appreciation for its food. Julia's move to France with Paul in 1948 punctured every fiction from her childhood. She discovered the true France. Its people weren't so mean, to start. French people seemed to treat her with the same respect they extended to their fellow citizens, looking upon Julia not as a foreigner but as a person. But France's most startling epiphanies arrived to her through food. Back in America, she didn't even know what shallots were. With Paul as her guide, though, she learned that cuisine in France was both high art and national sport. There was a palpable charge to the food there. She could taste the seawater in the Dover sole, which was more distinctive than the bland, broiled mackerel she had for Friday dinners in Pasadena. Parisian grapes had a soft, ephemeral sweetness, nothing like America's gracelessly cloying grapes. And she'd never quite had bread like a baguette, with its brittle crust and pillowy, pale yellow interior.

France showed Julia that food could be a portal to pleasure, not just a means for survival. Her interest in food grew so strong that by 1949, she enrolled in the famed culinary school Le Cordon Bleu at the suggestion of a friend. Her male classmates looked at her as some kind of trespasser, a woman in a man's world. But she bucked the sexist convention that only men should aspire to haute cuisine. Many Americans know what came next for Julia: She met two women, Simone (nicknamed "Simca") Beck and Louisette Bertholle, with whom she opened a cooking school called L'École des Gourmettes (later renamed L'École des Trois Gourmandes, or "The School of the Three Hearty Eaters") in 1952. It was Simca in particular who struck Julia. Simca was a fair, blonde woman with a stately demeanor. She hailed from Normandy and could speak at great length about her native region's cuisine. Simca and Louisette also involved Julia in a long-gestating project they had been working on, a French cookbook for American housewives. Who better than a real American, Simca and Louisette thought, to give that text its beating heart?

Julia eventually left France for America. She and Paul settled in Cambridge, Massachusetts, and Julia kept working on the book. The manuscript grew thicker than a bodybuilder's bicep. With time, a sharp-eyed Knopf editor named Judith Jones scooped it up and published the book as *Mastering the Art of French Cooking* (1961). The book opened up a thrilling possibility for Julia in America. A year later, she began filming the pilot for what would become *The French Chef*, a cooking show produced by Boston's public television station WGBH. It aired nationally for a decade. Julia established her celebrity through a cookbook, but she clinched it through television.

❧

JULIA CHILD'S ORIGIN STORY has been told so often, through so many media, that her life's plot points have congealed into an American myth. Her act of reverse immigration from France back to America fundamentally changed the way that her home country cooked, coaxing her home nation away from the tedium of Swanson TV dinners and Jell-O molds. In the process, she rewrote the script for stardom, living out a thrilling postwar fantasy where a home cook could become a household name.

Not everyone watched Julia on television because they wanted to cook. Many just wanted to watch *her*. Julia turned cooking into theater. Television put Julia's very American appeal on full display: her charm, her gaiety. Among Julia's most vital gifts was her ability to laugh at herself, as in one of her most enduring moments on television, when she half-heartedly tried flipping potatoes in a pan, only for most of them to spill onto the stove. She reassured viewers that they could always pick the potatoes up and put them back in the pan. Besides, if they were alone in the kitchen, who would even see? Julia was human, after all, a truth that's tempting to overlook when facing the gallery of impersonations she has spawned. Her quirks made her a target of parody, like the kind Dan Aykroyd played on *Saturday Night Live* in the late 1970s, yet over the decades, her greatness became indisputable. When the late Nora Ephron sought to cast the role of Julia for the film *Julie & Julia* (2009), it was only appropriate that she landed on the woman widely accepted to be America's greatest actress, Meryl Streep.

Still, cultural portrayals of Julia continue to accentuate her peculiarities. Sure, she was so tall that she once dreamed of being a basketball player; yes, her voice could travel scales in the span of a sentence. These perceived eccentricities, though, can obscure a very fundamental privilege she carried: Julia Child was American.

෴

JULIA HAD SPENT her California childhood actively avoiding the kitchen. Her mother, Carolyn, didn't cook much; when she did, those meals almost always required antacids. Thankfully, her family had a team of hired cooks. Julia belonged to what she would later call a "WASPy, upper-middle-class family" and grew up eating resolutely American dishes: roasted chicken with creamed spinach, mashed potatoes sweating with butter. She found them unspectacular. Cooking became a responsibility she couldn't forgo during her marriage. Just before she and Paul wed, she took cooking classes in Los Angeles. Her early meal attempts were resounding failures, like a nasty pile of calf's brains simmered in red wine. Once she and Paul settled in Washington, DC, Julia started to brave recipes she picked up from *The Joy of Cooking* or glossies like *Gourmet*. These cooking undertakings turned into hours-long ordeals with little payoff. She and her husband got used to going to bed hungry. France awakened the cook in her. When Julia wandered markets in Paris, she found curiosities like purple garlic and zucchini flowers. These ingredients lured her away from the canned goods of her Pasadena childhood. Le Cordon Bleu taught her to make spinach gnocchi and quiche lorraine. The fact that Julia was a late bloomer may have been a great virtue. As a recent convert to cooking, Julia could easily guide her audience—both readers and viewers—toward a life where cooking gave them purpose, just as it had for her.

⟆

JULIA DIDN'T EVEN own a television set when she first appeared before a camera in late 1961. Back in 1949, while she was still living in France, she'd begun hearing murmurs of this mysterious contraption causing a phenomenon over in America. But over a decade later, shortly after *Mastering the Art*'s publication in the fall of 1961, she received an offer to promote the book on the *Today* show with Simca, who came to New York from France to join her. Julia, then 49 years old, jumped at the opportunity. She and Simca had five minutes, and their self-assigned task was to prepare an omelet. Simca wasn't at ease in front of the camera, her English choppy once the camera began rolling. But Julia knew that wilting before the camera was not an option. She tried to have fun.

Deep down, she later confessed, Julia found the experience "simply terrifying." In any case, the segment widened her audience, as the show typically drew in four million viewers daily back then. Julia had already been a critic's darling—Craig Claiborne wrote that the book's recipes were "written as if each were a masterpiece, and most of them are," for example—but with her television debut, she was now on her way to becoming an idol for the masses.

Cooking shows were still grasping for a cogent identity back then. Personalities who preceded Julia tried to mix entertainment with education to varying degrees of success. James Beard hosted the first nationally aired cooking show, NBC's *Elsie Presents James Beard in I Love to Eat*, from 1946 to 1947. Beard's training as an actor seemed like more of a liability than an asset, resulting in an antsy screen presence. In 1947, the British chef Dione Lucas, the first female graduate of Le Cordon Bleu, started hosting *To the Queen's Taste* (later renamed *The Dione Lucas Show*) on WCBS in New York; it aired nationally, five nights a week, into the 1950s. But her detractors found her to have an air of stuffy British propriety. She was, in a word, foreign.

A mere handful of immigrant women had cooking television shows in that era beyond Lucas. Some, like Elena Zelayeta, hosted short-lived shows with local rather than national audiences. In the mid-1950s, the South African–born Poppy Cannon became known as the "can opener queen" as the host of an afternoon cooking segment of NBC's *Home* show. She tried her best to appeal to American viewers with French recipes reliant on convenience foods. Cannon would prepare vichyssoise, a French soup, from frozen mashed potatoes, a leek, and Campbell's cream of chicken soup. In the eyes of network executives, though, even these short-cuts made her recipes too "sophisticated" for American viewers, causing NBC to let her go shortly after.

American television was in need of a personality who could eliminate any sense of intimidation from French cooking. Julia radiated cheer, and unlike either Lucas or Cannon, she was American. In February 1962, the team at WGBH called Julia in for a cooking demonstration during *I've Been Reading*, a fixture of WGBH's Thursday night lineup. By then, *Mastering the Art* was in its third printing. She would again prepare an omelet, though this time she'd have thirty minutes, not five. The show tended to be dryly informative, and it featured mostly male academic guests, who were like its host, Professor Albert Duhamel. No one at WGBH was quite prepared for Julia. Just days before the taping, she called the producer, Russ Morash, and asked for a hot plate. It struck him as a ridiculous demand. Others on set had questions: How would they light a woman so tall? Would they be able to wrangle that voice into submission? But Julia commanded the screen anyway. She whisked two eggs and ladled them into a pan rubbed with butter. Julia managed to create a scene of utter bedlam in thirty seconds, pushing and pulling the pan from her body as if arm-wrestling a ghost. People on set were transfixed. Viewers had a similar reaction: Over the next month, a throng of callers to WGBH asked when the tall lady with the offbeat voice would return. The calls became so frequent that Bob Larsen, WGBH's program manager, began toying with the idea of giving Julia her own show. The team made the offer in April 1962, a few months before Julia turned 50. They decided to call the show *The French Chef*, which was short enough to fit on one line in *TV Guide*.

Truth be told, Julia didn't like it very much; she wasn't French, and she didn't really consider herself a chef.

Julia filmed her pilot episodes in a single day in June in a room in the auditorium of the Boston Gas Company. With Paul's help, she prepared pages of notes for her first day of shooting. They would shoot the episode live, with no leeway for retakes; the crew had the cameras for only a fixed amount of time. The initial episode began with a puddle of butter puttering in a pan in an extreme close-up. Moments later, eggs dropped into the pan. A fork handled by a pair of hands turned the glorious mess into an omelet. After Julia told the viewer about the omelet, the camera stepped back, revealing her face: "Hello. I'm Julia Child." When those three pilot episodes hit the airwaves in August, Julia nitpicked at them endlessly. She hated how she carried herself; she could see all of her rookie mistakes. Viewers disagreed. Fan letters began to flood WGBH's offices. Some appreciated Julia's mannerisms, the way her hands moved. Others loved her sense of intimacy, as if she was reaching out directly to the viewer. "I loved the way she projected over the camera directly to me," one admirer wrote. They all wanted more.

⁓

JULIA POSSESSED a unique qualification that allowed her to be a great teacher of French cooking for Americans: She carried no threat of the outsider. As Julia's fame grew, she understood that her American origins were a crucial component of why viewers listened to her. But imagine the inverse. Pretend that Julia was Juliette, that she'd grown up in the French Alps, that she'd come to America and tried to make a name for herself. Would she have been as famous? Julia pondered this herself. She thought, specifically, of her friend Simca, who'd been so instrumental to Julia's success. By 1964, *The French Chef* was airing in over fifty cities across the country, but Julia still found time to go back to France and visit Simca. Julia delicately avoided discussion of the show with Simca. The idea made Julia nervous, as if she had somehow done Simca wrong. Simca, who authored a number of cookbooks published in America, spent most of her life in France. "I felt that she was such a colorful personality, and so knowledgeable about cooking, that had she been American rather than French she would be immensely well known," Julia would later write. By then, Simca had been dead for years. Still, Julia wondered what could've been.

I Was a Good Fighter, Sister

Madeleine Kamman

B. NOVEMBER 22, 1930, COURBEVOIE, FRANCE

D. JULY 16, 2018, MIDDLEBURY, VERMONT, USA

ONE DAY IN March 1968, while Madeleine Kamman was leafing through the *New York Times*, she came upon a recipe she considered rubbish. It was for what Craig Claiborne referred to as "snails provençale on toast," or snails cooked briskly in a brew of tomatoes, garlic, shallots, butter, salt, and pepper and spooned over toast. Nonsense, Madeleine thought. She took Claiborne to task.

"Merci, merci, for advocating snails," her politely brutal missive to Claiborne began. "I have been an American for only eight years and still remember vividly and fondly the small sessions in my French home. We prepared them by the thousands, from scratch, and then there was a feast with Chablis." Madeleine went on to express her displeasure with Claiborne's recipe. As an alternative, she recommended a superior preparation from the French province of Languedoc. These were snails in a puree of braised lettuce kissed with hollandaise sauce, planted on a loaf of ficelle bread.

Madeleine's impassioned letter prompted Claiborne to pay a visit to her home in the Pennsylvania suburb of Huntingdon Valley, where her kitchen's walls were lined with copper saucepans made by her grandfather. "The Enthusiasm of Snail Addict Helps Turn a Meal into a Feast," the headline of Claiborne's profile of "Mrs. Alan Kamman" read. Her recipe for Cagaroulade de Montpellier ran in the May 23 edition of the *New York Times*, alongside another recipe for veal chops, also from Madeleine.

Madeleine was married and the mother of two young sons at the time of the story's publication. She taught cooking classes out of her home and in a nearby adult education center. It was only natural that she'd gravitate to the profession, she explained to Claiborne. Cooking coursed through her family's blood. Born Madeleine Marguerite Pin in November 1930, she was the only child of two laborers. She grew up understanding that cooking was more than women's work. It was an art.

Madeleine recognized this quality in her mother, Simone. Simone spent her days toiling away in a bicycle factory but still found time to prepare her daughter meals during her ninety-minute lunch breaks. Before returning to work, she'd peel potatoes by hand, fry them gently, and serve them to Madeleine with a bowl of mayonnaise puckered with lemon. Madeleine's aunt Claire Robert was another of the family's great chefs. Claire's two-Michelin star restaurant in Touraine, Hôtel des Voyageurs, had become a destination for Parisians. The family made routine pilgrimages there just to try her pâté of salmon and eel. Madeleine and her family moved to Touraine in June 1940 to escape the German army as its soldiers encroached upon Paris. Claire asked her 9-year-old niece to help in the kitchen, and Madeleine agreed, even though she was barely tall enough to see over the counter. Madeleine performed menial, but ultimately instructive, tasks. She would grind salt. She would peel ten pounds of green beans until her hands cramped.

She would hold the feet of rabbits and ducks that squirmed in her fingers as Claire slaughtered them. Madeleine came of age in the kitchen, inhaling every lesson Claire taught her. Claire could be short-fused, but Madeleine never saw Claire in terms of her anger. She was too enthralled with the woman's brilliance to care. When Madeleine wasn't working in the kitchen, though, she was always watching. As Claire kneaded pastry dough, Madeleine noticed how the older woman's face was suffused with calm, as if she'd found her life's calling in that moment. Another aspect of Claire also inspired Madeleine: Claire had a profound sense of justice. One day in 1943, Claire shielded two Jewish patrons from a prying police officer. She was angry that an outsider could intrude upon a site of refuge like her restaurant. Madeleine would later realize that Claire's moral integrity made her a feminist, even though Madeleine didn't have the words for it just yet.

ꞓ⸜⸝

AFTER THE WAR, Madeleine moved to Paris, where she studied languages at the Sorbonne. Cooking still beckoned: She attended both Le Cordon Bleu and L'École des Trois Gourmandes in the 1950s, working under Julia Child's collaborator Simone "Simca" Beck in the latter. Madeleine was a reservations manager for Swissair's Paris bureau when she met her future husband, Alan Kamman, in the summer of 1959. He was an executive at the Bell Telephone Company. Madeleine found Alan odd. Alan milled about for five minutes near her desk, repeatedly asking her to confirm his reservation. He then spent ten more minutes trying to ask her out to lunch.

Alan's peculiar charms worked on her. After marrying him in February 1960, she moved with him to Pennsylvania. She gave

birth to two sons, Alan Daniel in 1962, then Neil in 1966. Pennsylvania wasn't much like France. The language was different, the
music, practically everything. Even the buildings looked strangely
homogenized. But America offered culinary bounties. Madeleine
loved the lush farms of the Pennsylvania countryside, where she
picked vegetables on weekends. She could eat a whole lobster with
butter in America, not a measly claw like she was used to in France.
To ease her loneliness, she started to cook. Madeleine began
teaching out of her home and at Philadelphia's Adult Education
School in 1962, just after the birth of her first son. She showed students how to make dishes like rum raisin soufflés. Though Madeleine initially tried to teach recipes with exact measurements, her
students weren't learning much. So she decided instead to emphasize technique, taking time to explain chemical reactions between
ingredients. Having this foundational knowledge would allow her
students to express themselves in the kitchen. Following a recipe?
That wasn't cooking, Madeleine thought. That was just reading.

CLAIBORNE'S ARTICLE HELPED Madeleine secure a deal for a cookbook, which she began writing in 1969. That same year, the family moved to Lexington, a town on the outskirts of Boston. She
continued to teach as she wrote her cookbook. In September
1970, she established a cooking school, the Modern Gourmet,
in the nearby city of Newton. There, she taught nine different
courses. One explored French cuisine—students would make
egg-raised cakes, mousses, and crêpes—while another focused
on French provincial cuisine, covering regions like Alsace, Bur-
gundy, and Provence. But Madeleine also taught courses on
American cooking, which she admired for its diversity. "Yes,

there is an American gastronomy!" a 1970 class description in the *Boston Globe* read. "American dinners can be much more than meat and potatoes and this course will demonstrate the ethnic influences exerted on American cooking." Madeleine's cooking started evolving in this period, adapting to her American surroundings. She could take blueberries, a fruit that seemed ubiquitous in America, and whip them into a Bavarian cream that reminded her of her French home. She could look at a dish like succotash, with corn and lima beans, and give it a French lilt by adding chicken stock, a dash of sugar, and heavy cream. She could make crêpes Americana, using cornmeal for the batter and stuffing the pockets with corn, diced shrimp, Rock Cornish hen, and pine nuts. She didn't love everything about American cooking habits, though. Madeleine never quite took to microwave ovens, for example. "I have tried food that has gone through the oven and the flavors don't blend," she told the *Boston Globe*. "You can quote me as saying it tastes very virginal."

Madeleine tried to orient cooks away from convenience with her first cookbook, *The Making of a Cook* (1971). "Cooks who believe that 'another French cookbook' is just what we *don't* need can be assured that this is a book of a different kind," Madeleine wrote in her introduction. "What we need to keep from French cuisine is the peerless techniques." Cooks could apply those rules, she argued, to ingredients common in America like brown sugar or bourbon. In spite of her affection for flexibility, Madeleine also cared deeply about technique. These two ideas weren't as oppositional as they may seem on paper. She believed that cooks should master bedrock principles before fiddling with them. Only after harnessing the basics could a cook give a recipe a personal touch. One way to grasp those fundamentals, she felt, was to study history. "Something terrible happened to onion soup after it crossed the ocean and came to America," she humorously opened her chapter on stocks and soups. "Unless we cooks hurry and do something about it, the taste of this famous dish will be lost forever." The chapter splintered into a brief lesson on the origins of this dish derived from flat Champagne and onions in eighteenth-century Paris. Madeleine then explained how to make stock, a necessity for any cook.

The book sold only modestly, and its fixation on technique didn't register with all critics. Some regarded it as more of an encyclopedia than a cookbook, with those endless treatises on mayonnaise emulsification and how butter reacts to heat. Though her local paper, the *Boston Globe*, praised Madeleine as an "exuberant and unfettered" author, Nika Hazelton of the *New York Times* found it a total snooze. "The techniques used determine many of the chapter arrangements, such as 'dry-heat procedures,' a good teaching device, but hardly one that makes cooking a joy," Hazelton wrote of the book in December 1971. To her critics, Madeleine was blanching the fun out of cooking. More worrisome than any of these complaints, though, were the comparisons to Julia Child. In the *Los Angeles Times*, Jeanne Voltz claimed that Madeleine "borrows techniques but not recipes from the Julia Child books." And so it began.

❧

MADELEINE AND JULIA were no strangers. They shared a connection with Simca, after all. It was Madeleine who pursued a friendship with Julia. The two women met shortly after Madeleine moved to Lexington in 1969, just as Julia was finishing her manuscript for *Mastering the Art of French Cooking, Volume Two* (1970). Julia invited Madeleine and Alan over to dinner, while Madeleine did the same for Julia and her husband, Paul. "Madeleine Kamman and her husband came to dinner several weeks ago," Julia wrote

Simca in November 1969. "She is, obviously, very ambitious, and someone said that she intended to push us off the map!" (Simca and Madeleine, meanwhile, seemed to be on cordial terms; Madeleine even included Simca in the acknowledgments for *The Making of a Cook*.) Once Madeleine started teaching at the Modern Gourmet, though, she made clear that she wasn't a fan of Julia. A student wrote to Julia claiming that Madeleine forbade her students from watching *The French Chef* and ordered them to destroy their copies of *Mastering the Art of French Cooking*. Madeleine wasn't just asking Americans to respect French cooking; others, including Julia, had already accomplished that. She was asking Americans to respect the cooking of French women, a more complicated fight. She had every right to her anger, considering that Julia took to the press to trash the very people whom Madeleine honored in her work. "French women don't know a damn thing about French cooking, although they pretend they know everything," Julia complained to the *Washington Post* in November 1970. Madeleine was, quite literally, a French woman who cooked. And she was no pretender.

❦

IT WAS EASY TO MISS Chez La Mère Madeleine, a restaurant hiding in an alleyway in Newton Centre. In 1973, Madeleine launched the venue as a summertime offshoot of the Modern Gourmet, staffed by her more advanced students. Because of this affiliation, most people called the restaurant by the same name as the school. It would not open itself up to the public for another two years. Madeleine altered its menu every few weeks. She pulverized and pureed two varieties of imported French mushrooms to make a soup. She made a terrine from hazelnuts and rabbit and served it alongside goose liver pâté. She served a scallop casserole with heavy cream and tarragon. Madeleine began the restaurant out of a desire to empower the women working under her. She noticed how strenuously female chefs had to work to prove their worth in traditional restaurant kitchens, while men were exempt from such unspoken codes. She looked to one titan of cooking, Paul Bocuse, as evidence of this imbalance. Craig Claiborne wasn't exaggerating when he referred to Bocuse as "the king of chefs" in a June 1975 profile. The status gave him seeming license to flaunt his sexist leanings openly. "Women lack the instincts for great cooking," Bocuse told Claiborne. "It follows in the same sense that there are so few great women architects and orchestra leaders. Women who become chefs are limited in their accomplishments. They have one or two dishes they accomplish very well, but they are not great innovators." To Bocuse, female chefs could not be artists. In another interview he gave to *Newsweek* that year, Bocuse suggested that the only place for women was in bed. Madeleine's work stood as a counterargument to such oafish assertions. Bocuse himself would acknowledge this shortly after, when he referred to her restaurant as the best in the United States. Her genius was indisputable. To earn the respect of the Bocuses of the world, though, Madeleine still had to play by the food establishment's tired rules.

Madeleine worked hard to increase her profile through the 1970s. She appeared as a frequent guest on *Good Morning!*, an enormously popular and widely syndicated television talk show filmed in the Boston area (it is best known today as the precursor to ABC's *Good Morning America*). And Madeleine authored another cookbook, *Dinner against the Clock* (1973). It was more commercially successful than her first, though very much an outlier in Madeleine's oeuvre, considering its embrace of convenience. She filled the book with speedy preparations, like broiled steak with blue cheese and caraway butter that cooks could make in the span of ten minutes. Her lucid voice and principled methods still shone in this context, though. "This volume does not pretend to be the definitive book on quick cookery, for there is actually no quick cookery," she wrote. "There are only methods of cookery that allow one to prepare certain foods in a relatively short time."

Dinner against the Clock was precisely the kind of cookbook both the mass market and the food establishment wanted from Madeleine. That same year saw the debut titles of two fellow immigrant women, the Italian food writer Marcella Hazan's *The Classic Italian Cook Book* and the Indian actress and food writer Madhur Jaffrey's *An Invitation to Indian Cooking*. Both drew positive reviews for the careful ways in which the authors made non-American cuisines legible to American audiences. But French food didn't need structured decoding for audiences in the same way that Italian or Indian did; *Mastering the Art of French Cooking* had done that years before. Instead, Madeleine's effort shared oblique similarities with other general-interest cookbooks released that season, like the food writer Moira Hodgson's *The Campus Cookbook: Nutritious, Low Budget Meals*, meant for budget-strapped students; Glenn Andrews's *Impromptu Cooking*, which encouraged timid cooks to become confident with ad-libbing in the kitchen; and Bob Reinhart and Dick Woods's *The Cramped Quarters Cookbook*, on cooking in small kitchens. Like *Dinner against the Clock*, these books advised cooks to make do with what little they had. Perhaps it's no surprise that these titles have largely faded from public memory, while Hazan's and Jaffrey's books endure. This is not a reflection of the quality of these general cookbooks but rather a reminder of how fiercely of their time they were. For cookbook publishing in that era, accessibility reigned supreme.

Critics in the 1970s sure liked *Dinner against the Clock*. Nika Hazelton, the *New York Times* writer who had dinged *The Making of a Cook* for being too dense, was kinder to Madeleine's sophomore effort, hailing this "excellent book" as "one of the best I've seen in years." The book also won a coveted Tastemaker Award in the specialty cookbook category. But Madeleine herself thought it was "good-quality trash" in that it captured her sensibility but not her talent. Madeleine was souring on the food establishment and often found a tempting target in Julia. When an October 1974 article in the *Washington Post* characterized Madeleine as "an enemy" of Julia and Simca, Madeleine wrote to Julia saying that she was conspiring to bring down another woman. Julia did not respond. From that point forward, Julia instead had all letters that Madeleine wrote to her automatically forwarded to her lawyers.

Madeleine's focus on her work never wavered, even through her frustrations. She scaled her school to such a point by 1975 that she hired four auxiliary instructors. When it came to the corresponding restaurant, Madeleine found an early cheerleader in the *Boston Globe*'s food and wine critic, Anthony Spinazzola. He visited the restaurant in July 1975, shortly before its public opening. Spinazzola wrote that Madeleine "is fierce in protecting her classical patrimony but flexible enough to adapt it to this time and place." Once the restaurant opened to the public, critics all seemed to agree that it was revitalizing the Boston area's lethargic restaurant scene. Writing in the August 1976 issue of *Boston* magazine, critic Kathleen Fliegel bemoaned the dearth of great restaurants in and around the city. The lone exception, though, was Madeleine's restaurant, which was buoyed by a "single gifted personality, whose informing spirit permeates every aspect of the enterprise." Fliegel wrote of dishes like Madeleine's soupe aux escargots, with soft snails floating in a broth thickened with crème fraîche, and her apricot sherbet, the fruit's vibrant nectar accented by a raspberry sauce.

The restaurant conjured the France Madeleine once knew, a breathing document of a place whose memories were fleeting from her. She outfitted the restaurant's tables with pink and white linens and lined its red brick walls with copper pots. Madeleine went to great lengths to import ingredients, too: She got her mushrooms, $125 per kilogram, from a gatherer in France. (The restaurant wasn't cheap for the time, with weekend à la carte prices hovering in the $13 range for main courses.) Madeleine stood firm by certain rules: She never put a pinch of flour in any sauce. She never served more than sixty people in one evening, setting the pace of the restaurant's service intentionally slow. Madeleine believed that this leisurely tempo would let diners concentrate on their food. "This is the way we live in France, and this is the way we serve, and I won't have it any other way," Madeleine told Fliegel of her restaurant. Such nostalgia also animated Madeleine's opus, *When French Women Cook* (1976). If *Dinner against the Clock* was a strictly commercial play, *When French Women Cook* didn't kowtow to the pressures of the market. "I left France during the early days of 1960 and the France I left, my France, does not exist anymore; it has disappeared, slowly receding into time past," Madeleine opened the book. Her wistful tone saturated each page, creased with melancholy. "Where are you, my France," she asked, "where women cooked, where the stars in cooking did not go to men anxious for publicity but to women with worn hands stained by vegetables peeled, parched by work in house, garden or fields, wrinkled by age and experience. Where are you?"

The book's three-hundred-plus pages provided a firm answer:

These women were still alive in Madeleine's memory. Her writing would revive them. The book's eight chapters toggled between memoir and recipes, telling the story of French cuisine through eight different women Madeleine knew. She began with her great-grandmother, a mattress maker named Marie-Charlotte. Madeleine and Marie-Charlotte traveled to markets on Sunday mornings and bought hens with broken wings; Marie-Charlotte would poach the birds in vinegar sauce. Madeleine wrote of those summers during World War II in Claire's kitchen, too. She recounted the legends she'd heard of Eugénie, her maternal grandmother, who died when Simone was young. In the early 1940s, Madeleine trekked to the Alsatian village of Woerth where Eugénie once lived. There, she found Eugénie's treasured diaries and cookbooks, all written in German, containing stories of Eugénie's Jewish lover whom her disapproving father forced her to abandon.

The stories of these women revealed struggle; not all of them had happy endings. What bound the narratives, though, was the strength the women carried. The hardships that life handed these women inspired their creative output. The way Madeleine saw it, each woman recorded her resilience in recipes: Marie-Charlotte in her lemon crullers, Claire in her steamed calf's livers, Eugénie in her sauerkraut soup. Such women were the rightful authors of French cooking. The book read like a retort to both Julia Child's earlier charge that French women didn't know a thing about French cooking and Paul Bocuse's pronouncement that women had no artistic prowess in the kitchen. (In a sly gesture, Madeleine dedicated the book to Bocuse's grandmother and mother.) Bocuse, Julia, even Madeleine herself—everyone owed a debt to these women. With this book, Madeleine was redressing the injustice of time nearly erasing these women's art. Such a fate could easily befall any woman.

~

AS THE DECADE PROGRESSED, Chez La Mère Madeleine continued to receive stellar press. In December 1977, when the writer Laurie Devine of the *Boston Globe* gushed that it was "simply the best restaurant in Boston," Devine was essentially parroting accepted wisdom. The respect for the restaurant radiated beyond Boston. In writing about her restaurant, James Beard called Madeleine "a woman of firm convictions, a perfectionist who imbues her students with her single-minded dedication to the cause of good cooking."

None of this critical jubilation could stave off Madeleine's languor. Money was one issue. The restaurant may have become a critics' darling, but Bostonians just didn't get her food. Patrons would complain, for example, that they didn't understand why her pureed scallop mousseline didn't have chunks of scallops in it. At times, the city felt shockingly illiberal. Madeleine constantly battled the misperception that she was too snooty for Boston. Maybe, she surmised, Boston was just uncomfortable with a woman who spoke her mind. To Madeleine, few figures embodied Boston's orthodoxy more than Julia. In a letter she wrote to Julia in 1979, Madeleine told Julia that she could no longer handle Boston. Indeed, Julia's supremacy over the Boston food community reflected a greater national mood: Julia was beyond reproach, and criticizing her came with consequences. Former *New York Times* food writer John Hess and the culinary historian Karen Hess, who were married to each other, knew this reality all too well. In their book *The Taste of America* (1977), the couple harshly critiqued Julia, along with figures like Bocuse and Claiborne, for what the Hesses felt was an embarrassing lack of culinary acuity. The Hesses chided Julia for her trashing of French women, which they found sexist. To the Hesses, Julia's ascent to fame exposed the shortcomings of the American mind. "She is not a cook, but she plays one on TV," the couple wrote.

Madeleine, by comparison, was the real deal to the Hesses. They pointed to Madeleine's *The Making of a Cook* as a "serious work" on French cooking and questioned why the inferior *Dinner against the Clock* met more success. "One can only conclude that cookbook buyers do not really want to learn to cook, they want to look up a fancy recipe, and presto!, dazzle their guests," the Hesses judged. *The Taste of America* was read widely enough to cause consternation within the highest ranks of the industry. The book's contrarianism also made the Hesses unpopular with the food establishment. Madeleine, with her open criticisms of Julia, was flirting with a similar fate. "Her bluntness has not endeared her with the U.S. food establishment and her successes have come in spite of them, not with their aid," observed trade publication *Nation's Restaurant News* just before her move back to France. She was 49, "a rough age at which to start over again," the publication added. It was clear that Madeleine would be leaving a vapor trail of bitterness behind her in America.

Madeleine's husband, then a vice president at the consulting firm Arthur D. Little, stayed stateside and planned to visit her every third week. Their older son, Alan Daniel, was already in college, and their younger son, Neil, would accompany Madeline to France. So Madeleine sold the stock of her restaurant to her students. She got rid of some six hundred books. She took her grandfather's copper pots with her and traveled back across the Atlantic to a village called Annecy, in the southeast of France. Madeline outlined a systematic plan: She would set up a functioning cooking school and follow it with a three-star restaurant staffed entirely by women.

To her relief, she would be around French ingredients again.

Madeleine missed them in America, missed their purity. "I want strawberries that taste like strawberries, not formaldehyde," Madeleine told the *Washington Post* in July 1979. "I want unpasteurized milk for my cheeses. I want to work with fresh foie gras." The *Boston Globe*, which had once held up Madeleine as an exemplar of what the area's food scene could achieve, took her move as a sign of snobbery. "Too Good for Boston?" asked the headline of a March 1980 article by Alison Arnett. "She's created a legend of sorts in Boston, Madeleine Kamman has, famed for her audacity as well as for her exquisite cooking," Arnett opened the article. The word order was revealing: Madeleine's exquisite cooking was secondary to her audacity. "I am a feminist," Madeleine told Arnett. She added that very few people would've seen her as arrogant had she been a man "with a great big phallic symbol on my head," referring to a toque. Madeleine dared to be an artist in a man's territory, and no one took her seriously, she told Arnett. Madeleine wondered what people in the city would have to talk about once she left. "Does that sound unreasonable what I said about Boston?" she asked Arnett. "Do I sound like such a bitch?"

MADELEINE WOULD LAST just four years in France, not five as she planned. When she arrived in Annecy in the summer of 1980, she felt as if she'd stepped into an oasis at the foothills of the Alps. Surrounding her were peaches so red they looked as if they were bleeding, butter with the scent of sour grass, and rose quartz grapes. Annecy was an undisturbed little hamlet, free of the racket that drove her mad in Boston. There was nothing to distract Madeleine in Annecy, no one to criticize her, so at last, she could focus on her work. Madeleine started writing a fourth cookbook. She opened her cooking school in October of that year, deliberately keeping classes tiny; she usually taught thirty students in Boston, but in France, she would teach no more than six. The distance from America gave her clarity of purpose. "Only the French know how to teach French cooking," Madeleine told the writer Patricia Wells, who paid a visit to the school for a January 1981 article in the *New York Times*. "When you try to teach a cuisine that is not your own, there is always one dimension missing." Madeleine even recognized the limitations of her own hand in this regard. Her attempts at any dish from the American South would always feel inadequate, she told Wells, as if they were missing their heartbeat. But France didn't blunt Madeleine's sharp edges. Her classes were rigorous. One student would state that she had to pop an aspirin every afternoon during the two-week summer session. Her perfectionism earned her plaudits: The magazine *Bon Appétit* would hail Madeleine's school as "France's Best Cooking School" on the cover of its February 1982 issue.

With more time, though, the luster of Annecy wore off. Madeleine realized that France had more in common with America than she remembered: Most chefs at the top of restaurant hierarchies in France were, indeed, men. Food was still a man's game wherever she went. Plus, France's political climate made her uneasy; she was a Gaullist at her core, yet once the Socialist government of President François Mitterrand came to power, "the whole economy, everything, slipped back into the Middle Ages," she would later claim to *Cook's* magazine.

She never did open that fabled three-star restaurant, either. Madeleine decided to close her school in September 1983, citing an unreasonable tax upon her income. Unfortunately, she'd booked her classes through 1986, so she decided to give those would-be students their deposits back and return to America. Her collection of cookbooks, which she'd whittled down to three hundred, came with her across the Atlantic. This time, she settled in Glen, New Hampshire, a place she'd always liked. Madeleine spent the fall of 1983 teaching cooking across North America while gearing up for the release of her fourth book, *In Madeleine's Kitchen* (1984). As Madeleine toured the United States, one article in the *St. Louis Post-Dispatch* characterized her as a "mellowed" woman, a reformed firebrand whose failures in France humbled her. "Ooh la la, don't worry," she casually told a student who asked about the precise measurement of an ingredient. "Do what you want. Forget the recipe. Vary it with the vegetables and herbs you have in your garden."

In her fourth cookbook, Madeleine wrote candidly of her tribulations as a woman in Boston and beyond. "I became very controversial, which probably meant that I was in a place I was not supposed to be," she wrote of her Boston years. "I had transcended the limits imposed on women by generations of professional chefs and found myself succeeding in a so-called male profession." With an introduction by James Beard, *In Madeleine's Kitchen* dignified women's labor, just as Madeleine's previous books had. But she didn't restrict herself to French women this time. Instead, Madeleine celebrated "the enormously rich font of cuisine provided by all the women in the world" as she wrote in the early pages of the book. "One look at the cuisine of all nations will reveal that it exists everywhere: in the Orient, in the Islamic countries, through Africa, all over the Americas, and all over Europe." Her outlook—partly rejuvenated "by foreign and ethnic ingredients"—resulted in recipes like galantine of duck with Szechuan pepper and fresh, blanched green Madagascar peppercorns. Though the cookbook generated favorable reviews, with Marian Burros of the *New York Times* writing that Madeleine's "technical explanations are unrivaled," its text-heavy nature narrowed its appeal. Glossy cookbooks with high production values clasped attention more readily. This book got Madeleine a nomination for a Tastemaker Award, the same award she'd gotten for *Dinner against the Clock*, but she didn't win this time. She complained to the press that the awards went to coffee-table books with flashy photographs like that year's big winner, *Giuliano Bugialli's Foods of Italy* (1984) by the eponymous Italian food writer.

Madeleine then tried her hand at a medium other than writing, one that would give her an entirely different form of recognition: She filmed a "video cookbook" in 1983 called *Madeleine Kamman Cooks*. The two-and-a-half-hour VHS cassette sold for $89.95. As she had with *In Madeleine's Kitchen*, Madeleine brought a globally inclusive approach to these cooking segments: She made saffron, spinach, and beet pastas; she took cues from the Caribbean to make shrimp Martinique, a salad of sautéed shrimp with cantaloupe and avocados tossed in a dressing of lime juice and rum and topped with scallions. The videotape, which sold over ten thousand copies by November 1985, allowed Madeleine's gospel to reach viewers across the country. Her instructions weren't always easy, but critics found her screen presence disarming. "Now she is on video, a medium that activates her the way sugar activates yeast," observed *People* magazine in March 1985. "Cheerful and motherly in a hairdo that looks like a silver turban, she whisks the viewer along with the swift, Gallic cadences of her surprisingly girlish but confident voice."

After she filmed the episodes for the video, Madeleine opened a new version of her cooking school and its corresponding restaurant, L'Auberge Madeleine, in November 1984. The school and restaurant were situated in the middle of the woods in New Hampshire. She accepted eight American students for a regimented class that would last just under a year. No matter what Madeleine accomplished, the comparisons to Julia Child were unrelenting. After all, Julia sealed her stardom on television, the very medium Madeleine was now entering. "Negotiations are underway to bring Kamman to PBS sometime this year," noted *People* in its review of *Madeleine Kamman Cooks*. "She has the ingredients to be TV's next Julia Child."

❧

MADELEINE COOKS, an offshoot of the earlier videocassette series, was produced by Maryland Public Television and began airing on PBS in January 1986. On the show, Madeleine made "American fare with French flair," as one critic put it, including dishes like an "Oriental" salad with turkey, orange, and kiwi in a Szechuan peppercorn dressing. Madeleine had no delusions about her stint on television. In 1989, she would refer to her show as "me on the lowest level I can go." Still, the show maintained a steady enough viewership to last until 1991. In this period, Madeleine published two more cookbooks. *Madeleine Cooks* (1986) was a tie-in to the television show, with recipes drawing inspiration from around the globe: Tunisian-style broiled chicken, American roast duck with cranberries and kumquats, a Provençal rice salad. *Madeleine Kamman's Savoie* (1989), meanwhile, was proudly French, focusing on the cuisine of the region of Savoie in southeastern France. She wrote at great length of Savoie's history, its culture, and its people. That same year, an enticing offer to serve as the director of the School for American Chefs at Beringer Vineyards pulled Madeleine away from New Hampshire to Napa Valley, California. Madeleine spent most of the 1990s teaching and working on one final cookbook, *The New Making of a Cook* (1997), an update to the 1971 text. *The New Making of a Cook* exceeded a thousand pages and distilled her technique-driven sensibility more fully than any of her previous cookbooks, while incorporating recipes responsive to trends of the era, like low-fat cooking. The book fared well, netting her the James Beard Award for Book of the Year in 1998, and the foundation also gave her its Lifetime Achievement Award that same year. By that point, however, members of the food media seemed to agree that Madeleine did not become the star her talents could have made her. The food writer Molly O'Neill profiled Madeleine in January 1998, just two years before Madeleine taught her final class and retired for good. "Despite a public television series, tireless teaching, and prolific writing, celebrity status has always eluded her," O'Neill wrote. "Ms. Kamman remains a cook's cook." Madeleine recognized that she was an acquired taste. "I wasn't cut out for celebrity," she told O'Neill. Time, it seemed, tempered her anger. "I was a good fighter, sister," Madeleine continued. "Now, I cultivate peace and forgiveness."

⁓

IN MADELEINE'S LIFETIME, journalists were eager to append her with adjectives that now read as sexist dog whistles: abrasive, arrogant, feisty, imperious, temperamental, and, perhaps the most damning descriptor of all, difficult. The food media was usually less interested in Madeleine's many achievements than in her professional disagreements with Julia. It seemed that the press often did the patriarchy's bidding, pitting the two women against each other. In the long run, this framing arguably had a more damaging effect on Madeleine's legacy than on Julia's. "We note now, too, that Madeleine Kamman is no icon," mused scholar Sara Lewis Dunne in 2006. Dunne predicted that "no genuinely mournful television wakes" would mark Madeleine's passing as they did for Julia. The premonition, however cruel, turned out to be correct. When Madeleine died in July 2018 after a decade of deterioration from Alzheimer's, there were no Food Network paeans to her. The food media's ugly characterizations of Madeleine may have prevented her progressive, avowedly feminist message about French cooking from reaching more Americans. But in airing her grievances with the industry so openly, Madeleine gave permission to a generation of younger women to follow her lead, to be angry, to agitate in public. Today, perhaps the path to celebrity would be less rocky for a woman like Madeleine, at least one who carries the privileges of being white and European. But Madeleine herself knew that chasing fame was the American way. She wanted no part of that circus. "America has a tendency toward stardom," she told the author David Kamp in 2006, well after her career had come to a close. "I never wanted to be a star, and I resisted it very strongly by saying what I thought all the time. I'm not a very popular person. But you know what? So what!"

As Words Come to a Child

Marcella Hazan

B. APRIL 15, 1924, CESENATICO, ITALY

D. SEPTEMBER 29, 2013, LONGBOAT KEY, FLORIDA, USA

WHEN SHE WAS 7, Marcella Polini fell on the beach and broke her right arm. It was 1931, and she and her Italian family were living in the Egyptian city of Alexandria. The employees at the city's Italian hospital, named for Benito Mussolini, jacketed her arm in a cast that stretched from her shoulder to the tips of her knuckles. They told her to return in a week. The pain didn't subside after a few days, though, and she couldn't stop crying. The color of her hand began to dull. Her doctor removed the cast, revealing a gangrenous arm that resembled a rotting peach. The doctors suspended her arm up high, tied to the rod of a mosquito net attached to the bed. The swelling did not recede. Her injury grew larger, fiercer. Marcella's doctor told her mother, Maria, that he had no choice but to amputate Marcella's arm. Maria refused. She'd heard promising things about an orthopedic surgeon named Dr. Putti in Bologna, so she booked the first boat to Italy the next morning. Dr. Putti told Maria that repairing Marcella's arm would call for a miracle. After repeated surgeries, Putti and his team managed to salvage most of Marcella's arm, though she couldn't extend it beyond a ninety-degree angle. Her hand would assume an ungainly permanent posture from that point forward, refusing to fully straighten. As she grew older, Marcella trained herself to write with her left hand, putting herself through the ritual of growing up all over again. Her multiple surgeries forced the family to move back to Cesenatico, the fishing town where she had been born, located in the Italian region of Emilia-Romagna. Marcella was ashamed of that claw at her side and had to put up with the taunts of her classmates in grade school. When she became interested in boys, she did all she could to hide her disability, sheathing her arm in shawls that matched the color of her dresses. Marcella feared what would happen if she ever married and had a baby. Maybe she'd accidentally drop her child. But that hand was still functional. At least she could grip a knife with it.

⌁

FOR THE FIRST FEW DECADES of her life, Marcella was more of an eater than a cook. Before World War II broke out in Italy, good food surrounded her, so much that she took its pleasures for granted. Marcella would spend her days idling away at gelato parlors. She'd frequent shacks that sold piadina, a yeastless flatbread crisped over a terra-cotta griddle, the smoke giving the nutty dough some tang.

The war changed the tenor of Marcella's day-to-day life. She was just 16 in September 1940 when she and her family moved to a farmhouse on Lake Garda, in a town north of Cesenatico called Desenzano. The sole source of heat was a wood-burning stove. The kitchen became a sanctuary for Marcella during that brutally cold winter as she and her family members fed the stove.

The family initially hoped Desenzano would insulate them from the war's horrors; instead, the neighboring town of Salò became the de facto capital of Mussolini's fascist republic. All Marcella could think about was when the next air raid would strike, whether she'd survive it, and if she'd be able to find anything to eat afterward. The German army, allies of Mussolini, sequestered most people's food. Marcella's parents ground whatever wheat they had into flour to make bread; they snuck some corn from the farm to make polenta. Salt was especially scarce. Zia Margò, her maternal aunt who lived in Venice, would send the family bags of salt boiled down from lagoon water. Marcella and her parents would keep a portion of the salt for themselves, bartering the rest to survive. One time, they swapped some salt for a piglet. Marcella's parents gave her the task of preparing a gruel to fatten up the piglet for slaughter. She searched for mulberry leaves in her vineyard, finding that the leaves had been chalked with dust from bombs. She washed the leaves with vigor, until no trace of the explosives remained. She then chopped the leaves and boiled them with water and polenta flour.

In the event of air raids, Marcella and her parents took their dinner plates with them as they went to a nearby shelter, careful not to let plaster from the bombs fall on their food. The horrors of her present supplanted the images of her past. Marcella could barely remember what it was like to eat before the war began: to eat in pursuit of pleasure, not in a bid for sustenance.

～

MARCELLA AND HER PARENTS emerged from the war physically unscathed. They finally returned to Cesenatico in May 1945, following the surrender of the German army in Italy, but they discovered that their house had practically been destroyed by dynamite. Her father, Giuseppe, and a few bricklayers he knew rebuilt the house. It took Marcella time to readjust to the life she once knew, but she found small comforts in food. She was once again surrounded by familiar ingredients: puckered tomatoes, plump persimmons, Albana grapes that looked like golden teardrops. During the holiday season that winter, Marcella savored cotechino, a creamy boiled sausage made from the pig's hide. She had eaten it only once during the war.

Over the next few years, Marcella made her education her primary focus. By 1954, she ended up getting dual doctorates in the natural sciences and biology from the University of Ferrara, which she reached by train. In her final years of school, she found a job teaching math and biology to aspiring elementary school instructors in the town of Rimini, a few miles south of Cesenatico. She met Victor Hazan through a friend in 1953, when she was still in school. Marcella found him charismatic, though in an unusual way. He looked like a teenager to her, this wiry man with a mop of black hair. Most Italians were garrulous, their thoughts gushing out of them. Victor, though, was a quiet man who spoke in spare sentences, giving force to each word. Victor had a complicated relationship with Italy. Though he was born in the town of Cesena, not far from Cesenatico, he and his parents, who were Sephardic Jews, moved to New York in the spring of 1939, just before the war reached Italy. An illness caused him to abandon plans to study literature in college. Instead, Victor worked for his father's fur business. He returned to Italy after nearly a decade and a half in New York, hoping to reacquaint himself with the home he left behind. What stimulated Victor, more than anything, was food. He could speak of the seafood of the Romagna coast, the tastes of its sole and monkfish, as if nothing else in the world mattered. And Victor cooked often. Upon settling in Italy, he purchased a copy of food writer Ada Boni's tome *Il talismano della felicità,* or *The Talisman of Happiness* (1928), and embarked on ambitious cooking projects. To make a dish of Roman-style snails with tomatoes and anchovies, he captured snails, starved them, and then subjected them to a pan of water so hot that they wiggled out of their shells. For another recipe, he sautéed sweetbreads with butter, onions, and prosciutto before boiling them in a broth of veal bones and meat scraps, serving them with fresh porcini mushrooms he'd cooked in olive oil, garlic, and parsley. Marcella didn't have anything close to that kind of relationship to cooking. She knew only how to make gruel for pigs.

⌒

VICTOR DIDN'T HAVE A JOB when he and Marcella wed in February 1955 in Cesenatico. Marcella's meager income from teaching was barely enough to sustain them. Weeks later, though, Victor's parents persuaded him to return to New York. A job would be waiting for him at his father's fur business. He returned to New York that summer while Marcella stayed behind in Italy, preparing for the move. At the end of the summer, she boarded the SS *Cristoforo Colombo* alone for a ten-day journey to New York. She was hopeful, perhaps naively so, that day in September 1955 when Victor picked her up from the pier and hailed a taxi from Manhattan to his apartment in Forest Hills, Queens. From the car window, New York seemed utterly arresting to Marcella: a city flanked by two rivers, with buildings so tall that they seemed to brush the sky. But the cab soon made its way to Queens, a borough that felt like a different universe. Marcella hated it. The apartment building that Victor's parents owned looked like a shapeless slab of bricks. Marcella stepped inside the elevator, a contraption she'd never encountered, and felt as though its walls were choking her. Victor's fifth-floor apartment wasn't very welcoming, either. The bedroom had a bulky bed and a bookcase slathered in green paint. There was a television set, another unfamiliar invention. Marcella was especially startled to see that she and Victor had a refrigerator of their own. In Cesenatico, Marcella was used to sticking food in an icebox during the summer; in the winter, she'd set a box made of wire netting outside a window. In that moment, Marcella felt the weight of all she'd left behind in Italy: her family, her job, her life.

Another hurdle came with feeding herself. Eating out regularly wasn't an option. It was too expensive, and Marcella had a stubborn stomach. Victor took Marcella to a café in her first few days in America, hoping to introduce her to a hamburger. When he poured ketchup over the meat, Marcella was appalled. She could not comprehend the American impulse to pollute a dish with such sweet sludge. The coffee tasted like water that had been used to clean a coffee pot. She ordered a "coffee cake" under the mistaken impression that its batter would be laced with coffee. Instead, it had the clobbering taste of cinnamon, a spice she despised, and enough sugar to fill a candy store.

There was only one way for Marcella to survive in this country: learn to cook. American supermarkets flummoxed her, with their produce and meats suffocating in plastic. The poor tomatoes were subjected to chemical malpractice in America—gassed, transported over a long distance, then hastened back to life like zombies. Some foods were even *frozen*, to her shock. But the words of Ada Boni, the author whose cookbook Victor used so often back in Italy, ferried her back to the home she so missed. As she read the instructions in Boni's recipes, Marcella pictured her mother, her grandmothers, and her father in the kitchen. Cooking, she would later write, made her feel "as though I were telling a story I had heard as a little girl in another land."

She began modestly, with soups made from potatoes and

leeks, or cannellini and parsley. She worked her way up to frying, sheathing slices of zucchini in pastella, a batter of flour and water. Marcella had some real duds in those rookie days, like the breaded veal cutlets she served with a side of oversalted canned peas tossed in butter and diced ham. Thankfully, Victor was an honest critic. The two spent their nights sitting at their dining table cautiously consuming Marcella's experiments. With time, Marcella realized there had always been a cook inside her. Her skills had just been searching for articulation; displacement gave them shape. When she set her mind to the task, cooking came to her "as words come to a child when it is time for her to speak," she would later say.

❧

ONE IMPEDIMENT kept Marcella from adjusting to America: English. The language sounded odd to her. She could not make sense of where one word stopped and the next began. As summer turned to autumn in 1955, she looked to that funky machine, the television, to teach her English. She watched Brooklyn Dodgers games: Pitcher, batter, ball were some of her first words. Victor then enrolled Marcella in a six-week intensive English program at Columbia University, a borough away in Manhattan, but her English barely improved. The other students already had some working knowledge of the language, unlike Marcella. In spring 1956, Marcella and Victor left the lonely enclave of Forest Hills and moved to upper Manhattan, close to Victor's work. The move rejuvenated Marcella. She even managed to find a job doing dental research, in spite of her unease with the English language. English was all she heard anyone speak for the hours in the office, opening up a new avenue for her to understand the language.

Marcella quit her job in early 1958 when she became pregnant. The couple's son, Giuliano, was born on the first day of December. As the years passed, New York started to make both Marcella and Victor miserable: Marcella was stuck in her apartment with her child, while Victor found work unfulfilling. On a whim one day, Victor suggested that they move back to Italy. Marcella agreed—at least she would be able to speak in her mother tongue again. In June 1962, the family of three boarded a plane to Milan. Back in Italy, Victor steadied himself with work as a copywriter at advertising agencies, allowing him to exercise his gifts as a writer. Marcella, meanwhile, had a tough time finding work as a teacher, having fallen behind in the profession during her years in New York. Instead, she lost herself in cooking. She bought red beets the size of oranges and served them with salt, wine vinegar, and olive oil. She prepared frittatas with asparagus. She cooked mackerel in olive oil, garlic, and rosemary. Being in Italy gave her clarity as a cook. Her taste memories, the ones she had grown so reliant upon in her kitchen in America, were real.

The family ended up spending only five years in Italy. Victor's parents, looking to retire, lured him back to New York with an attractive promise. They wanted his help with selling the fur business. If Victor found a buyer, he, too, would be able to retire. Marcella complied, and they set off once again for New York in 1967.

⟨⟩

PEARL'S WAS THE GATEWAY. The Chinese restaurant, named for its proprietor Pearl Wong, opened in 1967 in mid-Manhattan and became a favored hangout for the city's theater crowd. After repeated trips there with her father-in-law, Marcella became a fan, too. Wong's inspired takes on Cantonese home cooking intrigued Marcella. She promptly enrolled in a Chinese cooking class taught by Shanghai-born Grace Zia Chu, author of *The Pleasures of Chinese Cooking* (1962). After the first session, however, Chu abruptly announced she'd soon be taking a sabbatical in China. The other students, wondering what they'd do without her, got to talking. One asked Marcella what she tended to cook at home. "Normal food," Marcella said. When a classmate asked her what that meant, she replied that normal food was risotto with porcini mushrooms. Normal food was tagliatelle alla bolognese; it was Venetian sautéed calf's liver with onions. During the next session, that same student asked Marcella if she had any teaching experience. Certainly, Marcella replied. She'd taught back in Italy, after all. A few sessions later, that student gave Marcella the names and phone numbers of six other women who wanted to learn Italian cooking from her. "American women are crazy," she told Victor after returning from class. "Look what they asked me." But Victor encouraged Marcella. She had proven herself to be an able teacher in Italy, and she clearly loved cooking. It's not as if she had a job, either.

Sure. She'd do it. It was October 1969 when Marcella started hosting classes once a week out of her apartment. She bought separate sets of knives and cutting boards for each student. Her students somehow squeezed themselves into her tiny kitchen, where Marcella showed them how to prepare pasta, risotto, soup. Marcella made one point clear in her classes: There was no monolithic Italian cuisine. "Italian cooking" was a phrase that captured the diversity of regional tradition: Neapolitan linguine with clams, Florentine soup of beans and black cabbage. Some of her students were quite squeamish, however. A few were unaccustomed to consuming lamb kidneys, for example, while others didn't want to touch raw squid. Marcella saw each class as its own fight: If she could get just one student to stir squid into her risotto, then she'd won a small battle. The classes stretched from October 1969 to June 1970, the equivalent of a scholastic year. Though she had initially been resistant to the idea, Marcella realized she liked teaching cooking. She wanted to keep going. That August, Victor wrote to the *New York Times* food section, asking the paper to include her class in its list of cooking schools. They were too late; the list had already gone to the printer.

It was just a temporary setback. A few weeks later, Marcella received a phone call from a stranger. He was from the *New York Times*, he said, and he wanted to interview her. She obliged, inviting him over for lunch on a weekday when Victor would be around. Marcella didn't quite catch this man's name. Maybe Greg? It was Craig Claiborne, Victor told her. Knowing the stakes were high, Marcella decided to make a meal that would impress him. She prepared upside-down artichokes, tortelloni with Swiss chard and ricotta, veal rolls jammed with pancetta and Parmesan cheese, a salad of sliced finocchio, and, for dessert, cold oranges marinated with sugar.

Marcella treated Claiborne like a guest coming over for a meal, not a journalist. Her charms worked on him. "There Was a Time She Couldn't Cook..." read the headline of a half-page story in the *Times* on October 15, 1970. It ran with a photo of Marcella leaning over the table as Victor beamed before his plates of food. The article ran with four recipes: two for the tortelloni and the artichokes she served him at that meal, plus others for chicken breasts Siena-style and spaghetti with thin slices of eggplant. Claiborne attached Marcella's phone number to the article. A swarm of prospective students called. Marcella wouldn't have to worry about staying busy from that point forward.

A year later she received a call from Peter Mollman, an editor at Harper & Row, who had seen a listing for her cooking school in the *Times*. He'd just taken a trip to Italy and was yearning to re-create some of the meals he'd eaten there, but he was having trouble finding adequate recipes. Mollman asked Marcella if she'd ever thought of writing a cookbook. No, she replied, as she could barely write in English. But Victor, overhearing the conversation, insisted that writing in English wouldn't be a problem. He'd be able to translate for her, for his English was smoother than hers. A contract came days later.

America was long overdue for a cookbook like Marcella's. Back in the 1950s, Ada Boni's cookbooks became bibles for American housewives, especially middle-class ones hoping to sprinkle their dinner parties with global flavor. Boni's *The Talisman Italian Cook Book* (1950), the American translation of her *Il talismano della felicità* (1928), featured recipes that many Americans were likely ignorant of: fish brodetto in the style of Rimini, pork chops in the style of Modena. Still, many Americans saw Italian food through the prism of restaurant food. Nominally Italian restaurants had been around in cities like New York since the late nineteenth century, though they mostly catered to Bohemian classes. Italian cooking, like its people, could face great prejudice in early twentieth century America. In 1939, for example, a *Life* magazine story on the baseball star Joe DiMaggio, the California-born child of Italian immigrants, noted that he "never reeks of garlic," as if the scent would mark him a pariah. To broaden their appeal, restaurateurs in the twentieth century began serving Italian-inspired preparations like manicotti or spaghetti and meatballs. They bore, at best, a passing resemblance to the dishes Marcella had known and cherished in Italy. In the realm of the home, meanwhile, Americans clung to convenience foods. Shortly before World War II, for example, the Italian immigrant chef Hector Boiardi created Chef Boyardee, a canned pasta. In 1961, the San Francisco–born entrepreneur Vincent DeDomenico started selling Rice-A-Roni, a package of rice, vermicelli, and dried soup.

Cookbook authors struggled to show American home cooks that there was more to Italian food. The American edition of English food writer Elizabeth David's *Italian Food* (1958) highlighted the regional nature of Italian cooking, yet it was more of a success in the United Kingdom, where it had come out in 1954, than in the United States. The American writer Waverley Root had similar aims as David with *The Cooking of Italy* (1968), but Nika Hazelton, writing in the *New York Times*, dismissed Root's interpretation of regional Italian cuisines as "strange." Marcella's work was clear-cut. Both she and Victor approached her assignment with determination. She bought ball-point pens and a pile of spiral notebooks; he purchased a typewriter. She spent her days testing and writing recipes, using American cookbooks of the era as her guideposts. Once Victor returned home, he would look the recipes over. The pair discovered that they had complementary working styles. Marcella was impulsive; Victor was patient, curious. He threw her endless questions: How much butter does this recipe need? Why are the measurements for the mayonnaise recipe missing? Are you supposed to snap off the ends of the green beans? Marcella listened and then tested recipes over and over again. Once Victor deemed the recipes satisfactory, he committed them to the page.

The pair completed the manuscript for *The Classic Italian Cook Book: The Art of Italian Cooking and the Italian Art of Eating* in February 1972. They thought they were done with their work, but within two weeks, an editor sent back a copy crowded with notes, castigating them for the repeated use of the word *piquant* and expressing confusion about the difference between mussels and clams. After Marcella and Victor answered those queries, another editor saddled them with yet another truckload of notes.

Marcella and Victor enlisted the talents of an illustrator named George Koizumi for the book's interior. Koizumi's graceful, detailed drawings would supplement the techniques that Marcella wrote of in her book: how to twist tortellini on a finger, how to cut pappardelle with a fluted pastry wheel, how to pare the green off artichoke leaves. But Harper & Row didn't bother to consult Marcella and Victor for the cover, which had a red, green, and white motif to mimic the Italian flag. Marcella and Victor felt the design was uncharacteristically jingoistic. Italians weren't really flag-wavers—not since Mussolini's fascist rule, anyway. The publisher met them halfway and agreed to get rid of the green, and the book was released in the spring of 1973. With 250 recipes, the book focused on the cuisines Marcella knew best, those of Emiglia-Romagna and Tuscany. Still, she stressed the regional variety of cooking traditions in the country. "The first useful thing to know about Italian cooking is that, as such, it actually doesn't exist," she opened her introduction. "The cooking of Italy is really the cooking of its regions, regions that until 1861 were separate, independent, and usually hostile states." Marcella struck a romantic, at times even erudite tone. She wrote of the "mountains of orange, cream-colored, and nut-brown wild mushrooms" that populated Italian markets in the fall and spring. She made references to Italian history and literature. "When the *polenta* was done, there was a moment of joy as it was poured out in a streaming, golden circle on the beechwood top of the *madia*, a cupboard where bread and flour were stored," she wrote in one passage describing the making of polenta in Italian country kitchens. "Italy's great nineteenth-century novelist, Alessandro Manzoni, described it as looking like a harvest moon coming out of the mist."

In a survey of that spring's cookbooks for the *New York Times*, the writer Raymond Sokolov admitted that Marcella's book was by no means the "encyclopedic" Italian cookbook that America still needed, but nonetheless a "fine stopgap." The hard-to-please *Times* food writer John Hess was more effusive. Writing in November 1973, Hess called Marcella's book one of "the best new working cookbooks" of the season. Hess also gave Marcella a *Times* profile the following month, documenting her methods for making pasta by hand. In a year-end roundup for the *Times*, Nika Hazelton suggested that Marcella's recipes "will come as a revelation to the frequenters of what so often laughingly passes as an Italian restaurant in the U.S.," a sign that Marcella was succeeding in her mission.

If the reviews for the book were almost uniformly enthusiastic, Marcella was dismayed when she embarked upon her book tour. Harper & Row didn't seem to be doing much to draw attention to the book. This gave Victor a bold idea. In an attempt to improve the book's distribution, he wrote a letter to Julia Child, asking how they could generate more publicity for Marcella's book. Julia, sensing no threat in Marcella, took to Marcella kindly. She introduced Marcella to her editor at Knopf, Judith Jones. Jones was a formidable figure in cookbook publishing at the time. She'd already done wonders for Julia after taking on *Mastering the Art of French Cooking* (1961). By 1973, Jones was editing another ascendant culinary star, Madhur Jaffrey, the Indian-born actress and food writer whose *An Invitation to Indian Cooking* had come out that spring. Jones knew how to craft an author's image, so long as they possessed talent. Marcella had it in spades. Initially, Marcella found Jones quite charming. Her husky voice, for example, enchanted Marcella. It made her seem so American. Jones helped Marcella wiggle out of her contract with Harper & Row. She secured Marcella the renowned literary agent Robert Lescher. After careful finagling on Lescher's part, Harper & Row transferred the rights of Marcella's book to Knopf. Knopf reissued

The Classic Italian Cook Book in February 1976. They replaced the garishly patriotic jacket with a more elegant, earth-toned cover. Marcella then began promoting her cookbook all over again. She attended industry parties where she schmoozed with the food establishment. But Marcella sometimes felt like a girl from a small town in such settings. She was a private person, and self-promotion went against her nature.

～

AS THE DECADE progressed, Marcella became a bigger name. She was so marketable that Bloomingdale's created a boutique in its storefront on Fifty-Ninth Street called Marcella Hazan's Italian Kitchen, stocking it with her homemade Bolognese pasta and extra-virgin olive oil from Tuscany. Her classes, meanwhile, began to attract celebrities from both the culinary world and beyond: James Beard, *New York* magazine restaurant critic Gael Greene, the actor Joel Grey.

Always, though, Marcella wished she could take her students to an actual Italian market, not the grocery stores she had to settle for in New York. To remedy this issue, she established a school for American students in the Italian city of Bologna in 1976. She would later say it was the only project she'd worked on in her career that was entirely her idea, not the fulfillment of someone else's wish. The city's tourism arm even invested in Marcella's school, building her a kitchen that matched specifications set by her. She was, quite literally, a culinary ambassador for Italy.

Back in America, though, her work wasn't finished. As Marcella's visibility heightened in America through the mid-1970s, she still faced confusion about what exactly Italian food was. Her young son, Giuliano, was in grade school at that point. An employee of his school called asking if Marcella could cater an event, hoping Marcella would prepare Swedish meatballs or tuna casserole. Marcella was frank: She didn't know how to make these dishes. They weren't Italian. (She agreed to bring a dozen bottles of Coke instead.)

It was clear that Marcella had to move the needle even more. So she wrote a second cookbook, *More Classic Italian Cooking* (1978), seeking to represent "the authentic language of the kitchen that is spoken in Italy today," as she wrote in the preface. Marcella traveled throughout Italy for the book, documenting recipes with the aid of a tape recorder. "I took down recipes the way one takes down unwritten folk songs and stories," she wrote. She included a wide range of recipes: spaghetti frittata, polenta shortcake, black-grape ice cream. Illustrations by the artist Marisabina Russo accompanied some of Marcella's instructions, showing readers how to slice veal against the grain or grate Parmesan. The book was the first Marcella worked on from beginning to end with Judith Jones, and the relationship between the two women crumbled as they collaborated. Marcella's directions were imprecise, Jones complained. She should've told readers to stir the onions as they sautéed so they didn't burn in the pan. Jones didn't understand what was so Italian about cauliflower gratin in béchamel sauce. When, Marcella wondered, did Jones become the arbiter of what was and was not Italian? Fortunately, none of this tension affected the book's reception. Critics appreciated the book's ambition. To *Kirkus Reviews*, the book went "further afield in quest of some regional specialties" than its predecessor had. "Too often excellent first cookbooks are followed by inferior second efforts that suggest the author is merely capitalizing on the earlier product," Mimi Sheraton of the *New York Times* wrote. "But this seems to be just the opposite." The book would win Marcella a prestigious Tastemaker Award in the foreign cookbook category the following year.

Around the time of *More Classic Italian Cooking*'s release, a flood of Italian cookbooks entered the market. Some were exhaustively researched volumes, like the Florence-born cooking teacher Giuliano Bugialli's *The Fine Art of Italian Cooking* (1977). In his book, Bugialli chronicled cooking traditions that stretched as far back as the 1300s. Others had more of a specialized focus. Edda Servi Machlin's *The Classic Cuisine of the Italian Jews* (1981) showed American readers an oft-ignored slice of Italian cooking; the American Italophile Carol Field's *The Italian Baker* (1985) celebrated Italy's breads and baked goods. Even Victor himself entered the fray when Knopf published his *Italian Wine* (1982), an acclaimed guide to the country's wines. Jones was Victor's editor, too.

The relationship between Marcella and Jones never quite recovered from their work on *More Classic Italian Cooking*, but the two again collaborated on *Marcella's Italian Kitchen* (1986). Marcella claimed that Knopf didn't print enough copies upon release, hampering its success. Next, at the advice of her agent, Marcella revised and combined her first two cookbooks into *Essentials of Classic Italian Cooking* (1992). She was disappointed by her puny advance and, upon publication, found that Knopf yet again printed too few copies. According to Marcella, Knopf also refused to submit the book for consideration for the James Beard Awards. Jones told her that the book didn't qualify, since those awards were only for new books, and Marcella's book wasn't new. So Marcella submitted the book on her own, and it ended up winning the category of Best Italian Cookbook. By this point, she'd had enough of Jones and Knopf, and with the aid of her agent, Marcella extricated herself from her contract. In Marcella's era, the food establishment often punished women with "unruly" behavior; look at Madeleine Kamman. But Marcella's contentious personality often served as evidence of her exactitude, not a reason to discount her. She ingratiated herself with the country's tight-knit food establishment rather than questioning its imbalances too openly. When Marcella sparred with Judith Jones, she wasn't punching up. The two women were on a level playing field. Marcella had earned the right to advocate for herself, and she had Victor's support.

She'd do just fine without Jones. The advance that her new publisher, HarperCollins, gave her for *Marcella Cucina* (1997) was a legendarily high $650,000, steeper than any that had been reported for an American cookbook. Marcella continued to command the establishment's respect, too. The book won her a James Beard Award in the Mediterranean category. More awards followed: In 2000, the foundation gave her its Lifetime Achievement Award and inducted her first cookbook into its Cookbook Hall of Fame. Marcella kept writing into the last decade of her life. She spent her final years in the placid town of Longboat Key, Florida. She would publish one more cookbook in her lifetime, *Marcella Says* (2004), plus a memoir, *Amarcord: Marcella Remembers* (2008), detailing her childhood, the beginnings of her career in food, and her disagreements with Jones. Marcella and Victor maintained their writing partnership until her death in 2013, at age 89, due to complications from emphysema and arterial blockage. One last book, *Ingredienti: Marcella's Guide to the Market* (2016), a handbook to shopping for specialty ingredients like fennel and sunchokes, was published posthumously under both Victor and Marcella's names. The notion of a husband writing for his wife may give some people pause, but Marcella was, by all accounts, delighted to have Victor's help. "Victor does not take me out of the page and put himself in," Marcella once said. "My students say when they read my books, it is like listening to me."

There was little indication that Victor ever sought to take credit for Marcella's work, either—in fact, the opposite may have held true: When Marcella died, the *New York Times* characterized Victor as Marcella's "muse," her "usually unacknowledged translator and co-writer." He gladly relinquished the stage to her.

Long after Marcella became the face of Italian cooking in America, though, she remained honest about the fact that she fell into food. She was at the right place at the right time. Her skill was not a matter of dispute, nor did she appear to be unhappy. Factually speaking, her talents fit the market's demands in the 1970s, when America needed an author who could make Italian cuisine legible to home cooks. It just so happened that Marcella was uniquely suited to the challenge, even if taking it on wasn't initially part of her plan.

"Darling, I never did in my life anything that I was not asked to do it," she would tell an interviewer in her characteristic broken English. "It was not my idea, never."

Her Own Quiet Rebellion

Julie Sahni

B. OCTOBER 16, 1945, KANPUR, BRITISH INDIA

START WITH THE NAME. Her mother had been planning to call her Deepa, but the girl arrived on October 16, 1945, the night of Diwali. Because of this auspicious holiday birth, her family decided to affix the name of Lakshmi, Hindu goddess of prosperity, to her name: Deepalakshmi Ranganathan Iyer. But when the girl was just nine months old, a few convent-educated aunts of hers christened her with the French name Jolie. It sounded tender, like a pigeon's coo. Some people couldn't quite say Jolie, though, and tended to flatten that first vowel. Thus was her name altered by mispronunciation into Julie.

At the age of 5, Julie began attending an Arya Samaj, or Hindu reform, school in the North Indian city of Kanpur. Classes there trained her to be a perfect housewife. She learned how to knit, how to take care of a sick man, how to make brittle dosas. As she grew older, she became extraordinarily proficient at cooking. Padma, her mother, told Julie not to cook too much at home. Otherwise, Padma warned, the family cook may run away.

JULIE WAS A SMALL GIRL at 9, barely tall enough to reach her bicycle. Starting in the summer of 1955, she'd have to bike to the nearby mandi in Kanpur every day to gather all the vegetables she could carry. "Woh ladki phir ayee," the shop owners would say in Hindi as they watched her approach the market. *That girl has come again.* Her older sister, Reena, had to prepare lunch. It was Julie's task to cook dinner. She spent her evenings making phulkas, watching the whole wheat breads inflate on burners like birthday balloons. During those summers, Julie and her three sisters lived on their own. Julie's father, Venkataraman Ranganathan Iyer, gave the family's servants a vacation. He compensated his daughters for their work with the same salary he provided the family's laborers. Using brooms made from twigs, the girls cleaned old-fashioned latrines, with toilets that resembled craters in the ground. They swept the entire four-room house twice a day. They tended to the garden. Those summers weren't easy, but those early routines shaped Julie. There was dignity in labor, she realized.

In the Ranganathan household, education came first. Julie's progressive family believed in creating equal opportunities for women and men, and this began with school. Her parents had wed when Padma was still a teenager, having only finished eighth grade. Though custom dictated that Padma halt her education after marriage, Julie's father wouldn't allow it. Padma continued studying, eventually obtaining two graduate degrees.

Perched at the top of the caste ladder as Tamil Brahmins, the Ranganathans were an unorthodox family. They encouraged their children to pursue the arts. Neither of Julie's parents had the freedom to practice art in pre-Independence India. Because their children came of age after Indian independence, they made sure Julie and Reena learned Bharatnatyam, a form of classical dance with roots in South India. Dancing became the main focus of Julie's childhood. To say she was skilled would be an understatement; she was a prodigy. By the time she was 14, she was performing on her own before audiences of thousands. She knew how to seize their attention: One false move, she understood, and the magic would fade. Julie moved often due to the nature of her father's job as a botanist who worked with India's Ministry of Defence. No matter where they lived, though, Julie and her family repeated a ritual. Once they arrived at their new home, they built a horseshoe-shaped chulha, or stove, from scratch. They decorated the stove with rice flour and uttered a prayer before filling a boiling pot with lentils or rice. They waited for the water to escape the pot's rim, making contact with the surface of the stove. The ceremony functioned as a sort of baptism. A house could never be a home without a functioning stove.

With her parents' blessing, Julie traveled the world as a dancer, performing in thirty-two countries, mostly in Europe and the Middle East. By the time she reached her late teens, though, she began to wonder if dance would really provide her a sustainable career path. Julie resolved to pursue dancing on the side, then, while setting her sights on architecture. Architecture made sense for her. She knew how to paint; she knew how to draw. It was 1962 when she successfully applied for one of thirty seats at the competitive architecture program at the University of Delhi's Ramjas College. Julie's choice of study was nonconformist: Most of her peers were men.

As a student, she would meet the man she would later marry, a physicist named Viraht Sahni. The two encountered each other at a party. Viraht was a student at the Indian Institute of Technology in Bombay. Though he and Julie lived in different cities, they visited each other frequently. Julie did not give up dancing entirely through college. Her talents allowed her to achieve a degree of fame, in fact. A photo of her dancing even graced the cover of Delhi's *Times of India* in November 1963. Increasingly, however, she wanted to learn more about the art of cooking. Between 1966 and 1967, when she was still in college, Julie began studying cooking in her spare time under Mrs. Balbir Singh, author of *Mrs. Balbir Singh's Indian Cookery* (1961). Singh's book, which focused on the cuisines of North India, had been a hit in the United Kingdom. Singh brought the sensibility of her book to her New Delhi classes, giving Julie an early model for how to teach North Indian cooking in a methodical fashion. But as long as Julie stayed in India, cooking would remain little more than a pastime for her.

Once she finished school, she began to feel that her independent streak didn't have a home in India. She thought seriously about where she might move instead. Maybe she could go to America. She'd been dreaming of the country ever since she saw *A Summer Place*, a movie starring Sandra Dee. Its story revolved around a protagonist who became pregnant out of wedlock but found support in her family. Julie loved the sentiment behind the movie: the idea that America made room for women who disobeyed social norms. Going to America wasn't out of the question for Julie, either. America's passing of the Immigration and Nationality Act in 1965 eliminated national quotas that had previously strangled Indian immigration to the United States. She was at a particular advantage as an educated professional. With this in mind, she decided to apply for graduate school scholarships to study urban planning in America, eventually receiving a scholarship to Columbia University in New York. Fortuitously, her husband-to-be, Viraht, was already pursuing his graduate studies in the city, too. After years of dating apart, the couple began talking to Viraht's parents about marriage. Julie's future in-laws insisted upon changing her first name per family tradition, but Julie hesitated. Viraht, sensing Julie's discomfort, put his foot down. The world knew her as Julie. Her name would stay as is.

⌒

WHEN JULIE ARRIVED in New York in 1968, she and Viraht lived in a cramped apartment in downtown Brooklyn, their kitchen the size of a coat closet. It was certainly a curious time to be Indian in America. America was in the throes of a minor obsession with India thanks to the popularity of the Beatles and their association with the Indian musician Ravi Shankar. Still, Julie sometimes found that American imaginings of India were astonishingly regressive. Quite a few Americans believed it was a land of snake charmers and half-naked people running around a lawless land. Maybe they got such ideas from the Walt Disney film *The Jungle Book,* with the shaggy-haired boy named Mowgli dressed in a carrot-colored loincloth. Whatever the reason, Julie heard scary stories from Indian immigrant friends who told her that strangers would spit on them in America. Julie was well aware that she could be catnip for such ugly attacks: She was short, she was a woman, she was brown. It was somewhat serendipitous, then, that she wasn't subject to such overt expressions of prejudice. Sure, she got some stares when she wore a sari to class at Columbia, but she could handle those.

Julie spent those early years in America focusing on her career. Upon graduating from Columbia with a master's degree in urban planning, she went on to work for the City Planning Commission in 1970. Her job involved writing legislation for open spaces and land-fill, along with recommending improvements to subway infrastructure. The work was both rewarding and fatiguing. To busy her mind in her off hours, she concentrated on cooking. Julie really didn't know how to cook too many dishes beyond what she'd learned in India and, unfortunately for her, Viraht wanted anything *but* Indian food. To appease her husband, Julie turned to three cookbooks in particular: Irma S. Rombauer's *The Joy of Cooking* (originally published in 1931 before a series of subsequent expansions); Simone Beck, Louisette Bertholle, and Julia Child's *Mastering the Art of French Cooking* (1961); and Craig Claiborne's *The New York Times Cookbook* (1961). Julie appreciated the careful way these authors wrote their recipes. Television helped Julie, too. She marveled at Julia Child's ability to make cooking appealing to the masses.

To expand her repertoire, Julie began taking night classes in Chinese cooking, which she would end up studying for two years. Her teachers, all from mainland China, taught her how to jelly duck blood, for example, along with the nuances between Cantonese and Peking roast duck. But Julie would soon find that her instructors and classmates wanted to learn from *her*. They would badger her with questions about Indian cooking, asking her about the difference between cooking chicken in a Chinese wok used for stir-frying and an Indian kadhai. Everyone was struck by the direct way Julie described these distinctions when asked. They suggested Julie teach cooking herself. The proposition planted an idea in her head.

❦

INITIALLY, ONLY TWO STUDENTS signed up for the inaugural classes of the Julie Sahni Cooking School, which Julie established in 1973. She eventually persuaded a colleague and an intern from her day job to join the class. Indian cooking was about to take off that year in America, though. The actress and food writer Madhur Jaffrey's debut cookbook, *An Invitation to Indian Cooking* (1973), came out that year. The book had been shepherded into the world by Judith Jones, who was Julia Child's editor at Knopf and Marcella Hazan's editor later in the decade. A film actress of international repute, Jaffrey caught the eye of the New York food establishment in 1966, when Craig Claiborne profiled her for the *New York Times*. "Indian Actress Is a Star in the Kitchen, Too," a glitzy headline read, laying the groundwork for Jaffrey's fame to flower in the following decade. "To me the word 'curry' is as degrading to India's great cuisine as the term 'chop suey' was to China's," Jaffrey groused at the beginning of her book. Jaffrey had good reason to reject the curry label. Recipes for "curry," a glop of spiced gravy, populated American cookbooks as early as 1824, facilitating America's conflation of Indian cuisine with that word. The muddling would only intensify later in the nineteenth century, when an Indian chef named J. Ranji Smile came to the United States. The press crowned Smile the "King of the Curry Chefs." His mystique had an abiding impact: American journalists continued to write of Indian cuisine from an uncomfortable remove, with Jane Holt of the *New York Times* describing curry as a "rare Oriental ragout" in 1941.

A group of Indian cookbook authors in the second half of the twentieth century worked hard to undo the mischaracterization that curry was the extent of what India's cooking had to offer. Dharam Jit Singh's *Classic Cooking from India* (1956) was one of the first cookbooks for Americans to clarify that "Indian food is not just 'curry' and Indian cooking depends on a personal measure of spices." The Indian-born, Wellesley-educated writer Santha Rama Rau followed with *The Cooking of India* (1969), a cookbook filled with recollections of Rau's Indian childhood. Rau, echoing Singh, lamented how "Western minds" reduced Indian cuisine "to the comprehensive and meaningless category 'curry,'" or "a floury, yellow cream sauce that can be used indiscriminately with meat or fish or chicken, and served with rice," as she wrote.

With *An Invitation to Indian Cooking*, Jaffrey worked from a template similar to Rau's, her cookbook a crossbreed between autobiography and instruction. Her recipes included pullaos of rice with lamb, shrimp with dill and ginger, and green peppers stuffed with keema. Many were dishes she'd grown up with in Delhi. But one book could do only so much to turn public opinion. In the early 1970s, Julie—like Singh, Rau, and Jaffrey before her—found that Americans could seemingly understand Indian food only through the framework of curry. Julie wanted to change such impressions, but she struggled to get crucial spices and herbs for Indian cooking in New York. Though neighborhoods like Jackson Heights in Queens and the East Village in Manhattan had a good number of Indian restaurants, Indian grocery stores were harder to come by. To circumvent these problems, she often asked her family to send her ingredients from India. Her mother canned sweet mango pickle, or achaar, in jaggery and shipped it by mail, but in transit, it swelled to the size of a football. The achaar nearly exploded upon contact, filling Julie's Brooklyn apartment with the perfume of pickled fruit. Julie knew sourcing ingredients would be a challenge for students, too. She was also aware that Indian scents and tastes might daunt many of them. Barraging them with too much information at once wouldn't work. Instead, she welcomed her students into this new universe softly. She held six weekly sessions, in which her students learned how to cook gobi sabzi, or tender cauliflower smacked with ginger and green chile, and ten-ingredient pullaos. Julie also provided lessons on customs around eating in India. She encouraged her students to eat with their hands, for example. Their food should be soft enough to break with three fingers.

The classes caught on: Within months, more students signed up through word of mouth. Julie no longer had to beg her coworkers to join. Her cooking school hummed along until the fall of 1974, when she got a call from a mysterious woman. Only later in the call did the woman reveal herself to be Florence Fabricant, a writer for the *New York Times*. She wanted to pay a visit to Julie's class for an article in the paper. The encounter resulted in a November 1974 profile of Julie, which ran with three recipes. Fabricant positioned Indian cooking as a puzzle for the reader. "While Indian cooking depends heavily on spices, it is the careful use of these magic ingredients that can render the various specialties of the subcontinent pungent or peppery, fragrant or soothing," the article opened. Fabricant went on to mention that Julie's class emphasized "classic" Indian cuisine, which specifically referred to the foods of Kashmir, Punjab, and Uttar Pradesh in North India. In that piece, Julie made clear that food was just a hobby. "I don't give my course to make money," she told Fabricant. Her career in urban planning was in full swing at that point. Yet Fabricant foresaw a different future for Julie. "Mrs. Sahni's passion is food and cooking," Fabricant observed. "Some day, it may become her vocation rather than a pastime."

For Julie, Fabricant's piece marked a turning point. After the article's publication, she found herself inundated with requests from would-be students. Her classes were fully booked for two years. This put her in a bind, as she now had to balance the pressures of a popular class with her "real" job. By day, Julie was heading a Planning Department task force charged with standardizing sidewalk cafés in the city. Once the sun set, though, she would be showing students how to make lamb rogan josh, with thick garlic cream blanketing the meat. In 1975, following Fabricant's article, Julie began ruminating on the idea of writing a cookbook. She thought of the other women, teachers like herself, who had made the same jump. Through the city's cooking school network, for example, Julie found a kindred spirit in Marcella Hazan. Marcella faced struggles of her own in trying to free Italian cuisine from the dungeon of red sauce. She reminded Julie that change couldn't possibly happen overnight. Getting her audience to respect Indian cooking would require patience.

⌇

"JULIE SAHNI WAS RAISED to be an achiever," wrote Patricia Wells in the *New York Times* on Valentine's Day in 1979. "When she was growing up in New Delhi during the 1940s, it was not just hoped, but expected, that she would make something of herself." If Florence Fabricant's 1974 piece brought Julie into the public eye, this article by Wells pushed her right in front of the food establishment's spotlight. Wells told readers that Julie had excelled as a dancer, architect, and city planner. "But what Mrs. Sahni really wants to do is cook," Wells observed. "And so, rebelling in her own quiet way, she maintains her professional life while keeping alive her culinary passion." Wells made an offhand mention of "an upcoming cookbook" from Julie. Julie hadn't yet spoken publicly about her aspirations to write a cookbook and didn't have a book deal at the time of the story's publication. In fact, she didn't even have an agent. After the article, though, three publishers contacted her, offering her varying amounts of money up front. Money didn't matter to Julie. She was more concerned with writing a book of integrity, one that would last beyond her death. The most appealing call came from an editor at William Morrow named Maria Guarnaschelli. Julie signed her book contract without having even set foot in the William Morrow headquarters. More changes were on the horizon as she wrote the book. In early 1979, she found out she was pregnant, meaning she would go on paid leave from her job. Julie would obtain her American citizenship in October 1979, just one month before the birth of her son, Vishal Raj.

She found time to write through all of this. At 541 pages, *Classic Indian Cooking* (1980) was a mammoth effort. Julie made certain choices that distinguished her book from previous works on Indian cooking in America. For one, there was little memoiristic writing as there had been in Rau's and Jaffrey's cookbooks; Julie saw her book as a teaching book. "There is no mystical secret behind Indian cooking," Julie assured readers in the opening pages. "It is, in fact, the easiest of all international cuisines." She stressed Indian cooking's beauty and diversity in equal measure: "It is the crushed cardamom smothering tender young chickens, garlic perfuming lamb with cream sauce, bruised carom lacing fish fillets, and pistachios sweetening the cream sauce for foamy cheese dumplings," she wrote. Complementing this text were line drawings by Marisabina Russo, who'd illustrated Marcella Hazan's *More Classic Italian Cooking* two years earlier. In Julie's book, Russo's art showed readers how to butterfly a leg of lamb and peel broccoli spears.

Julie devoted the book's first ninety pages to Indian cooking's principles, walking through its spices, seasonings, special ingredients like ruh (flower essence) and vark (silver foil), equipment, and techniques. She offered methodical explanations for how to powder asafetida, for example, or how to brown-fry onion, garlic, and ginger root. Julie also explained some discrepancies between regional diets, noting that Hindu Brahmins from

West Bengal ate fish, unlike Brahmins in many other states. Bengali Brahmins, she said, considered fish to be the vegetables of the sea. This scene-setting was necessary for the book's 160 recipes. Most were North Indian, though Julie made the occasional detour outside of the region. She went down to South India with the snap of tamarind-soaked Mysore rasam; she headed to West Bengal with dahi machi, fish fillets poached in spiced onions and yogurt. The book was not regionally exhaustive, and it didn't pretend to be. How could it possibly be for a country with as many diffuse cooking traditions as India?

The American press immediately recognized *Classic Indian Cooking* as a book of great value. Writing in the *New York Times*, Mimi Sheraton hailed it as one of "two exceptionally fine and much needed volumes on Oriental cooking" to be released in 1980, the other being Shizuo Tsuji's *Japanese Cooking* (1980). Sheraton praised Julie's recipe instructions, "models of clarity" that illuminated a cuisine with "beguiling breads" and "tantalizing relishes" that jolted the American palate. (The review was not all positive. "Mrs. Sahni's writing style is not one of the book's strengths," Sheraton wrote, "but the subject matter is fascinating enough to carry the day.") A year later, Sheraton would include the book in her recommendations for anyone looking to build a "classic cookbook library." It was the only Indian cookbook on that list. Others in the press swiftly slotted the book into a prestigious canon. "The publisher thinks this book will rank with Irene Kuo's *The Key to Chinese Cooking*, Marcella Hazan's *Classic Italian Cooking*, and other basic cookbooks," mused Walter and Claudine Cowen in the Autumn 1981 issue of the *Virginia Quarterly Review*. "We agree." The book's critical reception suggested that Julie was dismantling the stereotypes around Indian cuisine, just as she strove to do. Her efforts on the ground, however, proved much more difficult. While on her book tour, Julie held cooking demonstrations at malls and department stores across the country. The sessions were often demoralizing. She could feel the lack of enthusiasm from audience members. Julie consoled herself with Marcella's wisdom: If she could shift one person's cooking, then her work had meaning.

Julie juggled book publicity against the trials of motherhood and marriage. Soon after, she and Viraht would divorce. "We were not compatible," she would tell the newspaper *India Abroad* years later. (In that article, the writer noted that she was "reluctant" to discuss her marriage.) Even after the divorce, though, she still kept the surname Sahni.

⁓

FOLLOWING THE PUBLICATION of *Classic Indian Cooking*, Julie stepped away from urban planning for good. She was itching to write another cookbook. Realizing she couldn't just pursue cooking as a leisure activity, Julie gave herself entirely to food. Patching together an income proved more cumbersome than she anticipated, however. She continued teaching and, to make ends meet, she also began a career as a freelance food writer. Her first published article, on the magnificence of Burmese food, appeared in the October 1982 issue of the food magazine *Cuisine*. (The magazine, which folded in 1984, was one of five leading food glossies of the era, the others being *Bon Appétit*, *Gourmet*, *Food & Wine*, and *The Pleasures of Cooking*.) As the decade moved forward, Julie wrote about varied topics, like Anglo-Indian cuisine for *Food & Wine* and savory and sweet chutneys for *Bon Appétit*. While maintaining her freelance career, Julie chiseled away at a second cookbook. It would contain the vegetarian recipes that were cut for space from the first book. Julie did the bulk of her writing in the wee hours of the night, after Vishal Raj had fallen asleep. Those were trying years, financially and emotionally. She taught the occasional cooking class at Bloomingdale's just for the money. No longer having a steady paycheck meant that Julie couldn't spend too extravagantly, either. She couldn't dine out at pricey restaurants, for example. On a day in 1983, though, an older student of hers invited her to a Bangladeshi and Indian restaurant called Nirvana. The restaurant sat in a penthouse on the top floor of 30 Central Park South. The mirrors reflected sweeping views of the park; fresh roses were on each table. Julie thought the restaurant was gorgeous. Unfortunately, the food wasn't quite to her taste. The pair ordered many dishes, like bonfire-red tandoori chicken and roshogolla, a dessert of mounds of milk in rosewater. Julie politely critiqued each one. Her companion listened to her assessments intently.

Near the meal's end, Julie was surprised to learn that her student had been stealthily recording their dinner conversation. He was an employee of the restaurant, he confessed, and he took her class to see if she possessed the right qualifications to be the restaurant's new executive chef. Shamsher Wadud, a Bangladeshi immigrant, had founded Nirvana in 1970. He belonged to a generation of New York restaurateurs who were Bangladeshi in origin but ran nominally Indian restaurants. In the late 1960s, Wadud had eaten at one such "Indian" restaurant, a place called Kashmir, and found the quality horrid. He created Nirvana in an attempt to heighten the standards for Indian food in New York. Though Nirvana developed a positive reputation in the New York dining world, Wadud also had well-documented run-ins with the law and the mafia.

Though Julie wasn't aware of the restaurant's association with crime, she had other reasons to be reluctant. For one thing, she'd never worked at a restaurant before. In addition to this obvious impediment, she was pretty busy with teaching, writing another cookbook, and raising a child. Determined to rise to the occasion, though, she stopped teaching and joined Nirvana as its executive chef in December 1983, when she was 37. Julie thus became the first Indian woman to hold the post of executive chef at a New York restaurant. Julie found a way to retool Nirvana's menu to reflect her own home cooking ethos, incorporating influences from beyond North India. She included lobster meat cooked in coconut milk, chile, and fresh ginger, a recipe from the Malabar Coast; she offered a shrimp preparation from West Bengal, tossing the shellfish in a light sauce of cinnamon, cloves, scallions, and mustard paste. Julie started out at Nirvana as a consultant, clocking in twelve hours a week, but she soon lobbied her way to a full-time position. Her name was on the line, after all. The job became demanding quite quickly: Shortly after she began at Nirvana, Wadud told Julie he wanted to launch a sister restaurant, Nirvana Club One, atop Times Square. It would be a discotheque to rival Studio 54 and Limelight, two prominent nightlife destinations in the era. Nirvana Club One opened in April 1984 with a menu identical to that of Nirvana Penthouse. Reviews were rhapsodic for both venues. A May 1984 review in *Gourmet* by Jay Jacobs hailed the original Nirvana restaurant as "one of the most romantic" in Manhattan. Americans were surely still eager to cast Indian cuisine in colonial terms, the review proved: The write-up contained references to E. M. Forster's *A Passage to India* and noted how the "handsomely printed Nirvana menu isn't quite as long as the Bhagavad-Gita." (An article in *New York* magazine the following month struck similar notes, proclaiming how "sitar music shivers and weeps, and the air smells of spice.")

Nirvana's perceived exoticism did not distract the American food media from Julie's talent. Her scrupulous approach came through in the menu's mulligatawny, the soup that Jacobs called "a silky, golden piece of work—sturdy yet subtle, heady with uncountable aromas, and vastly gratifying," and the murgh vindaloo, "a hellaciously fiery specialty of Goa for which boneless morsels of the bird are marinated in a three-alarm curry sauce aggravated by a substantial quantity of chilies." Six weeks after opening, Nirvana Club One received a two-star review in the *New York Times* from Marian Burros, who lavished praise on Julie's aloo samosa and malai kofta, small orbs of vegetables in cream. Burros believed the restaurant to be superior to its antecedent, while calling Julie "one of the finest Indian cooks in New York."

Critics seemed to be unaware of any dysfunction behind the scenes. For one, Julie had trouble gaining the respect of her chefs, most of them men. They seemed unaccustomed to listening to a woman in the kitchen. Her life also began operating at a freakishly frenetic pace: She split her time between Nirvana Penthouse and Nirvana Club One, and she would sometimes finish her shifts at 2:30 in the morning. Then she had to find the time to keep writing that follow-up to her first cookbook. All the while, Vishal Raj was in the care of a nanny. Julie didn't have time to visit India, though her mother Padma often came to see Julie in New York. Julie would record her mother's recipes during those stays.

Classic Indian Vegetarian and Grain Cooking (1985) was, like its predecessor, over five hundred pages long. The book contained recipes for eggless "scrambled eggs" made with a kind of fresh cheese called chenna, pullaos of paneer and sweet peppers, and lassi made from ripe papaya. In this book's opening, Julie took a more personal tone than she had in *Classic Indian Cooking*. She began by narrating the memory of her sister Reena's wedding in South India and the twenty-two-course vegetarian feast that followed. The cookbook impressed the food media. The book "leaves you dizzy, wondering where to start," wrote

Linda Greider in the *Washington Post*. *Classic Indian Vegetarian and Grain Cooking* happened to arrive the same year as Jaffrey's *A Taste of India* (1985), a regional survey of Indian cooking. Journalists indulged in comparisons between the two women. "Of the two, Mrs. Jaffrey's book is the more immediately appealing, filled with gorgeous color photographs of handsomely presented dishes, as well as scenes from Indian markets, kitchens and village and urban life," Nancy Harmon Jenkins wrote in the *New York Times*. Julie's cookbook had no photographs, only line drawings.

Julie was proud of *Classic Indian Vegetarian and Grain Cooking*. It was crucial, she reminded herself, that she attach her name to projects that reflected well on her. Both Nirvana Penthouse and Nirvana Club One continued to attract great crowds and high-profile celebrities: Duran Duran, the Pointer Sisters, Sean Lennon. The restaurants represented the last gasp of the disco era in all its beauty and excess. But by the following year, Julie decided that she preferred to focus on teaching and writing. In May 1986, Julie announced she would be severing ties with both venues, bringing her career in restaurants to an end. Maybe Julie had unknowingly kick-started a trend, however: Later that year, Madhur Jaffrey became a consultant for Dawat, an Indian restaurant in the Upper East Side. The move sparked some speculation that Dawat was trying to replicate Julie's run with Nirvana. As the *New York Times* restaurant critic Bryan Miller wrote in his tepid one-star review of Dawat, Julie was the first example of Indian restaurants hiring "famous consulting chefs who, aside from giving culinary advice, also stir the stockpot of publicity." Julie emerged from Nirvana with her name intact. She resumed teaching. She began leading annual pilgrimages to India, establishing Julie Sahni's Gourmet Tours in 1994. She also appeared sporadically on television shows, like the Food Network's *Chef du Jour* in the late 1990s. She went on to write half a dozen more cookbooks, including *Moghul Microwave: Cooking Indian Food the Modern Way* (1990), in which she extolled the virtues of Indian cooking with the microwave, too often denigrated as an instrument of a lower class. It would garner her a nomination for a James Beard Award, her only nomination from the foundation to date.

The food establishment gave Julie plenty of other recognition throughout her career. The International Association of Culinary Professionals named her one of the three best cooking teachers in the world in 1998. The organization also bestowed its Best International Cookbook Award upon her book *Savoring India: Recipes and Reflections on Indian Cooking* (2001) and, in 2020, gave *Classic Indian Cooking* its Culinary Classics Award. In 2007, the James Beard Foundation named *Classic Indian Cooking* to its list of 20 Essential Books to Build Your Culinary Library; also on this list were Simone Beck, Louisette Bertholle, and Julia Child's *Mastering the Art of French Cooking: Volume One* (1961) and Marcella Hazan's *Essentials of Classic Italian Cooking* (1992).

In many respects, Julie is a pioneer. Her work as a writer, restaurant chef, and teacher has advanced the cause of Indian cooking in America. But she also exhibits a refreshing disregard for the limelight. She has renounced certain mandates of stardom that the industry often pushes upon immigrant women to survive in public memory: the idea that they must have a television show, for example, or consistently churn out cookbooks for the public to honor their genius. Perhaps this is why the American food media has downplayed Julie's legacy. Indian cooking still hasn't gained the same cultural cachet of European cuisines of comparable complexity, like Italian. As a consequence, the market continues to favor Indian cookbooks wrapped up in the language of promise: quick, easy, convenient. Julie's writing, reassuring but fastidious, rejected all of these bargains.

When it comes to Julie's restaurant work, the food media has been keen to assign men credit for what she achieved. After Julie left Nirvana, a score of chefs sought to distance Indian restaurant food from its working-class, Bangladeshi origins in the eyes of the affluent white establishment. Among those chefs was the Indian-born Floyd Cardoz, who died in 2020. In his obituary, the *New York Times* called him "the first chef to bring the sweep and balance of his native Indian cooking to fine dining in the United States" and "the first chef born and raised in India to lead an influential New York City kitchen," referencing his stint at Manhattan's Tabla in the 1990s and 2000s. Such statements neglect Julie's work the decade before; they also downplay the singularity of her achievement as a woman.

This elision reads like the erasure of a woman's legacy in real time. But Julie never worked in search of such institutional validation. Throughout her life in America, she thought often of what her parents instilled in her to prize personal fulfillment. "Long, long ago I learned it was not only important to excel, but also to be content," she would say. There was honor in the labor.

A Place for the Stateless

Najmieh Batmanglij

B. NOVEMBER 29, 1947, TEHRAN, IRAN

WHEN SHE WAS living in France as a refugee in the early 1980s, Najmieh Batmanglij began writing a love letter to her sons. One was still a toddler; the other wasn't even born yet. By then, she'd settled in a village called Vence with her husband, Mohammad, and their firstborn, Zal.

She'd fled to France in 1979 as a result of the Iranian Revolution, which warped her home country into a place she no longer recognized. Iranians once prayed at home and danced outside. After the revolution, they prayed in public and danced inside. This fundamentalist turn distressed her. She had no choice but to leave. Najmieh began to write out of a sinking suspicion that Zal and any future children she had would never set foot on Iranian soil. Maybe they would never eat breakfasts of fig jam and butter on fresh barbari bread as she had; maybe they would never taste the sweet chill of saffron ice cream sandwiches. Her love letter took the form of a French-language cookbook, *Ma cuisine d'Iran* (1984), with three hundred recipes from her Iranian home.

But as the book neared publication, Najmieh's adoptive

country began to perturb her. She noticed the way Zal's teacher at school talked to him, with a tone that suggested he was different from the other students. The reason was obvious: He was brown, while the other kids weren't. Najmieh had another son on the way. It became clear to her that France would be no place to raise her kids. Where else could she go? Iran was no longer an option. Her mind drifted to America, where she'd attended college back in the 1960s. Maybe it made sense to return. This time, though, she would be living there in exile.

‧‧‧

AMERICA WAS CERTAINLY not free from discrimination. By the time Najmieh arrived in Washington, DC, in 1983, her French cookbook was already off to the printers. But there was another cookbook simmering in her, this time a more substantial one, written in English. She tried to sell it. But when Najmieh sent out queries to major publishers, no one was interested. Some rejected her outright; others just didn't respond. She suspected these dismissals had more to do with the political anxiety around her than with her talent: The Iranian Revolution was a recent memory for Americans, while the Iran hostage crisis, which stretched from 1979 to 1981, cast an ugly pall over the country. How would American consumers respond to an Iranian cookbook?

With no publisher willing to buy her book, Najmieh took matters into her own hands. She and Mohammad established their own publishing house, Mage Publishers. *Food of Life: A Book of Ancient Persian and Modern Iranian Cooking and Ceremonies* (1986) would be Mage's flagship title. Today, both Iranians and non-Iranians in America regard *Food of Life* as a landmark text; few, if any, Iranian cookbooks in America have matched its scope. It was a rich document of recipes, for one: for whole stuffed lamb, for large red snapper loaded with tamarind, for pudding startled with saffron water. The project was also political by design, acknowledging how displacement breeds its own kind of hunger. Najmieh dedicated the book to her sons "and to all Iranian children living far from the country of their heritage by the course of political events." (Today, those sons of hers are stars in their own right: Zal is a renowned filmmaker, while Rostam is a musician who was a founding member of the indie band Vampire Weekend.) With *Food of Life* and seven subsequent cookbooks published by Mage, Najmieh became the country's most revered authority on Iranian cooking. She achieved this purely through her self-published writing, with no television show or restaurant to her name. Her intentions were selfless. She began writing for Iranians like her who found themselves unmoored after the revolution. Over time, though, cooking would help Najmieh clarify her own outlook, too. She made peace with the pain that the revolution brought her. "In exile, you become so much more conscious of your culture," she once explained, "and ours is so beautiful."

❧

NAJMIEH KHALILI WAS BORN in 1947 into a middle-class Muslim family of ten siblings. Food was the heartbeat of their home in downtown Tehran. Her father, Mohammad, was a religious scholar, while her mother, Zinat, became a bride at 15. They were financially secure enough to hire seasonal cooking help, so

Zinat had an army of cooks who would make tomato paste and jams from scratch. Najmieh very much wanted to learn to cook, but her parents forbade her from doing so. They told her that she could put on an apron and enter the kitchen only if she got a degree. So Najmieh followed orders: She studied. This mandate didn't stop her from carefully observing her mother and the family's cooks, though. Her maternal aunt excelled in pastries, making sheets of baklava seeping with syrup. But whenever Najmieh asked, her aunt refused to give the girl any of her recipes. Recipes represented a form of currency in Iran, a way for elders to preserve their power.

⁓

IN THE AUTUMN of 1967, Najmieh got her parents' blessing to travel to America. She would be going to Oklahoma to live with one of her brothers, five years her senior, who was studying engineering at a college in the state. She was 19 and clueless about international travel. She didn't know what a connecting flight was; she had never been in a hotel room alone. To make matters worse, she'd studied only a bit of English back in Iran but hadn't achieved anything close to fluency. Najmieh liked Oklahoma, finding comfort in the giving nature of "Okies," as she called them. But she would spend only a few months there, studying at her brother's college for a semester before moving to New Haven, Connecticut, where she had a distant cousin who was teaching at Yale University. In New Haven, Najmieh lived in a house occupied by female graduate students. She felt like a total outsider in this milieu. She abstained from drinking and smoking, two activities these women loved. Najmieh prayed five times a day; her housemates did not. She knew of no Iranian community in New Haven to keep her company. She was on her own.

At least she could cook in America. She joined a local co-op, getting boxes of produce, and convinced her mother to send her long-grain rice and notes for recipes. Her mother's packages took a few weeks to arrive, but once Najmieh received them, she'd make dishes like lubia polow, aromatic pots of rice with green beans. Zinat's directions rarely contained specific measurements. Still, these rough outlines were enough for Najmieh. Her memories of women cooking in Tehran guided her. Najmieh made sure to put the recipes in a scrapbook in case she ever needed them again.

After a few months in New Haven, Najmieh applied to different colleges in the area and eventually gained admission to Southern Connecticut State University, where she pursued undergraduate and graduate degrees in education. Najmieh went on to work as a substitute teacher for a year in the Boston area. She stayed in America for seven years in sum before returning to Iran to continue working as a teacher, two degrees and a scrapbook of recipes in hand. Once she arrived back home, her family couldn't argue with her anymore. Najmieh's mother let her into the kitchen.

∾

MOHAMMAD LOOKED LIKE a movie star. He had a handlebar mustache; he wore a T-shirt and roughed-up blue jeans. Najmieh took notice of him immediately at the party that night in 1977. Tehran was a loose, fun place to be back then. Women like her caked their faces in makeup; men dressed as if they lived in London or Paris. Mohammad had, in fact, done his schooling at the Architectural Association School of Architecture in London. Now back in Iran, he was working in construction with his brother.

Najmieh and Mohammad spoke throughout the duration of the party, though the conversation came to a halt when he suddenly fell asleep on her lap, exhausted from a wearying work project. All Najmieh could do was stare at him. She'd never seen a more beautiful man. Najmieh had a feeling she would marry Mohammad. But they would not wed until 1979, when Iran changed drastically. Ayatollah Khomeini overthrew the Shah, Mohammad Reza Pahlavi, in February of that year, sparking the Iranian Revolution. Family members told them that a revolution was no time to get married. They did it anyway in June. The couple had a low-key wedding with no more than thirty people in attendance, a small affair by Iranian standards; they served their guests javaher polow, or jeweled rice, a wedding dish with orange peels, almonds, barberries, and pistachios.

It was a joyous day, distracting Najmieh from the misery of life in Iran. Many of her friends started leaving the country, wanting nothing to do with the revolution. Pretty soon, Najmieh and Mohammad decided to follow suit. One of Najmieh's older sisters once lived in France, which was one of the few countries that didn't require extensive paperwork for Iranians at the time. The city of Nice, in particular, had become a hub for Iranian refugees. Though Najmieh didn't know a word of French, she packed her belongings in late 1979 to flee for Nice. She brought along that scrapbook of her mother's recipes, which she'd been adding to since her return to Iran in 1975, to buffer her against any sorrow. It was a difficult parting, full of uncertainty. Najmieh once dreamed of raising a family in Tehran. The image of her parents crying as she left stayed with her. Maybe she'd never see them again. Mohammad couldn't join her just yet, either, due to problems with his documents. There was an added complication to her departure: Shortly before leaving, Najmieh learned that she was pregnant.

⌒

EVERY DAY IN NICE, Najmieh walked alone down the Promenade des Anglais, sat on a bench overlooking the Mediterranean, and cried. Najmieh kept in touch with Mohammad and her parents via telex, a precursor of the fax machine. But this was no substitute for seeing them in person. So little made sense about her new life as a refugee: She couldn't speak the language. A baby was swelling to life in her belly. But she knew she would have to make France her home. Housing wasn't an issue, miraculously. Najmieh begged her way to a discounted room in a partially vacant hotel. At the suggestion of a concierge there, she posted an advertisement at the University of Nice for a French tutor. A doctoral student named Dominique answered. Dominique proved to be a faithful ally to Najmieh. To start, she found Najmieh an obstetrician to guide her through her pregnancy. She then taught Najmieh how to hail a taxi, how to place an order at a café—how to live as a French woman would.

Within a few months, Mohammad got clearance to travel to France, easing her solitude. After reuniting, he and Najmieh settled in the village of Vence, which Mohammad knew well. He'd visited in his days as a student and appreciated its quaint charms. Vence seemed to be pleasantly stuck in the past: It had only one library, one movie theater. Though there was a considerable population of Algerians and Moroccans in Vence, very few Iranians lived there, so Najmieh and Mohammed stood out among their white neighbors. But the women of Vence reminded Najmieh of Iran. They knew how to cook with love.

It was a neighbor's suggestion that Najmieh write a cookbook drawn from her mother's recipes. Najmieh had been in Vence for a few months by then, but she still missed home. She agreed to write the book. Maybe the project would give her a way to connect to Iran. Once she finally gave birth to Zal in April 1980, Najmieh began writing. It was a community effort she completed with the help of Mohammad and her neighbors. Mohammad wasn't working at the time; he was still a refugee without proper documents to secure a job. He could commit his energy to working on the book and raising Zal with Najmieh. Najmieh obtained ingredients like rosewater at the market in Vence. She found a local photographer named Serge Ephraim to take pictures for her book.

She tested recipes and typed them out on an Apple IIe computer, then a cutting-edge machine. Writing a recipe in French proved to be a challenge for Najmieh. How, for example, would she tell readers how to make something like what she eventually translated as "tah-tchine," a lightly torched dish of rice that resembled a cake? At first, it took her a full two weeks to translate one of her mother's recipes into French. As she wrote, Najmieh looked to the chef Roger Vergé's *Ma cuisine du soleil* (1978) for inspiration. In Najmieh's eyes, France had undergone its gastronomic revolution four decades before America. Vergé's book supported this truth: He had worked extensively in Algeria and Morocco before returning to France, utilizing North African and Middle Eastern ingredients. Books like Vergé's taught her how to write about cooking for a French audience.

With her neighbor's help, Najmieh generated interest from two publishers, one in France, the other in Switzerland. Fortunately Jacques Grancher, the French publishing house, had an immediate need to fill: It had put out cookbooks on the cuisines of various countries and was hoping to publish one on Iran, which it didn't have yet. Najmieh fit the bill. She visited the company's offices in Paris with Mohammad. Upon meeting Najmieh, the head of Jacques Grancher chafed at the length of her surname, advising that she shorten it to "Najmieh Batman." She complied reluctantly. In 1982, after months of testing recipes, Najmieh sent her publisher a floppy disk with the manuscript.

During their years in France, Najmieh and Mohammad found occasional time to travel to America. They visited family members spread across Boston, New York, and Washington, DC. These visits made them evaluate whether they should move to America for good. In spite of its virtues, Vence wasn't the kindest place for her children, as Zal's upsetting experiences in school reminded her. By early 1983, she also learned she had another child on the way.

Najmieh and Mohammad found themselves especially attracted to Washington, which would provide a stark contrast to Vence's homogeneity. Washington was a cosmopolitan sanctuary, flush with diplomats from every corner of the globe. They'd be right at home there. When the family made the move to Washington later in 1983, French customs officials looked at Mohammad with leeriness, asking what that lumbering machine called a computer was. They treated his documents with peculiar scrutiny. Najmieh thought that maybe she and Mohammad were making the right decision in leaving France. Hopefully they wouldn't face such prejudice once they reached America.

❧

JACQUES GRANCHER DIDN'T PUBLISH *Ma cuisine d'Iran* (1984) until after Najmieh arrived in Washington. The family moved into a two-bedroom house in the neighborhood of Georgetown. In November 1983, Najmieh gave birth to the couple's second son, Rostam. She then got to writing a more ambitious, English-language cookbook. At that point, Najmieh knew of very few Iranian cookbooks that had been published in America. She was vaguely familiar with Maideh Mazda's *In a Persian Kitchen: Favorite Recipes from the Near East* (1960), which contained recipes for baklava with rosewater, chicken with pomegranate syrup, and beef with fresh peaches—recipes that were "quickly accessible to the American housewife whose groceries come from the A&P and an occasional Greek store," as *Kirkus Reviews* claimed. The food establishment was a fan, too: In an August 1960 *New York Times* article, Craig Claiborne called Mazda's book "at once a fascinating collection of recipes and, for anyone interested in the foods of other lands, a pleasure to read." Mazda, who spent her childhood between Iran and what is now Azerbaijan, made a deliberate choice with her language, repeatedly referring to herself as "Persian" and to Iran as "Persia" in the book's introduction. The Persian designation evoked a sense of romanticism. She leaned into what she termed the "exotic" nature of Persian food, a tactic that may have made the book quite appealing to white Americans.

Regardless, Mazda's cooking certainly felt closer to the Iran that Najmieh knew than whatever she read in the writer Nesta Ramazani's *Persian Cooking: A Table of Exotic Delights* (1974). Ramazani's cookbook called for ingredients like soy sauce in dishes of eggplant kuku and chicken kebabs, additions that struck Najmieh as inauthentic. It was another author, however, who had the most success with raising the visibility of Iranian cuisine in America during the 1970s, and it just so happened she was neither Iranian nor American. The American edition of the Egyptian-born author Claudia Roden's *A Book of Middle Eastern Food* (1972) represented a breakthrough in books about Middle Eastern cooking. Roden had initially published the book in the

United Kingdom, her adoptive country, in 1968. From Roden's perspective, the United Kingdom once saw the Middle East as a land of "sheep's eyes and testicles." Roden's book would provide a corrective to such stereotypes. Her recipes spanned the region; she incorporated a variety from Iran, including one for eshkeneh shirazi, a yogurt soup flavored with fenugreek, and another recipe for lamb with apples and sour cherries. She, like Mazda before her, called these recipes Persian, not Iranian. Her book was such a hit in the United Kingdom that the Knopf editor Judith Jones published it in the United States in 1972. Establishment attention followed, with James Beard fêting it as "a landmark in the field of cooking." Still, it was a general Middle Eastern cookbook, not one specifically about Iran.

Besides, that book had come out in 1972, well before the Iranian Revolution in 1979. Najmieh would be writing in a different political landscape than Roden had. Around the time Najmieh moved to Washington, American media was rife with images that stoked anti-Iranian sentiment. During the 444-day hostage crisis that began in 1979, ABC News aired a nightly show, *The Iran Crisis: America Held Hostage*, that depicted Iranians burning American flags and protesters chanting "Death to America, Death to Carter," referring to then-president Jimmy Carter. Americans likewise often held anti-Iranian rallies in the early 1980s. Among the most lasting photographs from the era showed a protester in Washington, DC, holding a sign that read "Deport All Iranians! Get the hell out of my country!"

No wonder US publishers didn't want to touch Najmieh's book. Doing so was too great a financial risk. The query letters she sent publishers between 1983 and 1984 were met with either courteous rejection or silence. But she and Mohammad tried not to let this setback deter them. Instead, Najmieh pondered if starting an independent venture might make sense. If the market didn't have room for her, fine; she'd just carve out that space for herself. Najmieh thought back to her experience with Jacques Grancher. She hadn't been terribly impressed with the publisher and was still somewhat irritated by his insistence that she shorten her name for commercial viability. If *he* was a publisher, she thought, why couldn't a true intellectual like Mohammad be one? Mohammad enrolled in a Georgetown University course on editing; Najmieh took one on design. As she got closer to finishing the book, she found that titling it became a point of stress. Should Najmieh refer to the book as Iranian or Persian? "Iranian" might lead readers to associate the book with turmoil. In contrast, "Persian" spoke to the majesty of a great civilization that existed long before Ayatollah Khomeini changed the face of the country. Deciding that both aspects were of equal importance, Najmieh reached a compromise: She would title the book *Food of Life: A Book of Ancient Persian and Modern Iranian Cooking and Ceremonies*. The subtitle was a sweeping embrace of the country's history, linking its Persian past to its Iranian present. She and Mohammad went to great lengths to reach out to Iranian audiences in America. To build passion for the project, they opened up the telephone book and found the names of roughly a thousand Iranians in America, mailing brochures with information about the book. Najmieh also solicited recipe testers by hanging up ads on Georgetown's campus asking for people who'd want to try Iranian food.

Once Najmieh completed the manuscript, she and Mohammad found a printer in Baltimore and printed seven thousand copies, pricing the book at $35. The nearly 250-page cookbook, eventually published in the spring of 1986, opened with notes of longing: Najmieh told readers how the scent of onions and garlic made her see the pantry of her childhood kitchen clearly once again. "Perhaps this book was inspired most by those perfumed memories," she wrote. Najmieh presented a wide gallery of recipes: rhubarb stewed with meat, long-grain rice studded with sour cherries, and rose petal jelly. These recipes didn't have headnotes, just spare explanatory passages that framed each chapter. She used the start of each section to discuss the crucial role of soup in Iranian tradition or the Iranian love for fluffy, thick egg kukus. *Food of Life* was a handsome production: forty-eight color photographs by Serge Ephraim, the same man who'd photographed her first book, accompanied the text. The calligrapher A. H. Tabnak wrote each recipe name in Persian script. Najmieh filled the pages with poems from Persian poets like Hafez and Omar Khayyam, who had died centuries ago, honoring her native country's cultural history.

Najmieh was bowled over by a positive review from *Publishers Weekly* in July 1986. Reviewer Penny Kaganoff praised the assortment of "uncomplicated recipes" that populated the book's pages, like lamb brochettes, carrot preserves, and baklava. But the book otherwise received little attention from the press in that first year. *Food of Life*'s success hinged on word of mouth. Najmieh and Mohammad visited bookstores and begged them to carry her book. Slowly, it found a devoted audience in the Iranian diaspora, recent arrivals like her who emigrated after the revolution. Some of those readers happened to belong to Najmieh's generation. They would write her letters, telling Najmieh that reading her recipes rekindled memories that their minds had almost washed away.

It still wasn't easy to be Iranian in America through the 1980s, even as the Iranian Revolution and the Iran hostage crisis became more distant in public memory. Najmieh taught her sons to take pride in their Iranian heritage. As Zal and Rostam grew older, Najmieh would coordinate with their grade school teachers to hold celebrations for Nowruz, the Iranian New Year. Najmieh found that these festivities irked the other Iranian parents at the school, though. They identified as American, not Iranian. Why, they wondered, would Najmieh announce that she was from Iran so publicly? But she wasn't ashamed.

〜

NAJMIEH'S FAN BASE began to widen beyond the Iranian diaspora at the turn of the decade. Book distribution networks like Ingram and Baker & Taylor started including Mage in their channels. She also sold her book directly to Borders, a bookstore chain that had locations across the country.

It helped that Najmieh put out a slightly updated version of *Food of Life* in 1990. The new edition included revised recipes and other tweaks based on suggestions from readers, along with even more color photographs. She also remarked upon her crossover appeal in the preface, where Najmieh acknowledged the original edition's warm reception "both by the expatriate community and by the general public," calling the book "an excellent introduction for our American friends to the Persian culture through the art of Persian cooking." Thanks to this revised edition, the food establishment got wind of Najmieh. In June 1990, the *New York Times* included Najmieh's book in a roundup of summer cookbooks. Writer Nancy Harmon Jenkins saw the intent of Najmieh's work clearly, observing how she wrote "nostalgically but unsentimentally. Readers will gain a sense of a cuisine that may have been buried under modern Iranian puritanism but is being preserved by exiles." In a November 1990 *Los Angeles Times* piece on noteworthy cookbooks (another one of which was Julie Sahni's *Moghul Microwave*), the writer Grace Kirschenbaum also applauded Najmieh's bravery as an exile writing under fraught political conditions:

> Ours is an age of political turmoil, with migrations and displacements of entire ethnic groups. Often such events result in extraordinary cookbooks that would never have been written in more tranquil periods. One of these is Najmieh Batmanglij's "Food of Life," now the definitive book on Iranian cooking: not just a recipe collection but a fond introduction to a culture and a fascinating cuisine— customs, folk tales, ceremonies, poetry, sayings and proverbs and excellent recipes.

The American food media understood the spirit of Najmieh's project, along with all she fought as an émigré writer. In the early 1990s, America's critical class was becoming more attuned to the prejudice that Iranians routinely faced in America. Some film critics were rightly unkind about Brian Gilbert's *Not without My Daughter* (1991), a movie starring Sally Field as an American wife trapped in Iran by her repressive Iranian husband. The film was also a commercial disappointment. Perhaps change was afoot. As America's spite for Iran faded over the next few years, Najmieh continued to get press. Najmieh appeared in her local paper, the *Washington Post*, in May 1992. In the eyes of reporter Candy Sagon, Najmieh was a woman with progressive political values who "manages to balance her traditional roots with modern reality." Sagon visited Najmieh in the kitchen, where she prepared a bountiful feast that included a yogurt and cucumber dip, grilled chicken kebabs, and a pot of basmati rice with orange peel, carrots, and raisins. The next day, Sagon followed Najmieh as she took Zal and Rostam to a pro-choice rally. "I wanted to show my sons that there are some serious issues that women are concerned about," Najmieh explained to Sagon. Around this time, Najmieh started working on a more robust update to *Food of Life*. Released by Mage in the spring of 1993, *New Food of Life*, as she called it, contained an array of new recipes and 120 photos. *New Food of Life* ushered in another wave of attention for Najmieh from the press. The *Washington Post* ran a long profile of Najmieh in March 1993 tied to the publication of the book. In that article, Najmieh would admit that she missed Iran, but she also told the paper of feeling tethered to America. Flying into Washington after a long trip, she would say, filled her with the same relief as going to Tehran once had. This country was now her home. "I love America," she told the paper. "It's a wonderful place for the stateless."

⁓

NAJMIEH WOULDN'T RETURN to Iran until 2015, when she began researching her eighth book, *Cooking in Iran: Regional Recipes and Kitchen Secrets* (2018). Over the prior decades, she had written a variety of cookbooks, not all of them explicitly Iranian; *Silk Road Cooking: A Vegetarian Journey* (2002), for example, explored the food traditions that sat along that historic trading route. She started writing *Cooking in Iran*, however, in a bid to subdue a recurring dream she had of going back to Tehran. When she finally did go, her experience was disorienting. The quirks of language, how to use a telephone, the currency: Iran was nothing like she remembered.

The book, over seven hundred pages long, began with the story of her arrival in Tehran, where she paid a visit to her parents' graves. She went on to record the recipes from regional pockets across the country. She got a few from restaurants, like the soup of lamb's head, feet, and tripe she ate in Tehran. Others she obtained from home cooks, like the recipe for jam made from pistachio hulls that she received from a family in the city of Kerman.

Like each of Najmieh's cookbooks, *Cooking in Iran* was published by Mage. Despite the veneration for Najmieh in some circles, no lucrative deals from larger houses have lured her away from Mage. Working under Mohammad's editorship has afforded her creative freedom. But the fact that Najmieh forged her path independently speaks to prejudices wired into the American market as far back as the 1980s. In that early period, Najmieh was effectively a one-woman industry, the lone diplomat of Iranian cooking in America. In shouldering this responsibility, she established a blueprint for writing about Iranian food in the country. It would take decades before major American publishers deemed Iranian cookbooks worthy of acceptance. Today, a younger generation of Iranian-origin authors in America is bearing the fruits of Najmieh's labor. They no longer have to self-publish these cookbooks as Najmieh has done for her entire career. The topics of the Iranian Revolution and displacement loom large in their work. It's tough to imagine a book like the Iranian-born author Naz Deravian's *Bottom of the Pot: Persian Recipes and Stories* (2018), in which Deravian describes fleeing Iran for Italy after the Iranian Revolution in the opening pages, existing without Najmieh's *Food of Life*.

But widespread recognition for Najmieh, from either the food establishment or the public, has come belatedly. Some may offer her writing's encyclopedic breadth as a reason for this: The perceived intimidation factor of her books, and *Food of Life* in particular, may have prevented immediate adoption of her work among more casual cooks. Yet there are more complicated factors at play. Najmieh wasn't writing for white Americans, at least not at first. She was writing for her own people. Nor was she just an immigrant; she was a woman writing in exile during a time of great hostility toward Iranians. Najmieh also made political expression central to her work, a daring choice considering so many consumers may, even now, see cooking as an anodyne, apolitical leisure activity. She began writing to salvage the national identity that the Iranian state tried to suppress following the Iranian Revolution. In her new American home, Najmieh chose to rebuild that very identity through food. Cooking was her gesture of resistance. Though *Cooking in Iran* may have represented a long-awaited homecoming for Najmieh, she did not write this book merely for her own gratification. The book was "for young Iranians and the struggle for the soul of Iran," she wrote. The fight was ongoing; it would not end with her.

The Taste of Papaya

Norma Shirley

B. AUGUST 13, 1938, SAINT JAMES PARISH, JAMAICA

D. NOVEMBER 1, 2010, KINGSTON, JAMAICA

I N 1979, Norma Shirley was fantasizing about a different future. "It's my dream to open another restaurant in Jamaica where Blacks would be the majority clientele," the 40-year-old chef told the American magazine *Essence*. At the time, Norma was working as the chef and manager of the Station restaurant in the Berkshires, a very wealthy, very white hamlet in Massa-chusetts. There, she cooked what she termed "French cuisine with a Jamaican accent," with dishes like suckling pig, pumpkin soup, and rice and peas. A former nurse and midwife, Norma was a headstrong woman. She was born in Jamaica but left her native country after adolescence, living in Scotland, Sweden, England, and eventually America. Feeling determined, she decided to give New York City a shot before returning to Jamaica, separating from her husband and moving to the city with her son in 1981. She hoped to open a restaurant there. But Norma quickly learned that she was a dime a dozen in the city, just another nobody who could cook. Norma faced a score of disadvantages in New York:

139

The city was one of the most competitive markets for restaurants in the world, to start. She was a single mother. She had no formal culinary training. And she was a Black woman whose cooking came from a part of the world that the white American food establishment didn't yet fully understand.

It took a few months for Norma to abandon her ambitions to open a restaurant in New York. Instead, she found fulfillment working as a food stylist and caterer for the media company Condé Nast. She honed her craft in this job, feeding models and photographers lunches of jerk chicken pasta salad, chilled cucumber soups, and stuffed snow peas. These light, refreshing dishes had a whisper of her Jamaican roots.

But after five years, she had the urge to return home. Norma moved back to Jamaica in 1986 and, over the next two decades, opened a spate of restaurants in cities all across the country— Kingston, Montego Bay, Negril, and Port Antonio. All venues bore her name. At these restaurants, Norma served highly stylized dishes that drew upon Jamaican flavors: Cornish hen with slabs of fried breadfruit, red pea bisque with a shock of brandy, rum and raisin cheesecake. Norma saw the same malleability in French cooking that Madeleine Kamman recognized just a few years before, applying the principles of French cooking to Jamaica's fruits, vegetables, and spices. Back in Jamaica, Norma was freed of a burden she had to carry in America: She no longer had to cook for white audiences. Instead, she could focus on cooking for the people of her island. She worked toward getting her fellow Jamaicans to see the beauty in their native ingredients. "Our soil is a very rich soil, and our fruits and vegetables just have a completely different flavor and taste," she once told a journalist in America. "For instance, papaya that comes in from Jamaica has a very sweet, succulent, sensuous taste to it, you know?" The way Norma saw it, Jamaican cuisine was not static. It was always finding new forms of expression. Norma sought to free the cuisine from the nostalgic trappings that some islanders were eager to keep it in. So many around her could not extricate dishes from the legacy of plantation food, with hearty breakfasts meant to sustain enslaved people before a grueling workday. But Norma would take a plate of stew peas, with pigtail or beef shin, and puree the peas so they became a bisque. She'd add brandy, peck it with cream, and plant a sprig of Italian parsley on top. Such gestures weren't meaningless aesthetic flourishes. Those choices were Norma's way of reframing a dish that affluent Jamaicans may have once turned up their noses at. Her cooking clarified Jamaican cuisine's innate excellence. Call her style nouvelle Jamaican; call it Creole. Whatever it was, Norma's food resisted easy classification, like the woman herself.

NORMA ELISE SMITH was born in 1938 in the yawning hills of Saint James Parish, located in the island's northwest. Jamaica was idyllic in her childhood. Her parents, Lucy Gibson and Verley Smith, would sometimes take her to visit Montego Bay, back when the city was untouched by tourists.

She belonged to a multicultural family: Norma's maternal grandfather was Scottish, while other relatives wed people of Chinese, East Indian, Italian, and Jewish ancestry. Those relatives brought their influences to the kitchen table. Norma would later remark that eating with them made her feel like Alice tumbling into Wonderland. She was just 9 when her parents left Jamaica and traveled to the United States in search of work, leaving Norma in the care of relatives. Her maternal grandparents owned a banana plantation where she'd spend her summers. Norma would walk into the fields and mingle with the workers, eating all that the land had to offer: guava, naseberries, mangoes. She didn't look down on these workers as other well-off Jamaicans did; she respected those who tilled the land. Her grandparents tried to forbid her from eating with the workers, but Norma refused to listen. When she returned to the house on those evenings, her grandparents would give her a flogging.

As a student at St. Hugh's boarding school in Kingston, Norma began contemplating a life outside of Jamaica. She had aspirations to become an architect or an interior designer, careers unheard of for girls like her in Jamaica in the 1950s. Her more realistic options included becoming a teacher, a secretary, or a nurse. So after graduating in 1954, Norma went off to study surgical nursing at Scotland's Southern General Hospital. Scotland was quite different from Jamaica. She figured this out upon finishing school, when she found work as a helicopter rescue nurse. Norma would travel to villages to pick up ailing patients. These people probably hadn't seen a Black woman before, she thought.

What Norma ate in Scotland intensified her feeling of being an outsider. The country felt like culinary backwater to her, a place of pallid meats, soggy peas, and sodden cabbage. Jamaica, meanwhile, had carrots and tomatoes and chayotes, or what Jamaicans like her called chochos, plucked fresh from the earth. Maybe she would have to learn how to cook. If she were to have a life outside of Jamaica, what other choice would she have? Starve?

⁓

NORMA RETURNED TO JAMAICA in the early 1960s. While working as a surgical nurse at the University of the West Indies Medical

School in Kingston, she met a man named Michael Shirley, who was training as a gynecologist. Michael had been raised and educated in England; growing up in Europe had exposed him to the cuisines of the world. The pair wed in 1965 and embarked on a honeymoon across Europe, where Norma developed a particular affinity for French cuisine. This experience nudged Norma closer to the kitchen. But she couldn't even boil water. Knowing this needed to change, Norma bought a pile of Julia Child cookbooks and studied them. With practice, she trained herself to look at six different chicken recipes and absorb all the information they had to offer. She'd borrow elements from each one to create a dish of her own. Always, Michael pushed her to be a better cook. With his encouragement, she began cooking with Jamaican ingredients like pig's tails and neckbones, seasoning them with her own ingenuity.

Norma still worked as a nurse and midwife in those years, though Michael's job had them bouncing around Europe. The family lived in Västerås, Sweden, for most of 1969. While there, Norma gave birth to a son, Delius. The family then decamped for Dulwich, just outside London. Europe would just be a stopover, though. When Delius was about a year old, the family moved to New York City, settling on Manhattan's Upper West Side. In New York, Norma served as the head of nursing at the Eastern Women's Center, an abortion clinic. But food's pull was growing stronger. She enjoyed hosting dinner parties for her and Michael's friends, filling her table with premium cheeses and meats. Her palate became more discerning, too: Norma started to hate mass-produced foods. For the first few years of Delius's life, she forbade him from having indulgences like a burger from McDonald's or even a peanut butter and jelly sandwich. Instead, Norma packed his lunch boxes with Brie sandwiches and foie gras, making him an oddity at school. Norma's workdays at the clinic kept her busy, but she often found herself unable to sleep at night. To calm her late-night disturbances, she wandered into the kitchen. The space soothed her. She had control when she cooked. The pots and pans didn't talk back to her, she would later say.

~

IN JUNE 1976, Michael found a job at the Berkshire Medical Center in Massachusetts, uprooting the family three hours north of New York. They moved to a house that straddled the neighboring towns of Lenox and Stockbridge.

When Norma got to the Berkshires, she felt as though she'd landed on a different planet. Her living situation wasn't exactly the trouble: The family moved into a two-hundred-year-old former barn, a house so big that using its fireplace might have required burning a whole tree. It was an ideal place to cook. The wood-paneled kitchen had an electric stove. She could grow fresh vegetables in their backyard garden. But there were other issues. The Berkshires weather felt strange to Norma. Though the lush summers reminded her of Jamaica, the winters were miserably cold. She couldn't relate much to the people, either; the rich ladies around her were content with spending their days at home. Norma initially held on to her job in New York. She followed an exhausting routine: She'd commute to the city and work for three days, sleeping in the apartment she kept there, then return to Stockbridge for long weekends. After a year, though, Norma left nursing for good. Becoming a housewife wasn't an option for her. Norma thought she might just die of boredom if she spent her days wondering if she should switch her drapes.

She knew she had to do something else with her time. An idea came to Norma on a Friday evening in summer 1977: She was in a cafeteria in Tanglewood, the site of a popular open-air music concert series in the Berkshires. The food disgusted her. *Anyone* could cook something better than what they served her, she thought. Norma certainly could. So she decided to start a small operation of her own, filling picnic baskets with her cooking for concertgoers. To advertise the venture, she had cards printed with the words "Gourmet picnics made to order" along with her home phone number, pinning them to bulletin boards around town. Anyone who called would stop by her house and fetch a basket with a wine glass, metal cutlery, and a plate of food. Doubt crept in. Maybe no one would bite, she worried. So she booked a trip to Boston for the weekend, trying to take her mind off matters. But requests unexpectedly piled up while she was away. Upon Norma's return to the Berkshires, she got to work. She bought peach baskets from the farmers' market and wine glasses from Bloomingdale's. Each basket, she decided, would contain chicken breasts stuffed with prosciutto and mushrooms; French bread filled with caviar, eggs, bacon, onions, and chives; a tomato salad; and chocolate mousse. Norma sold these feasts for the perhaps-too-reasonable price of $5. The only condition she had for her customers was that they return the basket, glasses, silverware, and plates undamaged.

Word of her basket business spread rapidly. Within a week, the calls about her service doubled. It was clear that Norma was fulfilling a need in her community. Norma taught herself how to scale her venture: She raised the price of her baskets to $8, then $10. By November, she went ahead and added dinner baskets. Her menu expanded accordingly. She offered carrot, leek, or red bean soups along with dishes like potatoes au gratin, chicken spiced with Jamaican Pickapeppa Sauce, and filet of beef with green peppercorns. The sheer variety showcased how much Norma had blossomed as a cook since marrying Michael a decade earlier. Her menu mainly reflected her love for the cooking of Western Europe. But that chicken with a jolt of Pickapeppa Sauce, so distinctly Jamaican, was an early sign of where her cooking could carry her in the years to come.

"Norma's instinct with a sauce is Heaven-given," observed the writer Milton R. Bass in a November 1977 article in the *Berkshire Eagle*, a local paper. The piece was full of praise, but Bass also made clear how much Norma stuck out in her lily-white surroundings. "If the person who answers has a British accent with a special little lilt to it, don't hang up," Bass wrote. "That's a real Jamaican you are hearing. Accept no substitute."

❧

THE STOCKBRIDGE STATION had many faces before it became a restaurant. Its days as an actual train station were long gone by 1965, when the building turned into a discotheque. A year later, it became a gift shop. In 1978, one of Norma's neighbors, an Italian actor named Terence Hill, decided to convert it into a restaurant. Hill, a star in the spaghetti westerns of Italian cinema, had moved to Stockbridge in 1975. Norma and her family arrived next door a year later. Her food impressed Hill so much that he asked Norma to serve as the restaurant's chef and manager. The Station restaurant opened in June 1978. The space, which could fit forty people, resembled a European café, with ferns, a grand piano, and a red brick fireplace. An open rail car, a remnant from an earlier era, doubled as a plant stand.

The restaurant began as a reservation-only establishment, open five days a week, with a lunch menu, a tea menu, bar service, and one set entrée for dinner. Norma characterized her evolving style as

"New England food with Jamaican flair." The only coffee she served was Jamaican Blue Mountain coffee, for example. She prepared dishes like Jamaican meat patties encased in pastry shells and curried shrimp on toast. It didn't take long for the restaurant, a novelty within its environs, to gain national recognition. In a feature for the April 1979 issue of *Essence*, reporter Stephanie Stokes noted the quietly subversive aspect of a Black woman cooking Caribbean food in a town "where Norman Rockwell lived and painted his view of America." Months later, in the summer of 1979, an article in *Gentlemen's Quarterly* fêted the unassuming restaurant as the find of the summer. Norma wasn't expecting such laurels so early on. She promptly bought twenty copies of that *GQ* issue, practically emptying the newsstand. That mention marked a turning point for Norma's career. The taste of fame made her more ambitious.

The positive press continued into the next decade. At the beginning of 1980, *Boston Globe* restaurant critic Anthony Spinazzola, who'd been a champion of Madeleine Kamman's Newton restaurant through the 1970s, gave Norma's restaurant a rave of a three-star review, heralding Norma as a chef who "does marvelous things in the kitchen." He showered particular praise on her scrod chowder, a silken blend of light cream, butter, fish, and parsley.

But as time elapsed, the demands of Norma's cooking career put a strain on her marriage. There was another troubling development she had to deal with: Norma began to feel distant from her actual homeland of Jamaica. One summer, her employees asked for the day off, telling her they wanted to see some reggae singer she'd never heard of. His name was Bob Marley, they told her, and he was Jamaican like Norma. She joined her staffers at the concert. The crowd was bigger than any other she'd ever seen for a musician in the Berkshires. Norma couldn't understand Marley's appeal at all, though. He was from a version of Jamaica she could no longer recognize.

❦

AFTER THREE YEARS of running the Station restaurant, Norma was ready for a new challenge. In 1981, she ceded control of the restaurant back to Hill. She separated from Michael. Norma's conviction drove her back to Manhattan. She figured it was a logical place for her to open a restaurant of her own. The clientele would be bigger than in the Berkshires, right? Norma, then 43, took young Delius and moved to a one-bedroom apartment on Sixty-Eighth Street and Broadway, just blocks from Central Park.

She helped her friend, a fellow Jamaica native named Yvonne Scherrer, open a restaurant called Devon House Ltd. on the Upper East Side. Scherrer's food resembled Norma's. She served variations on Jamaican food like a filet of beef massaged with Pickapeppa Sauce alongside capers, for example. These à la carte items could cost nearly $30, pricey for the era. Scherrer's restaurant was unique in many ways: For one, it was a fine dining establishment, flying in the face of the stereotype that Jamaican food wasn't worth dishing out money for. It was also located in Manhattan. In that period, Jamaican immigrants who owned restaurants in New York tended to be working-class immigrants in the Brooklyn neighborhoods of Flatbush, East Flatbush, and Crown Heights. Like Scherrer, Norma firmly believed that Jamaican cuisine was as fine as any other. But convincing New York's food establishment of that truth wouldn't be easy.

Despite her dogged efforts, Norma's goal to open her own restaurant in New York gradually started to seem like a fever dream. She didn't have many connections to the city's restaurant industry beyond Scherrer and couldn't find any investors. She began to lose hope, spending most of her time in her apartment, wasting away watching soap operas while she waited for Delius to return home from school. She would then fall asleep praying that morning would not come. What broke Norma from her spell of depression was a call from an assistant to Polly Mellen, who was then a high-ranking editor at *Vogue*. The magazine was set to do a shoot with supermodel and actress Brooke Shields, and the team needed a catered lunch for eight at the World Trade Center. The magazine's staff had heard that Norma was an excellent chef back in the Berkshires. Norma knew on the spot that she'd take the gig, but she put on an act, fibbing to the caller that she'd have to check her datebook to see whether she'd have room in her packed schedule. She didn't have any appointments, of course, but she was skilled in the art of pretend.

The initial shoot went so well that Mellen decided to hire Norma as a consultant. On shoots, Norma prepared light, tropical dishes that wouldn't suffer if they sat out for hours. She filled tables with gazpacho, baguettes soaked in garlic butter, and warm chicken breast salads with julienned carrot, potato, and slices of mango and papaya. These were visual feasts, too; presentation was crucial to Norma, so she often adorned her dishes with flowers. Catering and styling required taxing work hours, but Norma didn't mind at first. She wasn't much of a sleeper anyway. Norma would begin working as night lingered into morning. With the help of an assistant named Mischa Manderson Mills, Norma would bring her food to the Condé Nast building at around six in the morning. Her association with Mellen led to Norma catering for photographers like Hiro and Irving Penn, and for celebrities like Christie Brinkley and Raquel Welch. She soon branched into styling for *Gourmet*, the food magazine owned by Condé Nast. This work clearly made more sense for Norma than opening a restaurant in New York. But five years of working that job in that hectic city eventually wore on her.

Delius was getting older and would soon be leaving for boarding school in Massachusetts. Norma feared that she'd get lonely without her son. At 47, Norma wondered if it was time to go back home.

⌒

"JUST A FEW YEARS AGO, anyone with a serious interest in food discounted the Caribbean—an area that was visited for its climate and beaches but not for its cuisine," wrote Nancy Harmon Jenkins in a *New York Times* article published in April 1986, the same year Norma returned to Jamaica. But, Jenkins went on to declare, "The food of the Caribbean has become the hottest eating ticket in New York." Jenkins attributed this trend to a variety of factors: tourism to the region, a sudden demand for Caribbean cookbooks in America (though she did not name any), and the New York metropolitan area's significant Jamaican, Barbadian, and Cuban populations. The article captured the food establishment's attitudes toward Caribbean cuisine at the time, presupposing an affluent, likely white reader. For example, Jenkins cautioned that restaurants in "ethnic neighborhoods" might "intimidate the uninitiated." At least, she assured the reader, the food was "astonishingly cheap." Maybe Norma wouldn't have to fight as hard for respect back home. But that wasn't exactly easy, she'd soon realize.

Upon returning to Jamaica, Norma settled in Kingston, where she planned to open a restaurant called Norma's on Belmont Road. She dipped into a pool of $10,000 she had in personal savings and hired her friends to wait tables. Norma knew early on that she didn't want to cook for tourists. Jamaicans came first. But Jamaicans didn't quite get Norma's food, which she termed "nouvelle Jamaican." They didn't understand what a jackfruit salad was doing on the menu, for example. The restaurant was just a stone's throw away from Embassy Row, which attracted the city's upper and middle classes. But some patrons didn't comprehend why Norma would employ her friends as waitstaff; so many wealthier Jamaicans were used to treating service workers as subordinates. Norma kept cooking anyway. With time, her efforts began to make an impact. She had more luck reaching Jamaicans who had, like her, studied abroad, only to find themselves home once again after completing school. Diners like them took to preparations like her curried lobster with a flambé of mango and her roast loin of pork with prunes and tangerine marmalade.

In early 1992, she opened her second restaurant, Norma at the Wharfhouse, in a town just west of Montego Bay called Reading. She mounted the project with the help of Delius, now an adult; he left a finance job in America to be with his mother again. The restaurant was housed in a three-hundred-year-old former sugar factory. There, Norma offered even more of her clever takes on Jamaican cooking. She made smoked marlin with mango salsa; she baked crab shells and stuffed the cavities with crabmeat, Scotch bonnet chiles, and toasted bread crumbs. This restaurant would put Norma back in front of an American audience. In November 1992, *Vogue* writer Richard Alleman referred to her as "the Julia Child of Jamaica" in a piece recommending hotels and restaurants across the Caribbean. Norma was initially thrilled by the comparison to Julia. She excitedly told her mother, who lived in New York, about the news. But her mother shot back with skepticism when she heard the reference to Julia: "Isn't she dead?"

❧

AS JENKINS HAD PREDICTED in the pages of the *New York Times*, America's food establishment was starting to show a bit more respect toward Caribbean cooking in the 1980s and 1990s. These developments did not constitute a revolution by any means, though. Some growth was reflected in the publishing landscape, with cookbooks like *Ma Chance's French Caribbean Creole Cooking* (1985), by Saint Martin's Jeanne Louise Duzant Chance, and *Island Cooking: Recipes from the Caribbean* (1988), by Jamaica native Dunstan A. Harris. The closest America may have come to a breakout Jamaican cookbook in that period was the Jamaican-born Helen Willinsky's *Jerk: Barbecue from Jamaica* (1990). "To eat jerk is to feel the influences from which it developed," Willinsky declared in the opening pages, stressing Jamaican cooking's global nature. "It is as if you can hear the African, Indian, and calypso cultures that produced it."

Had she wanted to, maybe Norma could've emerged with a cookbook that showed American readers Jamaican cuisine in all its splendor. It's impossible to tell: She never published any cookbooks of her own, though she hinted at one in various interviews throughout the 1990s. Stray recipes of hers did, however, appear frequently in American cookbooks with many contributors, evidence of her authority on Jamaican cuisine. For example, the food writer Sheila Lukins featured Norma's jerk pork ribs—slathered in soy sauce, orange juice, allspice, thyme, and Scotch bonnet chiles—in *All Around the World Cookbook* (1994), wherein Lukins referred to Norma as "an extraordinary, talented woman." A recipe for Norma's shrimp Jamaica appeared in Frances McCullough and Barbara Witt's *Great Feasts without Fuss* (1995), a cookbook of recipes from revered white chefs like Diana Kennedy, the British-born expert on Mexican cuisine, and Paula Wolfert, a Brooklyn native who specialized in Mediterranean cuisine. Norma's recipe called for simmering the shrimp in a puree of butter, scallions, garlic, Scotch bonnets, thyme, and chicken stock.

Norma didn't need a cookbook in order for the American food establishment to hold her in high esteem; her restaurants accomplished that for her. The American food media was similarly smitten: In the 1990s, her cooking caught the attention of America's "Big Three" food magazines, *Food & Wine*, *Bon Appétit*, and *Gourmet*. Her stateside profile rose even higher in 1994, the year she lent her name to Norma's on the Beach, a Miami Beach restaurant operated by Delius and his business and life partner, the chef Cindy Hutson. The pair openly told the press that they rode Norma's coattails in naming the restaurant, knowing her clout would bring the establishment more buzz. Though Norma's actual involvement in the operation was minimal (she would ship coffee, produce, and fish from Montego Bay over to Miami), the menu shared Norma's sensibility. Fried ravioli stuffed with crabmeat, jerk pork loin with rum raisins: These dishes bore a mark that was undeniably Norma's.

In September 1995, the James Beard Foundation asked Norma to host its first Jamaican meal, another promising sign that Norma's work was shifting the American food establishment's perspective on Jamaican food. Hosting meals at the Beard House served as an emblem of honor. At the dinner, she stuck jerked chicken breasts on skewers; she poached a fillet of red snapper in spices and topped the fish with chayote. Even the drinks were Jamaican: Red Stripe beer, Jamaican Blue Mountain coffee. Meals at the Beard House were exclusionary by design; Norma's dinner, like most others held at the venue, cost $75 for members and $95 for guests. But in those days, much of America synonymized Jamaican food with cheap food, an excuse for not taking the cuisine seriously. Norma's cooking challenged such assumptions. "In the last few years, Jamaican cuisine has overtaken the city," declared *New York Daily News* writer Whitney Walker in a piece featuring Norma's Beard House dinner. "But where once you'd stumble across a roti stand in Queens, or a jerk house in the Bronx, now Jamaican restaurants are trading in their plastic forks for silver." Jamaican food, Walker suggested, was shedding its working-class associations, and Walker credited Norma with being "the leader of the trend." Norma carefully avoided the language of elevation when speaking about her specific interpretation of Jamaican cuisine, though. She was a firm believer in Jamaican cuisine's inherent worth. Norma acknowledged that a dish's lack of aesthetic polish could sometimes prevent outsiders from seeing the cuisine's possibilities. But that prejudice wasn't unique to Americans—she'd noticed that this absence of visual flair could lead Jamaicans to underestimate their own cuisine, too. Her primary goal was to get Jamaicans to see their food with pride. To do this, she took an ingredient like ackee, the national fruit of Jamaica, and gave it unexpected treatments: She would fold it into an ackee soufflé, or whip up an ackee bisque. Norma could imagine endless possibilities beyond traditional dishes like ackee and salted codfish.

⌒

THOUGH NORMA DIDN'T have her own cooking show, television helped her build her fame in America. She filmed three episodes of the popular cooking show *Great Chefs of the World*, broadcast on the Discovery Channel, beginning in 1998, along with an episode of its spinoff series, *Great Chefs of the Caribbean*. The shows positioned her as a figure of enormous influence. "She has come to personify the cooking of not only Jamaica, but the whole of the Caribbean," the narrator of *Great Chefs*, Mary Lou Conroy, told viewers.

In these segments, Norma articulated her vision of what she termed a "new world" cuisine that didn't confine itself to Jamaican borders. Norma arranged three broiled baby lamb chops on a nest of callaloo in one episode, sprinkling the plate's edges with parsley. In another, she put curried nuggets of lobster in a papaya boat. But Norma's fleeting appearances on television could do only so much to change the American food establishment's outlook on Jamaican cooking. In 1999, when Delius and Cindy's restaurant Ortanique opened in Coral Gables, Florida, the *Esquire* food critic John Mariani put the restaurant on his list of the country's best new restaurants. The recognition came with a caveat: "Jamaica does not leap to mind when I think of great food," wrote Mariani, "so it's odd—and very welcome—to find one of the best new restaurants of 1999 drawing on that island nation for inspiration." Today, Mariani's inclusion of Ortanique reads as a patronizing conferral of legitimacy, casually insulting an entire island's cuisine. Whatever the case, Norma's work could not single-handedly undo the American food establishment's dismissal of Jamaican cuisine. She was just one woman.

ᔕ

NORMA'S CRUSADE to get Jamaicans to honor their own food continued into the last decade of her life. She opened more restaurants in her name: Norma's on the Terrace in Kingston, Norma's at the Marina in Port Antonio, and Norma's on the Beach in Negril. American magazines continued to acknowledge her talents. In 2000, *Condé Nast Traveler* named Norma's on the Terrace to its "Hot List," which recognized sixty noteworthy new restaurants across the globe. Six years later, Norma authored a dinner party menu for an issue of *Bon Appétit* dedicated to the Caribbean. Her spread contained recipes for sautéed chayote with garlic and herbs, guava-stuffed chicken with caramelized mango, and a sweet potato, onion, and apple gratin.

The American press often latched on to the phrase "the Julia Child of Jamaica" when discussing Norma, occasionally calling her "the Julia Child of the Caribbean." A similar rhetorical trap has ensnared so many women throughout history: Some have called Marcella Hazan "the Julia Child of Italian food," or Julie Sahni "the Julia Child of India." Such analogies cast these women in Julia's shadow, suggesting they will always struggle to attain her level of name recognition. At any rate, Norma wore these grand appellations with a smidge of hesitation. "Oh, God, no . . . I don't see myself as the Grand Dame of Caribbean cooking," she told Jamaican newspaper the *Gleaner* in 2003. "It sounds pretentious but I thank the people who believe I am. I am just a quiet person who enjoys cooking and would love to give Jamaican people a little more understanding of what cooking can do for them." Some onlookers in America understood Norma's intentions. The author and scholar Jessica B. Harris, for example, in her cookbook *Beyond Gumbo: Creole Fusion Food from the Atlantic Rim* (2003), wrote that Norma's cooking "hints at the way of the future, blending the tastes of the past with the aesthetics of the present."

Norma cooked less often in her final years. When she was nearing 70, afflicted with diabetes, she stepped away from her restaurants. But her star did not dim. In one of her final television appearances, on the Canadian Food Network series *At the Table with . . .* , Norma talked about the joy of starting a cooking school to pass on her gifts to others. "Don't be afraid of the food," she told one student in the episode. "It's not going to bite you."

Norma died of pneumonia at age 72, shortly after opening a final restaurant, Grog Shoppe in Kingston. Her death sent the nation into a period of mourning. "Her love for our country kept her here, although international fame could have taken her to foreign lands to take advantage of her talents in the culinary arena," read a letter to the editor in the *Gleaner* just after Norma's death. It's indeed tempting to envision a different version of Norma's story, one in which she stayed in New York. Had she worked at it, would she have succeeded in America? It was in Jamaica, after all, where Norma could express her culinary voice without filter. She blended cuisines out of pure passion, and her cooking inspired enough devotion for her to make a living out of running restaurants. In America, Norma was a Black immigrant woman. There is little guarantee that she would've had an easier time in today's American restaurant industry, where access to capital is still so often inextricable from whiteness. And the false impressions of Caribbean food that stymied Norma in America persist in the current era. "The aspect of West Indian food most often misrepresented is a belief that it is only a rustic, unrefined cuisine," the Jamaican restaurateurs Michelle and Suzanne Rousseau wrote in the introduction to *Provisions: The Roots of Caribbean Cooking* (2018). Norma spent her entire career dispelling that myth with her cooking of precision.

At a certain point, this thought exercise becomes futile: Pondering how Norma would have fared in America does a disservice to her legacy. Making food for white Americans was never her chief aim. She went home for a reason.

Afterword

T HERE'S A LONG LIST of immigrant women who could have qualified for this collection. Before settling on the seven women you've just met, I thought of writing about the British chef Dione Lucas, one of the first women to have her own televised cooking show in America, even before Julia Child. There was the Eritrean chef Desta Bairu, the chef of Mamma Desta, the pioneering Ethiopian restaurant in Washington, DC, in the late 1970s. Or the Palestinian chef Rawia Bishara, whose restaurant Tanoreen is a Brooklyn institution. I could go on. All of these women deserve their own biographical essays, at the very least. If I don't write about them, I hope others will. (Consider this an invitation.)

The seven brilliant immigrant women in this book—Chao Yang Buwei, Elena Zelayeta, Madeleine Kamman, Marcella Hazan, Julie Sahni, Najmieh Batmanglij, and Norma Shirley—worked hard to preserve their creative inclinations under the pressures of a system that dictated they make their talents, their voices, and their food as palatable to the masses as possible, and for commercial gain. Such constraints did not always hinder them from achieving full expression, though. This book is my attempt to uncloak the extent of their contributions. I have tried to vault these seven women to the same canon that James Beard, Julia Child, and Craig Claiborne now belong to, or what the writer Molly O'Neill referred to as the nation's "gastronomic trinity." (Some of these women don't need any assistance;

Marcella Hazan remains a revered figure by many.) The seven women in this book helped popularize flavors that challenged the nation's dominant palate. They also established new aesthetic standards in cooking for generations of chefs and food writers to come. Proper credit, however, did not always follow for these women and their labor. I can only hope that future narratives of culinary history in America will build on this scholarly motivation, honoring these immigrant women instead of looking past them.

As you traveled through these chapters, you may have noticed a gradual progression in the intentions of these women. With time, they no longer had to presuppose a majority white, affluent audience. Consider my final two subjects: Najmieh Batmanglij wrote self-published cookbooks for the diaspora of Iran, while Norma Shirley went home to cook for the people of Jamaica. They bypassed more traditional routes so they could work for their own communities. Their imagined spectators were different from the privileged consumer whom the American food media so often centers. For both women, the audiences came. Maybe Najmieh and Norma suggest a way forward for food in America. It's an ecosystem in which immigrant chefs and food writers, particularly those of color, will no longer feel hamstrung by the obligation to create for a white, affluent audience—unless that is their self-stated objective. Instead, they can cook according to their artistic whims, and without compromise. But the American food establishment remains stratified along many lines, particularly class and race, thus preventing more radical or subversive work from reaching wider audiences. There are a few ways in which the landscape can become more equitable in the years to come. To start, the food establishment—where capital is concentrated—must continue to amplify those on America's socioeconomic margins. In this model, opportunities like cookbook deals and the chance to open restaurants would go more consistently to people without material privileges. The establishment must also keep on making concerted strides toward racial justice. As I conducted research for this book, for example, I encountered disproportionately few cookbooks or food memoirs authored by Black immigrant women throughout the second half of the twentieth century compared to books by women of other races. My sense was that this was due to a lack of access to publishing channels. Those voices certainly didn't always land on the food establishment or the food media's radar, either. The problem persists today. The American food media has sometimes treated Black talent tokenistically, championing them in times of crisis as a corrective to decades of silencing. This opportunistic fetishizing of Black voices—a form of gatekeeping born out of white liberal guilt—should not dictate who gets a platform. The shifts I envision for the food establishment can't happen, though, without a mechanism to keep the establishment in check. In a just world, the food media would fulfill the role of holding the food establishment accountable. But it's too often been unclear what separates the food media from the establishment. The food media must continue to work toward abandoning the symbiotic relationship it has had with the food establishment for so long and instead adopt a more adversarial approach to power.

In ruminating on this point, I find myself returning to one of the most difficult stories to part with in my early stages of writing: that of Desta Bairu. Bairu's cooking at the Washington, DC, restaurant that bore her name earned her passionate fans from the public and the food media. Following her lead, more restaurants that were Ethiopian in name sprouted across the nation's capital, and eventually the entire country. She is largely responsible for establishing a present-day scenario in which

Ethiopian and Eritrean flavors are a vital part of American dining. Though I had hoped to devote a chapter to her, there just
wasn't enough extant material that presented her speaking in
her own words. Imagine what this book would have looked like
had someone chronicled her story in her lifetime, or given her
the means to do so herself. There are countless other pioneers
whose stories few in the food media took the time to document.
The onus then falls on food journalists, like myself, to turn a
narrative gaze to those on the margins while they are still with
us, and to gain the trust of those sources. They include the chefs
who run what some may refer to as "mom and pop" restaurants
that mean a great deal to the communities who flock there, as
well as the line cooks, dishwashers, and other workers who do
not have the luxury of visibility even if their labor deserves cel-
ebration. Though I'm aware this is not a system-wide solution,
one effective way to reform this creaky structure I have outlined
is to remind yourself of the influence you have, however minimal
it may be, to determine tastes. In the reality that I (and, I sus-
pect, many readers) inhabit, consumers aren't completely pow-
erless. As long as that's the case, they, too, can be mindful when
deciding how to spend their money: where to eat, whom to buy
ingredients from, what publications to support.

Moving forward, perhaps the people outside the food establishment's orbit will push their way to its center, just as these seven
women did. Or maybe they will accomplish something even more
revolutionary: They will work outside the confines of this hierar-
chical establishment to build a new, entirely different future for
food unlike any America has ever seen—or tasted.

Acknowledgments

I AM, ABOVE ALL, indebted to each of the women in this book. Chao Yang Buwei, Elena Zelayeta, Madeleine Kamman, Marcella Hazan, and Norma Shirley: Thank you for producing such vital work that has outlived you. Julie Sahni and Najmieh Batmanglij: Thank you for trusting me, a young stranger, with your stories. And thank you, Julia Child, for your everlasting impact on American food culture.

I likewise have sincere gratitude to the friends and family members of the women in this book who aided me in my reporting: Mohammad Batmanglij, Victor Hazan, Alan Daniel Kamman, Neil Kamman, Mischa Manderson Mills, Rosemary Parkinson, Delius Shirley, and Michael Shirley. Many thanks to the scholars and journalists who have helped me in researching this book at various stages, too, including Gustavo Arellano, Scott Alves Barton, Mitchell Davis, Teresa Finney, Sara B. Franklin, Eric Geringas, Kristina Howard, Kristen Miglore, Andrea Nguyen, Dana Polan, Richard Sandomir, Matt Sartwell, Nach Waxman, Tom Williams, and Izabela Wojcik.

I'm endlessly grateful to my agent, William Callahan at Ink-Well Management, for hearing my voice as a writer long before anyone else cared to, and for giving me the confidence to write a book at all. And how lucky I am that he guided me to my editor at Norton, Melanie Tortoroli, who saw the sincerity of my intent as a writer during our very first meeting in November 2018, pushing me past my comfort zone at every step of the writing process.

(What a relief, too, to meet an editor who rightly insisted that this book did not need any recipes.) Thank you to Karen Wise for your sharp copyedits, and to everyone on the Norton team whose hands have touched this book, among them Lauren Abbate, Mo Crist, Becky Homiski, and Amy Medeiros. I am so thankful to Will Scarlett at Norton and and Hannah Gottlieb-Graham of ALMA Communications for publicizing this book with such passion. Thank you, too, to Amit Malhotra, whose design for the cover of this book captures its tone with such beauty, and to Sarahmay Wilkinson for your attentive art direction. I'm happy that writing this book gave me an excuse to work with a photographer I've long admired, Amir Hamja, who graciously took my author photo. And I'm not quite sure how to sufficiently thank my intrepid, precise fact-checker Charlotte Goddu, other than to offer her an apology for having to listen to hours of audio with my voice. (Thank you, Kameron Austin Collins, for introducing me to Charlotte.)

Though he may not realize it, my friend Shuja Haider first planted the idea for this book in my head, and I'm very glad he did. A hug to my beloved friends, both here and departed: Miguel Boluda, Laetitia Walendom, Lê Lan Anh, Amy Rose Spiegel, Thora Siemsen, Iva Dixit, Mallika Rao, Mala Chatterjee, Natasha Abadilla, Antonia Madian, and Sarah Thompson. I've been lucky to have your love in my life.

I owe a huge thank-you to all of my former colleagues at Food52, but a special one to Kenzi Wilbur for her extraordinary faith in, and patience with, me. This book would not exist had you not taken a huge gamble and hired me back in 2016. I am likewise grateful to my students at New York University, who have taught me a great deal about my own craft.

I could not have written this book without my friends in the food world who have supported me, in private and in public, during the many moments when this industry has broken my spirit. You know who you are. But a special thank-you to John Birdsall, Alicia Kennedy, Layla Schlack, Rebecca Flint Marx, Charlotte Druckman, Kia Damon, Eric Kim, Ifrah Ahmed, Natalie Pattillo, Seema Pai, Rachel Gurjar, Reem Kassis, and so many, many others who told me to keep writing even when I wanted to stop.

To my father, Sakti Sengupta: I'm not sure that the wound of your loss years ago will ever fully heal. But thank you for always nurturing the creative spirit in me. I miss you very much, and I wish you could read this book.

And, finally, I would never have had the urge to write this book at all if it were not for my mother and my best friend, Kasturi Sen, who has lived through more in one lifetime than most people do, who endured hardships in coming to this country as an immigrant that I will never fully understand, and whose cooking gave me life.

A Note on Process

YOU MAY BE wondering how I stitched these stories together. In writing this book, I sought to surface the inner lives of these women and to let my own voice fade as much as possible. Though I reported this book extensively through in-person, phone, and email interviews, I did not want to tell these stories from a journalistic remove, quoting others as I would for an article, especially if that meant constructing a portrait around the absence of a main character (as it may have for the women in this book who are deceased). Because of this objective, my first step in writing these essays was to find as much material that presented each woman speaking for herself. This wasn't too difficult when my subjects were alive. When dealing with deceased subjects, however, relying on extant texts required an embrace of the unreliable.

Chao Yang Buwei, Elena Zelayeta, Julia Child, Madeleine Kamman, and Marcella Hazan all left behind memoirs that captured their voices more fully than any other written source. While reading these memoirs, I curated the parts that felt germane to each woman's food story. I kept my eyes peeled for mentions of what they ate or cooked, the feelings they attached to these meals, and whether these memories had anything to tell us about the women they became. To round out my portraits of these women, I consulted their cookbooks, combed through newspaper and magazine archives, found video material where I could, and, when applicable, contacted their surviving family members, friends, and former professional collaborators. These first-person texts, however, have their limitations. Chao Yang Buwei's memoir, *Autobiography of a Chinese Woman*, provided me with the bulk of the information for my chapter on her. Yet her memoir contains few details about the meals of her youth in China. She does not tell readers much about the horrible food she ate in Japan, either. She also sprints from a place where she was a poor cook to a remarkably capable one. The book is scant on food detail at crucial junctures: She mentions a glorious spread of thirty-three courses that she cooked for the mourning meal after her adoptive father's death, but she names only one dish, her vegetarian "roast duck" made from pea starch.

Like Chao Yang Buwei, Elena Zelayeta also had a memoir, *Elena*. I drew on that text, along with her self-help book *Elena's Lessons in Living*, for most of this chapter. There are again lacunae, though. In both books, Elena skims over the period in her life when she went from a bride who couldn't boil water to a skilled cook. She likewise makes some of her decisions, like the one she had to open a restaurant just after the Great Depression, seem somewhat opaque. She doesn't touch much on the prejudice so many Americans had against Mexican immigrants in that same period, either. I have done my best to account for these lapses, writing of Elena's motivations without sacrificing narrative truth.

There's obviously no shortage of writing on Julia Child. I derived most of my interlude on her from Julia and her great-nephew Alex Prud'homme's memoir *My Life in France* (2006), along with Dana Polan's critical work *Julia Child's the French Chef* (2011) and Bob Spitz's detailed biography, *Dearie: The Remarkable Life of Julia Child* (2012). While reading all three works, I paid particular attention to instances in which Julia spoke about the hurdles she faced as she began her career on television and the dynamic between her and her friend Simca as her own fame grew.

Madeleine Kamman's memoir, *When French Women Cook*, presents a fundamental problem in that it fixates on her time in France before coming to America. It is not, in other words, a book that takes us through her years in Pennsylvania, Massachusetts, and New Hampshire, the period that is the focus of my chapter on her. I thus constructed the majority of my chapter on Madeleine from newspaper and magazine archives. Madeleine gave a wealth of interviews throughout her lifetime and, thankfully, she rarely held back when talking to the press. I also spoke to both of her sons, Alan Daniel and Neil, who put Madeleine's relationship with Julia Child in more generous context than the press had.

The biographical details in my chapter on Marcella Hazan, meanwhile, mostly come from her memoir, *Amarcord*, and I also corresponded with her husband Victor via email. The memoir contains essential information about these formative years in Marcella's life as she went from a timid newlywed to a respected author. As with all of Marcella's books, *Amarcord* comes with a caveat: Victor was also her writing partner. I assembled this portrait of Marcella while reminding myself that Marcella's voice in *Amarcord* was, to some degree, negotiated by her husband's, even though there are many indications that he knew her as intimately as she knew herself.

I built my chapter on Julie Sahni from phone and in-person interviews I conducted with her throughout 2019 and 2020, amassing hours of audio material. She told me many stories regarding the end of her marriage and the beginning of her life as a single mother that haven't squeaked into this book. You can attribute any narrative lulls in this chapter to Julie's own reluctance to dwell on these personal details. These are not my stories to tell, in part because they aren't quite relevant to understanding Julie's career in food. One day, I trust, she will tell these aspects of her own story in full.

I first met Najmieh Batmanglij when interviewing her for the *Washington Post* in October 2018. My chapter on her is based on conversations I had with her back then as well as throughout 2019 and 2020. Her husband and creative partner, Mohammad, was present for these conversations, too, and he added more color to some narrative details. You may notice that I have omitted the names of certain family members, like those of the older brother and distant cousin she encountered in America in the late 1960s. This was intentional, due to Najmieh's own reticence about sharing those names.

Writing my chapter on Norma Shirley was a challenge, given that she is now deceased and left behind no cookbooks or memoirs of her own. The lack of much first-person material forced me to patch together my chapter on her from archival materials, namely newspaper and magazine interviews. In addition, Norma's friend Rosemary Parkinson had conducted a number of interviews with Shirley in the hopes of writing her biography. Her public writings on Norma proved to be immensely useful, as was a twenty-minute 2008 episode of *At the Table with . . .* , a Canadian show featuring Norma, graciously uploaded online for me by the director of the episode, Eric Geringas. Conversations with Norma's ex-husband Michael, her son Delius, and her friend Mischa Manderson Mills also helped me give the narrative skeleton of that chapter some flesh.

As I wrote in my Introduction, my primary purpose with each of these chapters was to surrender the stage to these figures rather than to intrude. This book is meant to tease out how each of these figures saw themselves and how America saw them, where the two aligned and where they diverged.

Notes

Introduction

xi **a boy selling matchboxes:** Bob Kann, *A Recipe for Success: Lizzie Kander and Her Cookbook* (Milwaukee: Wisconsin Historical Society Press, 2007), 25.

xi **had come to the United States in the 1840s:** Ibid., 24.

xi **born in 1858:** Ibid., 102.

xi **in the 1880s:** Ibid., 24.

xi **a new rush of anti-Semitism:** Fred Wasser, "The Matzo Ball Matriarch of American Jewish Food," National Public Radio, April, 12, 2009. https://www.npr.org/templates/story/story .php?storyId=102913413.

xi **"It is a selfish motive that spurs us on":** Kann, *A Recipe for Success*, 24.

xii **fresh from Poland and Russia:** Ibid., x.

xii **German, Jewish, Eastern European, and American recipes:** Kann, *A Recipe for Success*, 57.

xii **174 pages:** Ibid., 56.

xii **pot roasts, creamed cod, and Boston-browned potatoes:** Ibid., 57.

xii **across more than forty editions:** Layla Schlack, "The Settlement Cookbook: 116 Years and 40 Editions Later," *Taste*, June 21, 2017. https://www.tastecooking.com/the-settlement-cookbook-116-years -and-40-editions-later/.

xii **many of which Kander herself revised:** Fred Wasser, "The Matzo Ball Matriarch."

xii **James Beard considered it one of his favorite cookbooks:** Ibid.

xii **Kander's aims were also somewhat patronizing:** Ibid.

xii **"Americanizing impulse":** Erika Janik, "The Settlement Cook Book," *Edible Milwaukee*, December 1, 2014. https://ediblemilwaukee .ediblecommunities.com/recipes/settlement-cook-book.

xiii **her death at 82 in 1940:** Kann, *A Recipe for Success*, 105.

xx **"consists of those people":** Nora Ephron, "Critics in the World of the Rising Souffle (Or Is It the Rising Meringue?)," *New York*, September 30, 1968, 35.

xxi **"gastronomic trinity":** Molly O'Neill, "Food Porn," *Columbia Journalism Review*, September 1, 2003.

xxii **"Big Three":** Deirdre Carmody, "New Flavors for Readers of Food Magazines," *New York Times*, May 23, 1994.

xxii **in 1990 with the establishment of the James Beard Awards:** Florence Fabricant, "Food Notes," *New York Times*, December 26, 1990.

A Note on Names

xxv **"When I sign my name in English, it is Buwei Yang Chao, but in China, I am Chao Yang Buwei":** Buwei Yang Chao, *Autobiography of a Chinese Woman* (New York: John Day, 1947), 321.

Mother Tongue: Chao Yang Buwei

1 **"I am ashamed to have written this book":** Buwei Yang Chao, *How to Cook and Eat in Chinese*, 2nd ed. (New York: John Day, 1949), xii.

1 **in her mid-fifties:** Anne Mendelson, *Chow Chop Suey: Food and the Chinese American Journey* (New York: Columbia University Press, 2016), 148.

1 **stirred dandelion:** Ibid., 151.

1 **jellied lamb:** Ibid., 83.

2 **"Shrimps Fried with Mushrooms":** Ibid., xii.

2 **"all the credit for the good points of the book is mine and all the blame for the bad points is Rulan's":** Ibid., xiv.

2 **She made the decision to study medicine abroad, in Japan:** Mendelson, *Chow Chop Suey*, 149.

2 **opened her own birth control clinic in China:** Buwei Yang Chao, *Autobiography of a Chinese Woman* (New York: John Day, 1947), 228.

2 **broke off an engagement to a cousin:** Ibid., 77.

2 **a love marriage to Yuenren without a formal ceremony:** Mendelson, *Chow Chop Suey*, 140.

3 **first systematically thorough cookbook on Chinese cooking:** Ibid., xix.

3 **the culinary glories of north China and the Jiangnan region below the Yangtze River:** Ibid., 157.

3 **ever since Chinese migrants arrived during the California Gold Rush of 1849:** Ibid., 17.

3 **phrases like "stir-fry" into the modern American lexicon:** Ibid., 107.

3 **Buwei was born with the name Lansien:** Chao, *Autobiography*, 9.

4 **"Let us take the photograph without the baby":** Ibid., 16.

4 **"bring along a little brother":** Ibid., 15.

4 **"What a wasteful man Confucius was!":** Ibid., 30.

4 **Perhaps, they predicted, she would even cause trouble beyond the home:** Ibid., 33.

5 **purposeless to go to America without knowing the language:** Ibid., 67.

5 **He suggested she study medicine:** Ibid., 89.

5 **She couldn't speak Japanese, either:** Ibid., 134.

5 **"And you will start making great strides towards greatness now":** Ibid., 103.

6 **Buwei arrived in Nagasaki, Japan, by sea in late 1913:** Ibid., 122.

6 **Its tiny houses barely rose from the ground:** Ibid., 132.

6 **She would beat the yolk with chopsticks:** Chao, *How to Cook*, 2nd ed., 133.

6 **Buwei cooked by trial and error:** Chao, *Autobiography*, 138.

7 **a breakfast of spiced roasted chicken, large prawns stewed in a pot, and hot biscuits strewn with sesame:** Ibid., 152.

7 **"That's right, Ch'uanti":** Ibid., 156.

7 **It was September 1920 when she met Yuenren:** Ibid., 166.

7 **Senjen Hospital, among the first medical practices in China begun by nonmissionary women:** Ibid., 159.

8 **An only child:** Ibid., 179.

8 **teach math at Tsing Hua College:** Ibid., 169.

8 **He once translated Lewis Carroll's *Alice's Adventures in Wonderland* (1865) into Chinese for pleasure:** Ibid., 187.

8 **He would visit Buwei in the hospital:** Ibid., 176.

8 **They married in June of the following year:** Ibid., 193.

8 **The pair agreed to forgo a proper ceremony:** "One-Time Rebel against Old China Traditions Relenting," *Longview Daily News*, February 17, 1958.

8 **"New-Style Wedding of New-Style People":** Chao, *Autobiography*, 193.

8   **Harvard offered Yuenren a chance to teach philosophy:** Ibid., 186.

9   **She still barely spoke the language:** Ibid., 201.

9   **America's complicated infatuation with Chinese food:** Samantha Barbas, "'I'll Take Chop Suey': Restaurants as Agents of Culinary and Cultural Change," *Journal of Popular Culture* 36, no. 4 (2003), 669.

9   **The country's first Chinese restaurants started sprouting following the 1849 California Gold Rush:** Paul Freedman, *Ten Restaurants That Changed America* (New York: Liveright, 2016), 213.

9   **from roughly four thousand to fifty-two thousand between 1850 and 1852:** Ibid., 215.

9   **years of long-simmering animus:** Mendelson, *Chow Chop Suey*, 63.

9   **"It is a fact of history that wherever the Chinese have gone they have always taken their habits, methods, and civilization with them":** David W. Dunlap, "135 Years Ago, Another Travel Ban Was in the News," *New York Times*, March 17, 2017. https://www.nytimes.com/2017/03/17/insider/chinese-exclusion-act-travel-ban.html.

10 **In 1892, for example, the Geary Act added a provision:** Mendelson, *Chow Chop Suey*, 65.

10 **The following decade, the Chinese Exclusion Act was renewed yet again:** Beth Lew-Williams, *The Chinese Must Go: Violence, Exclusion, and the Making of the Alien in America* (Cambridge, MA: Harvard University Press, 2018), 208.

10 **until the 1943 Magnuson Act:** Mendelson, *Chow Chop Suey*, 147.

10 **spreading rumors that ingredients mingled with vermin or opium:** Ibid., 77.

10 **chop suey, a tangle of meat and vegetables stir-fried in a thick sauce:** Freedman, *Ten Restaurants*, 219.

10 **the United States War Department incorporated two recipes for it:** Charles W. Hayford, "Open Recipes, Openly Arrived At: *How to Cook and Eat in Chinese* (1945) and the Translation of Chinese Food." *Journal of Oriental Studies*, 45, no. 1/2 (2012): 72.

10 **The cultural fixation on chop suey, a dish some believed originated at the hands of Chinese cooks in America:** Freedman, *Ten Restaurants*, 223.

10 **Chicago-based newspaper writer Jessie Louise Nolton wrote *Chinese Cookery in the Home Kitchen* (1911):** Andrew Coe, *Chop*

Suey: A Cultural History of Chinese Food in the United States (New York: Oxford University Press, 2009), 185.

10 **In *The Chinese Cook Book* (1917), Shiu Wong Chan:** Mendelson, *Chow Chop Suey*, 125.

11 **lifestyle magazines like *Harper's Bazaar*:** Sherrie A. Inness, *Dinner Roles: American Women and Culinary Culture* (Iowa City: University of Iowa Press, 2001), 104.

11 **newspapers like the *Chicago Tribune*:** Mendelson, *Chow Chop Suey*, 114.

11 **"China being a country of topsy-turvydom":** George Cecil, "Globe-Trotting in Far-Off Lands," *Catholic World*, May 1927, 176.

11 **Soup, fish, steak, egg salad:** Chao, *Autobiography*, 200.

11 **a journey that typically took days in that era:** "Official Guide of the Railways and Steam Navigation Lines of the United States, Porto Rico, Canada, Mexico and Cuba," compiled and edited under the direction of E. S. Allen and A. J. Burns, June 1921.

11 **third-floor apartment:** Chao, *Autobiography*, 202.

12 **spent her days knitting and shopping for pots and pans:** Ibid., 204.

12 **Her first daughter, Rulan, was born in April 1922:** Laurie D. Willis, "Rulan Pian, 91: Chinese Music Scholar, Harvard Professor," *Boston Globe*, January 1, 2014, https://www.bostonglobe.com/metro/obituaries/2014/01/01/rulan-pian-scholar-chinese-music-and-chinese-language-teacher-harvard/tMj1O7nqzBiahlctPuQubI/story.html.

12 **another girl, Nova, followed a year later:** Chao, *Autobiography*, 210.

12 **he accepted an offer for a research professorship at Tsing Hua University:** Ibid., 213.

12 **teaching anatomy and physiology:** Ibid., 246.

12 **The rich, she noticed, had access to resources about contraception that lower classes did not:** Ibid., 214.

13 **offering free services to those who couldn't afford a visit while charging more for affluent clients:** Ibid., 228.

13 **what she called a "community kitchen":** Ibid., 227.

13 **Changchow-style hot biscuits:** Ibid., 233.

13 **pudding flavored with lotus starch, rose candies, and drunken shrimp that somersaulted in her mouth:** Ibid., 232.

13 **shreds of snake meat and chicken crowned with white chrysanthemum petals:** Ibid., 239.

13 **she would bombard cooks with questions:** Buwei Yang Chao, *How to Cook and Eat in Chinese*, 3rd ed. (New York: Vintage, 1972), xxi.

13 **Lensey:** Chao, *Autobiography*, 244.

13 **Bella:** Ibid., 248.

13 **Yuenren's different jobs throughout the 1930s had them move to various cities in China:** Ibid., 259.

14 **The family lived through World War II:** Ibid., 273.

14 **then known as Langson in French Indochina:** Ibid., 275.

14 **a vendor at a train station on her way back into China in January 1938:** Ibid., 276.

14 **Yuenren received a visiting professorship at Yale:** Ibid., 290.

14 **the family moved back to Cambridge in 1941:** Ibid., 301.

14 **Yuenren appointed twenty instructors to teach Chinese to American soldiers:** Ibid., 313.

14 **she could cook any dish she'd ever eaten, drawing only from memory:** Chao, *How to Cook*, 3rd ed., xxi.

15 **Books that focused on Chinese cuisine were few and far between in that era:** Anne Mendelson, *Stand Facing the Stove: The Story of the Women Who Gave America the Joy of Cooking* (New York: Henry Holt, 1996), 252.

15 **The prominent publishing house Macmillan:** Mendelson, *Chow Chop Suey*, 149.

15 **With its spacious banquet hall outfitted with fish tanks and hanging lanterns:** Rachel Wharton, "Wok of Ages," *New York Daily News*, January 22, 2006, 32.

15 **She rubbed elbows with well-connected white intellectuals in Cambridge:** Mendelson, *Chow Chop Suey*, 150.

15 **It was Agnes who encouraged Buwei to write a cookbook:** Ibid., xiii.

15 **Yuenren joked that their kitchen resembled a chemistry research department:** Mary Hart, "Recipes Are a Visitor's Dish," *Star Tribune*, July 24, 1966.

16 **Writer Lin Yutang, a friend of the couple, was an early champion:** Mendelson, *Chow Chop Suey*, 148.

16 **his publishing firm, the John Day Company:** "Richard Walsh, Publisher, Dead," *New York Times*, May 29, 1960.

16 **raised by two Presbyterian missionaries in China:** Albin Krebs, "Pearl Buck Is Dead at 80; Won Nobel Prize in 1938," *New York Times*, March 7, 1973.

16   **critical and commercial juggernaut** *The Good Earth*: Mendelson, *Chow Chop Suey*, 145.

16   **committed to promoting harmony between China and America:** Ibid., 146.

16   **"Mrs. Chao's cook book is splendid and we must certainly have it":** Ibid., 153.

16   **a table of recipe names with Chinese characters:** Ibid., 159.

17   **an encouraging wave of cookbooks that looked beyond America's borders:** Edith M. Barber, "Foreign Food Intrigues Palates," *Battle Creek Enquirer*, January 13, 1946.

17   **"too remote to be fully understandable":** Countess Morphy, *Recipes of All Nations* (New York: Wm. H. Wise & Company, 1935), 7.

17   **Buwei made room for specialties from the Jiangnan region:** Mendelson, *Chow Chop Suey*, 157.

17   **red-cooked meats with dried lilies or pea starch noodles:** Chao, *How to Cook*, 2nd ed., 55–56.

17   **large "lion's head" meatballs:** Ibid., 67.

17   **the cold "saltwater" duck of Nanking:** Ibid., 104.

17   **She also inserted recipes from the country's north:** Mendelson, *Chow Chop Suey*, 157.

17   **soy jam noodles:** Chao, *How to Cook*, 2nd ed., 201.

17   **rinsed lamb of Peiping:** Ibid., 85.

17   **mutton-stuffed dumplings:** Ibid., 214.

17   **defined the process of stir-frying:** Jason Epstein, "Chinese Characters," *New York Times Magazine*, June 13, 2004. https://www.nytimes.com/2004/06/13/magazine/food-chinese-characters.html.

17   **"a big-fire-shallow-fat-continual-stirring-quick-frying of cut-up material with wet seasoning":** Chao, *How to Cook*, 2nd ed., xvi.

17   **referred to dumplings as "wraplings" and wontons as "ramblings":** Epstein, "Chinese Characters."

17   **Buwei's introduction was methodical:** Chao, *How to Cook*, 2nd ed., 3.

17   **clear-simmering:** Ibid., 41.

17   **shallow-frying:** Ibid., 44.

17   **pickling:** Ibid., 46.

17   **until more than fifty pages in:** Ibid., 51.

18   **letting readers use peanut butter in lieu of sesame jam:** Ibid., 85.

18   **"All the ingredients in my recipes are American":** Mary Hart, "Recipes Are a Visitor's Dish," *Star Tribune*, July 24, 1966.

18 **the flagship title for John Day's newly established Asia Press imprint:** Mendelson, *Chow Chop Suey*, 154.

18 **The passage of the Magnuson Act in December 1943:** Mendelson, *Chow Chop Suey*, 147.

18 *Asia and the Americas*, **a popular magazine owned by John Day:** Ibid., 146.

18 **"human appetites, human aspirations and all human ways":** Ibid., 154.

18 **"I would like to nominate her for the Nobel Peace Prize":** Chao, *How to Cook*, 2nd ed., xi.

19 **a manual of gastronomic diplomacy:** Larry Wissow, "Over the Coals," *Bennington Banner*, August 10, 1974.

19 **Preeminent food personality Ida Bailey Allen:** Mendelson, *Chow Chop Suey*, 160.

19 **authored over fifty books on cooking and homemaking:** *New York Times*, "Ida Bailey Allen, Cookbook Author," July 17, 1973.

19 **"probably the most literary and the most amusing cookbook ever written":** Howard Taylor, "Gay Chinese Cookbook," *The Philadelphia Inquirer*, May 13, 1945.

19 **writing under the pen name Jane Holt:** "Margaret McConnell, Editor, Food Writer," *New York Times*, July 8, 1976.

19 **"something distinctly novel in the way of a cook book":** Jane Holt, "News of Food," *New York Times*, May 10, 1945.

19 **She had been chipping away at an autobiography of sorts since 1913:** Chao, *Autobiography*, vii.

20 **Buck and Walsh agreed to print the book under John Day's Asia Press imprint:** Ibid., ix.

20 **"Since my wife has the last word, I shall have the foreword":** Ibid., vii.

20 **"has not always been a well-behaved translator":** Ibid., x.

20 **She was a typical Chinese woman:** Ibid., 3.

20 **"If you want to know what I really am, you should read the story of my life":** Ibid., 5.

21 **in 1947, the year the family moved west:** "One-Time Rebel against Old China Traditions Relenting," *Longview Daily News*, February 17, 1958.

21 **"Oriental languages":** Yuen Ren Chao, "Yuen Ren Chao: Chinese Linguist, Phonologist, Composer, and Author," conducted by

Rosemary Levenson, 1974, Regional Oral History Office, Bancroft Library, University of California, Berkeley, 1977.

21 **"the most delightful account of family living since *Life with Father*"**: Advertisement in *Chicago Tribune*, April 6, 1947.

21 **"Mrs. Chao may term herself a 'typical Chinese woman'"**: "Autobiography of a Chinese Woman," *Kirkus Reviews*. https://www.kirkusreviews.com/book-reviews/yan-yuenren-chao-duwei/autobiography-of-a-chinese-woman/.

21 **"She is amazingly *sui generis*"**: Harry E. Wedeck, "Buwei Yang Chao's Many-Sided Autobiography," *New York Times*, April 27, 1947.

21 **Far more successful was the second edition:** Mendelson, *Chow Chop Suey*, 161.

21 **the addition of a few recipes:** Chao, *How to Cook*, 2nd ed., iii.

21 **Peiping roast duck:** Ibid., 105.

21 **stirred crabmeat:** Ibid., 132.

21 **"in the few years since the publication of this book":** Ibid., iii.

21 **John Day struggled after Walsh suffered from a debilitating stroke in 1953:** Mendelson, *Chow Chop Suey*, 162.

22 **lacked the ability to break down techniques:** Ibid., 206.

22 **which became storied institutions in America:** Mendelson, *Chow Chop Suey*, 207.

22 **The Refugee Relief Act of 1953:** Alice L. McLean, *Asian American Food Culture* (Santa Barbara: Greenwood, 2015), xxii.

22 **both obtained their citizenship in 1954:** Madeleine Y. Hsu, *The Good Immigrants: How the Yellow Peril Became the Model Minority* (Princeton, NJ: Princeton University Press, 2015), 121.

22 **by 1960, that number grew to 237,292:** McLean, *Asian American*, xxii.

22 **innovations on the part of cookbook authors to make Chinese cooking more legible to American audiences:** Mendelson, *Chow Chop Suey*, 191.

22 **Grace Zia Chu's *The Pleasures of Chinese Cooking*:** Ibid., 200.

22 **the standard repertoire of Chinese dishes in American restaurants:** Gish Jen, "The Lives They Lived: Grace Zia Chu, b. 1900; West Meets East," *New York Times Magazine*, Jan 2, 2000. https://www.nytimes.com/2000/01/02/magazine/food-the-lives-they-lived-grace-zia-chu-b-1900-west-meets-east.html.

22 **bird's nest soup:** Grace Zia Chu, *The Pleasures of Chinese Cooking* (New York: Cornerstone, 1967), 130.

22 **shark's fin with Chinese cabbage:** Ibid., 142.

22 **She avoided including any Chinese characters in the text:** Mendelson, *Chow Chop Suey*, 208.

23 **gave wiggle room to home cooks:** William Grimes, "Grace Zia Chu, 99, Guide to Chinese Cooking," *New York Times*, April 19, 1999. https://www.nytimes.com/1999/04/19/nyregion/grace-zia-chu-99 -guide-to-chinese-cooking.html.

23 **the option to use a can of creamed corn:** Chu, *The Pleasures of Chinese Cooking*, 89.

23 **"hors d'oeuvres with an Oriental flavor":** Ibid., 146.

23 **"may well be the finest, most lucid volume on Chinese cooking ever written":** Grimes, "Grace Zia Chu, 99, Guide to Chinese Cooking."

23 **Chu cited Buwei's cookbook as one of her favorites:** Craig Claiborne, "Chinese Cook Will Teach Ancient Art," *New York Times*, September 14, 1961.

23 **Random House published the third, and final, edition of Buwei's cookbook in 1963:** Mendelson, *Chow Chop Suey*, 162.

23 **The Immigration and Nationality, or Hart-Celler, Act eliminated national quotas:** Hsu, *The Good Immigrants*, 11.

23 **Starting in 1966:** Dana Polan, "Joyce Chen Cooks and the Upscaling of Chinese Food in America in the 1960s," WGBH. http://openvault .wgbh.org/exhibits/art_of_asian_cooking/article.

23 **the first nationally syndicated cooking show hosted by a person of color in America:** Kathleen Collins, *Watching What We Eat: The Evolution of Television Cooking Shows* (London: Continuum, 2009), 93.

23 **blowing air into a duck carcass with a bicycle pump:** Polan, "Joyce Chen Cooks."

24 **slices of roast duck with pineapple:** Florence Fabricant, "Nixon in China, the Dinner, Is Recreated," *New York Times*, January 25, 2011. https://www.nytimes.com/2011/01/26/dining/26nixon.html.

24 **"Chinese Restaurants Flower Following Diplomatic Thaw":** Ralph Blumenthal, "Chinese Restaurants Flower Following Diplomatic Thaw," *New York Times*, July 27, 1972.

24 **Virginia Lee, a cooking teacher and native of Shanghai:** "Virginia Lee, Noted Teacher and Chinese Cooking Expert," *New York Times*, October 19, 1981.

24 **the beloved San Francisco Chinese restaurant the Mandarin:** Momo Chang, "Q&A with Cecilia Chiang of the Mandarin Restau-

rant," PBS, 2016. https://www.pbs.org/food/features/qa-cecilia
-chiang-mandarin-restaurant/.

24 **published her first book,** *The Mandarin Way,* **with writer Allan
Carr:** Mendelson, *Chow Chop Suey,* 220.

24 **The Ningbo-born, New York–based cooking teacher Florence
Lin's debut cookbook:** Emily Langer, "Florence Lin, Doyenne
of Chinese Cooks in America, Dies at 97," *Washington Post,* January 5, 2018. https://www.washingtonpost.com/local/obituaries/
florence-lin-doyenne-of-chinese-cooks-in-america-dies-at
-97/2018/01/05/78313500-f010-11e7-b390-a36dc3fa2842_story
.html.

24 **America's first Chinese vegetarian cookbook:** Mendelson, *Chow
Chop Suey,* 222.

24 **born in Shanghai and educated at Barnard College:** Ibid., 226.

24 **"resplendent book of Chinese cuisine":** "The Key to Chinese
Cooking," *Kirkus Reviews.* https://www.kirkusreviews.com/book
-reviews/irene-kuo/the-key-to-chinese-cooking/

24 **a guest of Mike Douglas and Johnny Carson:** Advertisement in
Arizona Republic, November 8, 1977.

25 **continued cooking into her eighties:** William Rice, "As the Year
4671 Arrives, a New Wave of Snobbery Tempts Eager Diners," *Washington Post,* February 1, 1973.

25 **A slim paperback:** Mendelson, *Chow Chop Suey,* 163.

25 **instead focused on topics like table manners:** Natalie Miller,
"Mrs. Chao Tells How to Order in Chinese," *Ithaca Journal,* July 31,
1974.

25 **"Since the publication of my** *How to Cook and Eat in Chinese,*
I have received numerous inquiries": Buwei Yang Chao, *How to
Order and Eat in Chinese* (New York: Vintage, 1974), v.

25 **the pervasive notion that tea is always served at meals:** Ibid., 48.

25 **Buwei died of a stroke seven years after its publication, at the
age of 91:** "National Obituaries," *United Press International,* March 3,
1981.

25 **faint coverage beyond the Bay Area:** "Deaths," *Associated Press,*
March 4, 1981.

25 **Yuenren died a year later, at 89:** "Dr. Y. R. Chao, Expert on Oriental
Languages," *New York Times,* March 2, 1982.

25 **until the mid-1980s before it fell out of print:** Mendelson, *Chow
Chop Suey,* 163.

25 **Martin Yan's *Yan Can Cook* began airing on American public television in 1982:** Natalie Haughton, "Celebrity Chef Martin Yan Takes You on a Chinese Tour," *Los Angeles Daily News*, February 7, 2008. https://www.dailynews.com/2008/02/07/celebrity-chef-martin-yan-takes-you-on-a-chinese-tour/.

25 **"His wife, Buwei Yang Chao, died in 1981":** "Dr. Y. R. Chao, Expert On Oriental Languages."

26 **"Patriotism is your mother tongue":** Chao, *Autobiography*, 181.

You'd Never Give a Thought to Pity Her: Elena Zelayeta

27 **that afternoon in 1934:** Elena Zelayeta, *Elena* (Englewood Cliffs, NJ: Prentice-Hall, 1960), 96.

27 **Mashed potatoes, a salad, and a dessert of packaged pudding:** Ibid., 110.

27 **Elena's Mexican Village:** Elena Zelayeta as told to Lou Richardson, *Elena's Lessons in Living* (San Francisco: Dettners, 1947), 27.

28 **she would dance before the crowd as a string orchestra thrummed behind her:** Zelayeta, *Elena*, 79.

28 **A mature cataract and a detached retina were to blame:** Ibid., 101.

28 **36 years old and seven months pregnant:** Ibid., 13.

29 **scrubbing her fingers against the leaves to catch any dirt or vermin:** Ibid., 110.

29 **Elena's parents had both been born in Spain:** Ibid., 6.

30 **Doña Louisa occasionally permitted:** Zelayeta, *Lessons*, 25.

30 **hanging red chiles:** Ibid., 26.

30 **stirring masa for the tortillas:** Ibid., 71.

30 **bruising cumin seeds in her mother's molcajete:** Ibid., 26.

30 **many decades after Mexico declared its independence from Spain in 1821:** Gustavo Arellano, *Taco USA: How Mexican Food Conquered America* (New York: Scribner, 2012), 7.

30 **"Down with the Spaniards!":** Zelayeta, *Elena*, 8.

30 **boarding school in Mexico City for three years:** Zelayeta, *Lessons*, 98.

31 **a train to San Francisco:** Ibid., 97.

31 **the pricey Argonaut Hotel:** Zelayeta, *Elena*, 8.

31 **They had come to the region in two waves:** Encarnación Pinedo and Victor Valle, *Encarnacion's Kitchen: Mexican Recipes from Nineteenth-Century California, Selections from Encarnación Pinedo's*

El cocinero español, trans. Dan Strehl (Berkeley: University of California Press, 2003), 5.

31 **then again during the Gold Rush in the mid-nineteenth century:** Erica J. Peters, *San Francisco: A Food Biography* (Lanham, MD: Rowman & Littlefield, 2013), 29.

31 **what would become a third wave:** Ibid., 35.

31 **890,000 documented Mexican immigrants:** Paula E. Morton, *Tortillas: A Cultural History* (Albuquerque: University of New Mexico Press, 2014), 76.

31 **"FOR RENT":** Zelayeta, *Elena*, 9.

32 **High School of Commerce:** Ibid., 19.

32 **working as a file clerk:** Zelayeta, *Lessons*, 75.

32 **a nice figure and pretty face:** Ibid., 58.

32 **her short stature, her face framed by thick-rimmed glasses:** Zelayeta, *Elena*, 20.

33 **a physician and surgeon from Nicaragua:** Ibid., 21.

33 **A fall 1923 visit to a doctor:** Ibid., 30.

33 **He hailed from the city of Mazatlán:** Ibid., 37.

33 **He proposed in June 1925:** Ibid., 40.

34 **Her mother's cooking anchored Elena that night:** Ibid., 48.

34 **recipes for casseroles and pies:** Ibid., 51.

34 **her parents had raised her to be her husband's subordinate:** Ibid., 53.

35 **a friend spotted him at a concert one night:** Ibid., 61.

35 **She stunned her father with her crisp salads and warm sopa:** Ibid., 53.

35 **In May 1926, Elena and Loren had a son:** "Obituary: Larry Zelayeta," *San Francisco Chronicle*, April 26, 2007, https://www.legacy.com/obituaries/sfgate/obituary.aspx?n=larry-zelayeta&pid=87560822.

35 **a live-in maid named Manuelita:** Zelayeta, *Elena*, 59.

36 **found a seven-room place on Green Street:** Ibid., 64.

36 **"so 'hot' that only a cast-iron throat and stomach can endure it":** Sherrie A. Inness, *Dinner Roles: American Women and Culinary Culture* (Iowa City: University of Iowa Press, 2001), 102.

36 **"Get rid of the Mexicans!":** Francisco E. Balderamma and Raymond Rodríguez, *Decade of Betrayal: Mexican Repatriation in the 1930s*, rev. ed. (Albuquerque: University of New Mexico Press, 2006), 1.

36 **over a million people of Mexican origin:** Alex Wagner, "America's Forgotten History of Illegal Deportations," *Atlantic*, March 6, 2017, https://www.theatlantic.com/politics/archive/2017/03/americas -brutal-forgotten-history-of-illegal-deportations/517971/.

36 **she rose at five in the morning:** Zelayeta, *Elena*, 65.

37 **green peppers bulging with Monterey Jack cheese:** Elena Zelayeta, *Elena's Secrets of Mexican Cooking* (Garden City, NY: Dolphin, 1973), 189.

37 **cream puffs filled with rum:** Zelayeta, *Elena*, 65.

37 **Elena changed the locks on the apartment:** Ibid., 68.

37 **They spent five months apart:** Ibid., 76.

37 **She turned to religion:** Ibid., 73.

37 **a spot in the King George Hotel:** Ibid., 77.

37 **Elena hired a painter, Darrell Pischoff:** Ibid., 79.

38 **"Straight from Old Mexico":** "Monthly Business and Professional Directory," *San Francisco Examiner*, September 1, 1935.

38 **Elena was happier than she'd ever been:** Zelayeta, *Elena*, 80.

38 **The first sign something was amiss:** Ibid., 84.

38 **Maybe she should've told Manuelita:** Ibid., 80.

40 **the tartness of the salad dressing:** Ibid., 89.

40 **in August 1934:** Ibid., 91.

40 **sinking beneath a $5,000 mountain of debt:** Ibid., 99.

40 **it even chased Manuelita away:** Ibid., 102.

41 **When she cracked eggs, she cradled her hands to catch the whites:** Ibid., 112.

41 **She smelled deep fat heating on the stove:** Craig Claiborne, "Blind Cook Is in City to Test and Taste National Fare," *New York Times*, August 15, 1960.

41 **fifteen-minute radio programs:** Zelayeta, *Lessons*, 99.

41 **deep-fry chiles rellenos without scalding herself:** Zelayeta, *Elena*, 112.

41 **She scrambled eggs:** Ibid., 115.

41 **tiny empanadas stuffed with creamed crabmeat:** Ibid., 122.

41 **teaching cooking at the San Francisco Center for the Blind:** Ibid., 124.

41 **Later that year:** Ibid., 139.

41 **thinking it might help her afford to buy a guide dog:** Ibid., 136.

41 **placing an ad in the *San Francisco Chronicle*:** Ibid., 130.

42 **She found two, Cornelia Farrell and Daisy Dennis:** Ibid., 137.

42 **bygone restaurant standbys:** Ibid., 87.

42 **Elena slid $500 into debt:** Ibid., 140.

42 **Pinedo's book was in Spanish:** Morton, *Tortillas*, 75.

42 **Pinedo documented the recipes of Mexicans living in nineteenth-century California:** Dan Strehl, "In Encarnación's Kitchen," *Encarnacion's Kitchen: Mexican Recipes from Nineteenth-Century California* (Berkeley: University of California Press, 2003), 19.

42 **Harriet S. Loury's *Fifty Choice Recipes for Spanish and Mexican Dishes*:** Arellano, *Taco USA*, 94.

42 **"alligator pear salad":** Keith J. Guenther Jr., "The Development of the Mexican-American Cuisine," *National & Regional Styles of Cookery: Proceedings: Oxford Symposium 1981* (London: Prospect, 1981), 273.

42 **May Southworth, who published a volume of 101 *Mexican Dishes*:** Arellano, *Taco USA*, 94.

42 **make tortillas from flour:** Ibid., 201.

43 **Bertha Haffner-Ginger, founder of the Los Angeles Times' School of Domestic Science:** Ibid., 94–95.

43 **"When made properly, there is great merit in this class of foods":** Bertha Haffner-Ginger, *California Mexican-Spanish Cookbook* (Bedford: Applewood, 1914), 19.

43 **Fabiola Cabeza de Baca, author of *Historic Cookery*:** Arellano, *Taco USA*, 113.

43 **Erna Fergusson, author of *Mexican Cookbook*:** Strehl, *Encarnacion's Kitchen*, 30.

43 **Cleofas Jaramillo, author of *The Genuine New Mexico Tasty Recipes: Potajes Sabrosos*:** Arellano, *Taco USA*, 113.

43 **"we like it best here in the United States":** Elena Zelayeta, *Elena's Famous Mexican and Spanish Recipes* (San Francisco: Dettners, 1944), 6.

43 **rabbit stew:** Ibid., 65.

43 **pork chops in peanut butter sauce:** Ibid., 61.

43 **chicken with chestnuts:** Ibid., 73.

43 **adding cinnamon to American chocolate would do:** Ibid., 120.

43 **"reasonable facsimile":** Ibid., 106.

44 **Some of these home economists had prior connections:** Zelayeta, *Elena*, 142.

44 **pay off the debts from her restaurant:** Zelayeta, *Lessons*, 93.

44 **she was able to get a guide dog named Chulita:** Zelayeta, *Elena*, 145.

44 **"famed authority on the culinary art from south of the border":** "Popular Dancers Enroll in 'Times' Cooking School," *Los Angeles Times*, October 29, 1944.

44 **"My friend Elena is blind":** Prudence Penny, "Elena's Famous Mexican Recipes Available," *San Francisco Examiner*, August 31, 1944.

44 **being treated at the South San Francisco Emergency Hospital:** Zelayeta, *Elena*, 157.

45 **Loren had been in a crash with a bus:** Ibid., 161.

45 **Loren would visit Elena in her dreams:** Ibid., 164.

45 **In April 1946:** Ibid., 166.

45 **a group of thirty blind students:** Ibid., 168.

45 **She spent four weeks teaching students:** Ibid., 174.

45 **"spiritual companion":** Prudence Penny, "Elena Does a New Book," *San Francisco Examiner*, September 4, 1947.

45 **"While this is not a cook book, it was, in a way, born in the kitchen":** Zelayeta, *Lessons*, 7.

45 **her mother's arroz con pollo:** Zelayeta, *Lessons*, 115.

45 **zucchini torte:** Ibid., 118.

45 **chiles rellenos:** Ibid., 124.

46 **It drew scores of admirers to her apartment:** Zelayeta, *Elena*, 193.

46 **television producer Richard Dinsmore:** Herb Caen, "Monday Medley," *San Francisco Examiner*, May 1, 1950.

46 **A makeup artist traced her eyebrows with a pencil:** Zelayeta, *Elena*, 205.

46 **The crew attached strings to her ankles:** Dana Polan, "It's Fun to Eat: Forgotten Television," in *How to Watch Television*, ed. Ethan Thompson and Jason Mittell (New York: New York University Press, 2013), 348.

46 **toggled between cameras:** Herb Caen, "Bay City Breeze," *San Francisco Examiner*, February 3, 1953.

46 **"Oh, darling! Let me see":** Bay Area Television Archive, "It's Fun to Eat with Elena," Accessed December 14, 2019. https://diva.sfsu.edu/collections/sfbatv/bundles/189406.

46 **began airing in April 1950:** "Television Schedule," *Los Angeles Times*, April 28, 1950.

46 **would air in the Bay Area:** "Program Hi-Lites," *San Francisco Examiner*, October 13, 1952.

46 **"This book is not a Mexican cook book":** Elena Zelayeta, *Elena's Fiesta Recipes* (Pasadena: Ward Ritchie, 1952), ix.

46 **Spanish-style turkey with chestnuts:** Ibid., 58.

46 **Mexican turkey meatballs:** Ibid., 59.

46 **The Christmas Eve fruit salads she knew in Mexico:** Ibid., 23.

47 **her featherweight chiles rellenos with thicker batter:** Ibid., 63.

47 **a frozen food business, Elena's Food Specialties:** Zelayeta, *Elena*, 226.

47 **waffles and fish sticks you could stow in your freezer:** Andrew F. Smith, *Food and Drink in American History: A "Full Course" Encyclopedia* (Santa Barbara: ABC-CLIO, 2013), 378.

47 **an authority on dining on the West Coast:** Jane Nickerson, "Thanksgiving Feast with Regional Flavor," *New York Times*, November 20, 1955.

47 **"always searingly hot, exotically and overly spiced, and heavy":** Zelayeta, *Elena's Secrets*, v.

47 **"the likes and dislikes of most Americans":** Charlotte Turgeon, "Favorite Dishes of Gertrude Stein and Others," *New York Times*, December 7, 1958.

47 **her turkey in green mole sauce:** Zelayeta, *Elena's Secrets*, 75.

48 **"good old American hot dogs":** Ibid., 29.

48 **She did not, for example, think cornmeal was an acceptable substitution for masa:** Ibid., viii.

48 **took over the post of food editor after Nickerson in 1957:** Bryan Miller, "Craig Claiborne, 79, Times Food Editor and Critic, Is Dead," *New York Times*, January 24, 2000.

48 **"may well be the definitive volume on the subject":** Craig Claiborne, "Blindness No Handicap to Author of New Book," *New York Times*, November 13, 1958.

48 **"artlessly written":** "Elena," *Kirkus Reviews*, Accessed December 14, 2019. https://www.kirkusreviews.com/book-reviews/elena-zelayeta/elena-5/.

48 **"One cannot help but wish":** "A Blindness," *Oakland Tribune*, December 11, 1960.

48 **she was asked to serve as a consultant for the New York restaurant La Fonda del Sol:** Evan Jones, *Epicurean Delight: Life and Times of James Beard* (New York: Fireside, 1990), 208.

49 **a high-end pan-Latin restaurant:** Andrew F. Smith, *The Oxford*

Companion to American Food and Drink (New York: Oxford University Press, 2007), 40.

49 **"There is no facet of the art beyond her grasp":** Claiborne, "Blind Cook Is in City."

49 **"I have always felt that Elena learns more about a person through her fingers than most people do with their full senses":** Elena Zelayeta, *Elena's Favorite Foods California Style* (Englewood Cliffs, NJ: Prentice-Hall, 1967), i.

49 **a restaurant chain and seasoning company:** Barbara Hansen, "Legacy of Elena Zelayeta," *Los Angeles Times*, June 6, 1974.

49 **"It takes adventuresome people to uproot themselves":** Zelayeta, *Elena's Favorite*, 178.

50 ***Mexican Cook Book:*** Jean S. Baker, "Mexican Cook Book on the Market Today," *Santa Cruz Sentinel*, May 21, 1969.

50 **"unique understanding of American kitchens":** Marian Manners, "Give the Cook a Book," *Los Angeles Times*, December 10, 1967.

50 **her husband, a Mexican diplomat, took a post at the United Nations Information Centre in Mexico City:** Paul Levy, "Elisabeth Lambert Ortiz," *Independent*, November 25, 2003. https://www.independent.co.uk/news/obituaries/elisabeth-lambert-ortiz-37521.html.

50 **"exotic chiles, herbs, and fruits of vibrant colors and aromas":** Diana Kennedy, *The Essential Cuisines of Mexico* (New York: Clarkson Potter, 2000), xii.

51 **duck in a green mole of pumpkin seeds, fish in caper sauce, and guava stuffed with coconut:** Raymond A. Sokolov, "Cultures of the World Depicted in Ounces, Cups and Spoonfuls," *New York Times*, October 5, 1972.

51 **insisting that making tortillas from scratch would be easy even for novices:** Pat Strauss, "America Goes Mexican," *Morning Call*, November 14, 1982.

51 **"will probably rank as the definitive book":** Kennedy, *Essential*, xvi.

51 **"the definitive volume on the subject":** Craig Claiborne, "Blindness No Handicap."

51 **died in March 1974:** Hansen, "Legacy of Elena Zelayeta."

51 **a convalescent home for months:** "Elena Zelayeta, Famed S.F. Cook," *Associated Press*, April 1, 1974.

51 **all of northern California:** Hansen, "Legacy of Elena Zelayeta."

51   **More figures in Mexican cooking would follow:** Arellano, *Taco USA*, 101.

51   **"recipes and happy philosophy live on":** Hansen, "Legacy of Elena Zelayeta."

52   **"Blind Cook to Feature Enchiladas":** "Blind Cook to Feature Enchiladas," *The Los Angeles Times*, April 10, 1945.

52   **"Blind Cook to Display Her Skill":** "Blind Cook to Display Her Skill," *Los Angeles Times*, March 6, 1955.

52   **"Blind Cook Tells Happiness Recipes":** Anne La Riviere, "Blind Cook Tells Happiness Recipes," *Los Angeles Times*, October 24, 1968.

52   **"What a wonderful place to be stranded":** Jan Silverman, "Viva, Elena!," *Oakland Tribune*, December 13, 1967.

Interlude: Julia Child, American Woman

53   **many stories about France as a kid growing up in California:** Julia Child with Alex Prud'homme, *My Life in France* (New York: Knopf, 2006), 13.

53   **an imperious conservative:** Ibid., 22.

53   **she called "Big John":** Ibid., 13.

53   **He abhorred the intellectualism:** Bob Spitz, *Dearie: The Remarkable Life of Julia Child*, (New York: Vintage, 2013), 42.

53   **The only people she knew from France were uptight spinsters:** Child, *My Life*, 13.

54   **looking upon Julia not as a foreigner but as a person:** Ibid., 16.

54   **She could taste the seawater in the Dover sole:** Ibid., 18.

54   **Parisian grapes had a soft, ephemeral sweetness:** Ibid., 24.

54   **she'd never quite had bread like a baguette:** Ibid., 17.

54   **by 1949, she enrolled in the famed culinary school Le Cordon Bleu:** Spitz, *Dearie*, 187.

54   **Her male classmates looked at her as some kind of trespasser:** Ibid., 191.

54   **the sexist convention that only men should aspire to haute cuisine:** Dana B. Polan, *Julia Child's the French Chef* (Durham, NC: Duke University Press, 2011), 5.

55   **with whom she opened a cooking school:** Spitz, *Dearie*, 225.

55   **"The School of the Three Hearty Eaters":** Child, *My Life*, 125.

55   **a fair, blonde woman:** Ibid., 114.

55   **Simca and Louisette also involved Julia in a long-gestating project:** Ibid., 231.

55 **a sharp-eyed Knopf editor named Judith Jones:** Spitz, *Dearie*, 300.

56 **away from the tedium of Swanson TV dinners:** Ibid., 6.

56 **living out a thrilling postwar fantasy:** Michael Pollan, "Out of the Kitchen, onto the Couch," *New York Times Magazine*, July 29, 2009. https://www.nytimes.com/2009/08/02/magazine/02cooking-t .html.

56 **Many just wanted to watch *her*:** Polan, *Julia Child's the French Chef*, 12.

56 **Television put Julia's very American appeal on full display:** As the critic Dana Polan wrote, Julia still "stands for a particularly American embodiment of boisterous fun." Ibid., 3.

56 **who would even see?:** Spitz, *Dearie*, 348.

56 **parody, like the kind Dan Aykroyd played on *Saturday Night Live*:** Ibid., 420.

56 **she once dreamed of being a basketball player:** Regina Schrambling, "Julia Child, the French Chef for a Jell-O Nation, Dies at 91," *New York Times*, August 13, 2004. https://www.nytimes .com/2004/08/13/dining/julia-child-the-french-chef-for-a-jello -nation-dies-at-91.html.

57 **those meals almost always required antacids:** Ibid., 41.

57 **"WASPy, upper-middle-class family":** Child, *My Life*, 3.

57 **nasty pile of calf's brains simmered in red wine:** Laura Jacobs, "Our Lady of the Kitchen," *Vanity Fair*, July 6, 2009. https://www .vanityfair.com/culture/2009/08/julia-child200908.

57 ***The Joy of Cooking* or glossies like *Gourmet*:** Child, *My Life*, 6.

57 **purple garlic and zucchini flowers:** Spitz, *Dearie*, 179.

57 **spinach gnocchi and quiche lorraine:** Ibid., 195.

57 **she'd begun hearing murmurs of this mysterious contraption:** Child, *My Life*, 72.

57 **to promote the book on the *Today* show:** Spitz, *Dearie*, 313.

58 **Simca, who came to New York from France:** Child, *My Life*, 229.

58 **their self-assigned task was to prepare an omelet:** Ibid., 231.

58 **"simply terrifying":** Spitz, *Dearie*, 315.

58 **"written as if each were a masterpiece, and most of them are":** Ibid., 313.

58 **James Beard hosted the first nationally aired cooking show:** Kathleen Collins, *Watching What We Eat: The Evolution of Television Cooking Shows* (London: Continuum, 2009), 27.

58 **In 1947, the British chef Dione Lucas:** Ibid., 49.

58 **the first female graduate of Le Cordon Bleu:** Ibid., 241.

58 **an air of stuffy British propriety:** Polan, *Julia Child's the French Chef*, 8.

58 **"can opener queen":** Collins, *Watching What We Eat*, 63.

58 **an afternoon cooking segment:** Lawrence Van Geider, "Poppy Cannon White, 69, Dead; Writer Was Authority on Food," *New York Times*, April 2, 1975.

59 **vichyssoise, a French soup, from frozen mashed potatoes, a leek, and Campbell's cream of chicken soup:** Collins, *Watching What We Eat*, 65.

59 **causing NBC to let her go shortly after:** Laura Shapiro, *Something from the Oven: Reinventing Dinner in 1950s America* (New York: Viking, 2004), 216.

59 **a fixture of WGBH's Thursday night lineup:** Spitz, *Dearie*, 4.

59 **By then, *Mastering the Art* was in its third printing:** Child, *My Life*, 236.

59 **It struck him as a ridiculous demand:** Spitz, *Dearie*, 3.

59 **How would they light a woman so tall?:** Ibid., 11.

59 **as if arm-wrestling a ghost:** Ibid., 13.

59 **made the offer in April 1962:** Ibid., 330.

59 ***The French Chef*, which was short enough to fit on one line in *TV Guide*:** Ibid., 333.

60 **in a room in the auditorium of the Boston Gas Company:** Ibid., 334.

60 **"Hello. I'm Julia Child":** Ibid., 336.

60 **"I loved the way she projected over the camera directly to me":** Ibid.

61 **By 1964, *The French Chef* was airing in over fifty cities across the country:** Child, *My Life*, 246.

61 **"I felt that she was such a colorful personality":** Ibid., 247

I Was a Good Fighter, Sister: Madeleine Kamman

62 **One day in March 1968:** Craig Claiborne, "Snail's Place," *New York Times*, March 24, 1968.

62 **"Merci, merci, for advocating snails":** Craig Claiborne, "The Enthusiasm of Snail Addict Helps Turn a Meal into a Feast," *New York Times*, May 23, 1968.

63 **Born Madeleine Marguerite Pin in November 1930:** Richard Sandomir, "Madeleine Kamman, Chef Who Gave Americans a

Taste of France, Dies at 87," *New York Times*, July 22, 2018. https://
www.nytimes.com/2018/07/20/obituaries/madeleine-kamman-87
-celebrated-french-chef-is-dead.html.

63 **Before returning to work, she'd peel potatoes by hand:** Madeleine Kamman, *When French Women Cook: A Gastronomic Memoir
with Over 250 Recipes*, 2nd ed. (New York: Ten Speed, 2002), 4.

63 **Hôtel des Voyageurs:** Ibid., 174.

63 **barely tall enough to see over the counter:** Linda Greider, "A Case
of Improving on the Classics," *Washington Post*, October 19, 1983.

64 **She would hold the feet of rabbits and ducks:** Kamman, *When
French Women Cook*, 176.

64 **Claire had a profound sense of justice:** Ibid., 179.

64 **studied languages at the Sorbonne:** Marian Burros, "Flinty,
Revered Teacher of Chefs," *New York Times*, August 4, 1993. https://
www.nytimes.com/1993/08/04/garden/flinty-revered-teacher-of
-chefs.html.

64 **She attended both Le Cordon Bleu and L'École des Trois Gourmandes:** *Philadelphia Inquirer*, "French Cooking Class Meets in Mrs.
Lloyd's Kitchen," October 15, 1968.

64 **working under Julia Child's collaborator Simone "Simca" Beck:**
Philadelphia Inquirer, "Free Instruction in French Cooking," September 26, 1968.

64 **when she met her future husband, Alan Kamman, in the summer of 1959:** Claiborne, "The Enthusiasm of Snail Addict."

64 **marrying him in February 1960:** Alan Daniel Kamman, phone
interview by author, December 12, 2019.

65 **Alan Daniel in 1962, then Neil in 1966:** Marilynn Marter, "A Preparer of Chefs," *Philadelphia Inquirer*, March 25, 1998.

65 **The language was different:** Kamman, *When French Women Cook*, 1.

65 **the lush farms of the Pennsylvania countryside:** Bill Citara, "Recipes and More," *San Francisco Examiner*, February 22, 1998.

65 **She could eat a whole lobster with butter in America:** Mary
Goodbody, "The Cook's Interview: Madeleine Kamman," *Cook's*,
July/August 1984, 13.

65 **Philadelphia's Adult Education School in 1962:** Bill Citara, "Recipes and More."

65 **just after the birth of her first son:** Marter, "A Preparer of Chefs."

65 **rum raisin soufflés:** *Philadelphia Inquirer*, "French Cooking Class
Meets in Mrs. Lloyd's Kitchen."

65 **she decided instead to emphasize technique:** Marilyn McDevitt
Rubin, "French Chef with Class," *Pittsburgh Press*, September 6, 1981.

65 **That wasn't cooking:** Carol Haddix, "The REAL Way French
Women Cook," *Detroit Free Press*, March 10, 1976.

65 **she began writing in 1969:** *Philadelphia Inquirer*, "Recipe for
Chicken Breasts," February 27, 1969.

65 **In September 1970, she established a cooking school:** Otile
McManus, "Teaching the Why of French Cookery," *Boston Globe*,
February 25, 1971.

65 **she taught nine different courses:** Otile McManus, "A Full Course
of Cooking Schools," *Boston Globe*, September 16, 1970.

66 **Bavarian cream:** Phyllis Hanes, "Teaching the Techniques: Showing How It's Done a French Way from Cordon Bleu Indian Puree
Blueberry Bavarian Cream," *Christian Science Monitor*, January 14,
1971.

66 **"I have tried food that has gone through the oven":** Gail Perrin,
"The Microwave Oven: Some Pros and Cons," *Boston Globe*, November 27, 1974.

66 **"Cooks who believe that":** Madeleine Kamman, *The Making of a
Cook* (New York: Atheneum, 1971), ix.

66 **"Something terrible happened to onion soup":** Ibid., 73.

67 **The book sold only modestly:** John L. Hess and Karen Hess, *The
Taste of America* (New York: Grossman, 1977), 135.

67 **"exuberant and unfettered":** Samuel Chamberlain, "The Objective: Teaching One to Cook," *Boston Globe*, December 19, 1971.

67 **"The techniques used determine":** Nika Hazelton, "Pleasing to
the Palate," *New York Times*, December 12, 1971.

67 **"borrows techniques but not recipes from the Julia Child
books":** Jeanne Voltz, "Cookbooks I'd Like to Give," *Los Angeles
Times*, November 21, 1971.

67 **It was Madeleine who pursued a friendship with Julia:** Noel
Riley Fitch, *Appetite for Life: The Biography of Julia Child* (New York:
Anchor, 1997), 352.

67 **The two women met shortly after Madeleine moved to Lexington in 1969:** Ibid., 351.

67 **"Madeleine Kamman and her husband came to dinner several
weeks ago":** Ibid., 352.

68 **Madeleine even included Simca in the acknowledgments:** Kamman, *The Making of a Cook*, vii.

68 **A student wrote to Julia:** Fitch, *Appetite for Life*, 352.

68 **"French women don't know a damn thing about French cooking":** Nancy L. Ross, "Mastering Julia's French Recipes," *Washington Post*, November 5, 1970.

68 **Chez La Mère Madeleine, a restaurant hiding in an alleyway:** Steve Weiss, "Madeleine Kamman 'Is' the Modern Gourmet," *Institutions*, August 15, 1977, 49.

68 **most people called the restaurant by the same name as the school:** Roy Andries de Groot, "In Search of the Greatest Restaurant in the United States," *Diversion*, April 1977, 39.

68 **It would not open itself up to the public for another two years:** Goodbody, "The Cook's Interview."

68 **altered its menu every few weeks:** "Modern Gourmet," *Where It's At: A Gustatorial Search for Fine Wines*, September 1976, 13.

69 **"the king of chefs":** Craig Claiborne, "Paul Bocuse, King of Chefs, Creates in an East Hampton Kitchen," *New York Times*, June 30, 1975.

69 **the only place for women was in bed:** Linda Bird Francke with Scott Sullivan, "The King of the Kitchen," *Newsweek*, August 11, 1975, 53.

69 **Bocuse himself would acknowledge this shortly after:** Kathleen Fliegel, "Dining Out: The Greatest Restaurant in, Uh, Boston," *Boston*, August 1976, 110.

69 **a frequent guest on *Good Morning!*:** Nina Allen, "Sampling Courses in Cookery," *Boston Globe*, December 30, 1975.

69 **an enormously popular and widely syndicated talk show:** WCVB 5, "WCVB's Station Timeline," May 12, 2005. https://www.wcvb.com/article/wcvb-s-station-timeline/8135747.

69 **broiled steak with blue cheese and caraway butter:** Madeleine Kamman, *Dinner against the Clock* (New York: Atheneum, 1973), 76.

70 **"This volume does not pretend":** Ibid., vii.

70 **the Italian food writer Marcella Hazan's *The Classic Italian Cook Book* and the Indian actress and food writer Madhur Jaffrey's *An Invitation to Indian Cooking*:** Nika Hazelton, "New and Old Angles to Cooking," *New York Times*, December 2, 1973.

71 **"excellent book":** Ibid.

71 **coveted Tastemaker Award:** Gail Perrin, "Jungle Cats Eat Well," *Boston Globe*, May 15, 1974.

71 **"good-quality trash":** Hess and Hess, *The Taste of America*, 135.

71 **"an enemy":** William Rice, "An Enduring Entente," *Washington Post*, October 3, 1974.

71 **Madeleine wrote to Julia saying that she was conspiring to bring down another woman:** Fitch, *Appetite for Life*, 367.

71 **scaled her school to such a point by 1975:** Nina Allen, "Sampling Courses in Cookery," *Boston Globe*, December 30, 1975.

71 **"is fierce in protecting her classical patrimony":** Anthony Spinazzola, "Let's Eat Out," *Boston Globe*, July 3, 1975.

71 **"single gifted personality":** Fliegel, "Dining Out: The Greatest Restaurant in, Uh, Boston."

72 **"I left France during the early days of 1960":** Kamman, *When French Women Cook*, 1.

73 **She began with her great-grandmother, a mattress maker named Marie-Charlotte:** Ibid., 22.

73 **she found Eugénie's treasured diaries:** Ibid., 220.

73 **Marie-Charlotte in her lemon crullers:** Ibid., 53.

73 **Claire in her steamed calf's livers:** Ibid., 196.

73 **Eugénie in her sauerkraut soup:** Ibid., 224.

73 **dedicated the book to Paul Bocuse's grandmother and mother:** Ibid., i.

74 **"simply the best restaurant in Boston":** Laurie Devine, "The Best Restaurants in Boston," *Boston Globe*, December 3, 1977.

74 **"a woman of firm convictions":** James Beard with Jose Wilson, "Who's Teaching the Great Chefs?," *Los Angeles Times*, October 12, 1978.

74 **why her pureed scallop mousseline didn't have chunks of scallops in it:** Harvey Steiman, "Madeleine Kamman: Champion of 'Women's Cuisine,'" *San Francisco Examiner*, May 13, 1981.

74 **the city felt shockingly illiberal:** Barbara Hansen, "Renowned Teacher and Restaurateur: French Cook Is Enjoying Success in Her 'American Phase,'" *Los Angeles Times*, February 28, 1985.

74 **the misperception that she was too snooty:** Patricia Wells, "Chef-Teacher Starts a New Life," *New York Times*, January 7, 1981.

74 **In a letter she wrote to Julia in 1979:** Fitch, *Appetite for Life*, 404.

75 **"She is not a cook":** Hess and Hess, *The Taste of America*, 355.

75 **"serious work":** Ibid., 135.

75 **The book's contrarianism also made the Hesses unpopular with the food establishment:** Bill Daley, "Karen Hess: Food Historian, Caustic Critic of American Food," *Chicago Tribune*, December 8, 2014. https://www.chicagotribune.com/dining/recipes/sc-food-1212 -giants-hess-20141208-story.html.

75 **"Her bluntness has not endeared her":** "Controversial Chef Bids 'Au Revoir' to the U.S.," *Nation's Restaurant News*, August 20, 1979.

75 **then a vice president at the consulting firm Arthur D. Little:** Alison Arnett, "Too Good for Boston?," *Boston Globe*, March 23, 1980.

75 **stayed stateside:** Neil Kamman, phone interview by author, December 19, 2019.

75 **visit her every third week:** Peggy Katalinich, "A Master Teacher in the French Mode," *Newsday*, February 19, 1986.

75 **Madeleine sold the stock of her restaurant to her students:** Goodbody, "The Cook's Interview."

75 **She got rid of some six hundred books:** Wells, "Chef-Teacher Starts a New Life."

75 **Madeleine outlined a systematic plan:** "Controversial Chef Bids 'Au Revoir' to the U.S."

76 **"I want strawberries that taste like strawberries, not formaldehyde":** Marian Burros, "With the Standard of St. Joan," *Washington Post*, July 15, 1979.

76 **"Too Good for Boston?":** Arnett, "Too Good for Boston?"

76 **When she arrived in Annecy in the summer of 1980:** Nao Hauser, "Woman with a Vision," *Cuisine*, September 1981, 40.

76 **There was nothing to distract Madeleine in Annecy, no one to criticize her:** Steiman, "Madeleine Kamman."

77 **started writing a fourth cookbook:** Barbara Gibbs Ostmann, "Cooking with 'La Mere Madeleine,'" *St. Louis Post-Dispatch*, November 2, 1983.

77 **She opened her cooking school in October of that year:** Wells, "Chef-Teacher Starts a New Life."

77 **in France, she would teach no more than six:** Steiman, "Madeleine Kamman.'"

77 **"Only the French know how to teach French cooking":** Wells, "Chef-Teacher Starts a New Life."

77 **pop an aspirin every afternoon:** Rubin, "French Chef with Class."

77 **"France's Best Cooking School":** "France's Best Cooking School," *Bon Appétit*, February 1982.

77 **"the whole economy, everything":** Goodbody, "The Cook's Interview."

77 **She never did open that fabled three-star restaurant, either:** Neil Kamman, phone interview by author, December 19, 2019.

77 **citing an unreasonable tax upon her income:** "Tidbits: Cooking School Cut," *Star Tribune*, April 17, 1983.

78 **Her collection of cookbooks, which she'd whittled down to three hundred:** Ostmann, "Cooking with 'La Mere Madeleine.'"

78 **a place she'd always liked:** Alan Daniel Kamman, phone interview by author, December 12, 2019.

78 **spent the fall of 1983 teaching cooking across North America:** Ostmann, "Cooking with 'La Mere Madeleine.'"

78 **"mellowed":** Ibid.

78 **"I became very controversial":** Madeleine Kamman, *In Madeleine's Kitchen* (New York: Atheneum, 1984), 3.

78 **"the enormously rich font of cuisine provided by all the women in the world":** Ibid., 6.

78 **"by foreign and ethnic ingredients":** Ibid., 10.

78 **galantine of duck:** Ibid., 121.

78 **Though the book generated favorable reviews:** Walker and Claudine Cowen, "Cookbooks," *Virginia Quarterly Review*, Spring 1986, 66.

79 **"technical explanations are unrivaled":** Marian Burros, "Cooking," *New York Times*, December 2, 1984.

79 **She complained to the press that the awards went to coffee-table books with flashy photographs:** Charlene Varkonyi, "Cookbooks Moving from Kitchen to Coffee Table," *Sun Sentinel*, December 11, 1985.

79 **filmed a "video cookbook" in 1983:** Marian Burros, "Now Showing on Nation's VCRs: Adventures in Videotape Cooking," *New York Times*, November 13, 1985.

79 **sold for $89.95:** Judith Barrett, "Gadgets for Gourmet Gift-Giving," *Boston Globe*, November 28, 1984.

79 **She made saffron, spinach, and beet pastas:** Video flyer, *Madeleine Kamman Cooks*.

79 **which sold over ten thousand copies by November 1985:** Burros, "Now Showing on Nation's VCRs."

79 **"Now she is on video":** *People* Staff, "Picks and Pans Review: The Video Cooking Series: Madeleine Kamman Cooks," *People*, March 25, 1985. https://people.com/archive/picks-and-pans-review-the-video-cooking-series-madeleine-kamman-cooks-vol-23-no-12/.

79 **in November 1984:** Patricia Tennison, "Madeleine Kamman's Encore for 1984," *Chicago Tribune*, October 4, 1984.

79 **situated in the middle of the woods in New Hampshire:** Linda Greider, "A Case of Improving on the Classics," *Washington Post*, October 19, 1983.

79 **accepted eight American students for a regimented class that would last just under a year:** Tennison, "Madeleine Kamman's Encore."

80 **"Negotiations are underway to bring Kamman to PBS sometime this year":** *People* Staff, "Picks and Pans Review."

80 **began airing on PBS in January 1986:** Bob Hoover, "Et Cetera," *Pittsburgh Post-Gazette*, December 11, 1985.

80 **"American fare with French flair":** Steve McKerrow, "Rating the TV Gourmets," *Sun*, October 17, 1987.

80 **"Oriental" salad:** Suzanne Hamlin, "Meet Madeleine, and Start Cooking," *Daily News*, January 22, 1986.

80 **"me on the lowest level I can go":** Peter M. Gianotti, "Recipe for Ratings: The Chefs Are All Over the TV Dial," *Newsday*, March 29, 1989.

80 **to last until 1991:** Tom Williams, email to author, November 26, 2019.

80 **Tunisian-style broiled chicken:** Madeleine Kamman, *Madeleine Cooks* (New York: William Morrow, 1986), 19.

80 **American roast duck:** Ibid., 160.

80 **a Provençal rice salad:** Ibid., 96.

80 **wrote at great length of Savoie's history, its culture, and its people:** Madeleine Kamman, *Madeleine Kamman's Savoie: The Land, People, and Food of the French Alps* (New York: Atheneum, 1989), xiii.

80 **an enticing offer to serve as the director of the School for American Chefs at Beringer Vineyards:** "Madeleine Kamman at Beringer Vineyards' School for American Chefs," *Wine Country International*, June/July 1990, 18.

81 **distilled her technique-driven sensibility more fully than any of her previous cookbooks:** Madeleine Kamman, *The New Making of a Cook: The Art, Techniques, and Science of Good Cooking* (New York: William Morrow, 1997), xvi.

81 **like low-fat cooking:** Ibid., xiii.

81 **netting her the James Beard Award for Book of the Year in 1998, and the foundation also gave her its Lifetime Achievement Award that same year:** Joe Crea, "Kamman Scores Top Honors at Beard Awards," *The Orlando Sentinel*, May 14, 1998.

81 **retired for good:** Janet Fletcher, "A Grande Dame Steps Down," *San Francisco Chronicle*, February 16, 2000.

81 **"Despite a public television series, tireless teaching, and prolific writing":** Molly O'Neill, "For Madeleine Kamman, A Gentler Simmer," *New York Times*, January 14, 1998. https://www.nytimes .com/1998/01/14/dining/for-madeleine-kamman-a-gentler-simmer .html.

81 **abrasive:** Charles Kenney, "The Cast-Iron Lady," *Boston Globe*, June 30, 1985.

81 **arrogant:** Ibid.

81 **feisty:** Rose Dosti, "Madeleine Kamman: A Controversial Cooking Teacher Who Says the Next Great Chefs Will Be American Men and Women," *Los Angeles Times*, June 7, 1990.

81 **imperious:** Steiman, "Madeleine Kamman."

81 **temperamental:** Linda Giuca, "She Taught," *Hartford Courant*, March 3, 1982.

81 **difficult:** Burros, "Flinty, Revered Teacher of Chefs."

81 **"We note now, too, that Madeleine Kamman is no icon":** Sara Lewis Dunne, "Julia Child," in *American Icons: An Encyclopedia of the People, Places, and Things That Have Shaped Our Culture: Volume One*, ed. Dennis R. Hall and Susan Grove Hall (Westport, CT: Greenwood, 2006), 143.

82 **a decade of deterioration from Alzheimer's:** Richard Sandomir, "Madeleine Kamman, Chef Who Gave Americans a Taste of France, Dies at 87," *New York Times*, July 22, 2018. https://www.nytimes .com/2018/07/20/obituaries/madeleine-kamman-87-celebrated -french-chef-is-dead.html.

82 **"America has a tendency toward stardom":** David Kamp, *The United States of Arugula: How We Became a Gourmet Nation* (New York: Broadway, 2006), 109.

As Words Come to a Child: Marcella Hazan

83 **When she was 7:** Marcella Hazan, *Amarcord: Marcella Remembers* (New York: Gotham, 2008), 1.

83 **rod of a mosquito net:** Ibid., 5.

84 **Maybe she'd accidentally drop her child:** Ibid., 87.

84 **At least she could grip a knife with it:** Kim Severson, "Marcella Hazan, Author Who Changed the Way Americans Cook Italian Food, Dies at 89," *New York Times*, September 29, 2013. https://www

.nytimes.com/2013/09/30/dining/Marcella-Hazan-dies-changed-the-way-americans-cook-italian-food.html.

84 **idling away at gelato parlors:** Hazan, *Amarcord*, 9.

84 **piadina, a yeastless flatbread crisped over a terra-cotta griddle:** Ibid., 16.

84 **in September 1940 when she and her family moved to a farmhouse on Lake Garda:** Ibid., 20.

84 **The kitchen became a sanctuary:** Ibid., 21.

85 **the neighboring town of Salò:** Ibid., 22.

85 **bags of salt boiled down from lagoon water:** Ibid., 23.

85 **She searched for mulberry leaves in her vineyard:** Ibid., 24.

85 **careful not to let plaster from the bombs fall on their food:** Ibid., 28.

85 **to eat in pursuit of pleasure:** Ibid., 38.

85 **Marcella and her parents emerged from the war physically unscathed:** Ibid., 42.

85 **returned to Cesenatico in May 1945:** Ibid., 39.

86 **puckered tomatoes:** Ibid., 41.

86 **cotechino, a creamy boiled sausage made from the pig's hide:** Ibid., 25.

86 **She had eaten it only once during the war:** Ibid., 44.

86 **By 1954, she ended up getting dual doctorates:** Ibid., 51.

86 **spoke in spare sentences, giving force to each word:** Ibid., 53.

86 **He returned to Italy after nearly a decade and a half in New York:** Ibid., 52.

87 **a dish of Roman-style snails with tomatoes and anchovies:** Hazan, *Amarcord*, 58.

87 **he sautéed sweetbreads with butter, onions, and prosciutto:** Ibid., 59.

87 **he and Marcella wed in February 1955 in Cesenatico:** Ibid., 65.

87 **she boarded the SS *Cristoforo Colombo* alone:** Ibid., 67.

87 **that day in September 1955:** Ibid., 68.

88 **In Cesenatico, Marcella was used to sticking food in an icebox during the summer:** Ibid., 70.

88 **hoping to introduce her to a hamburger:** Ibid., 71.

88 **poor tomatoes were subjected to chemical malpractice in America:** Tom Jaine, "Marcella Hazan Obituary," *Guardian*, October 6, 2013. https://www.theguardian.com/lifeandstyle/2013/oct/06/marcella-hazan.

88 **But the words of Ada Boni:** Hazan, *Amarcord*, 73.

88 **"as though I were telling a story I had heard as a little girl in another land":** Ibid., 103.

88 **She began modestly, with soups:** Ibid., 73.

89 **pastella, a batter of flour and water:** Ibid., 74.

89 **"as words come to a child when it is time for her to speak":** Ibid., 73.

89 **She watched Brooklyn Dodgers games:** Ibid., 75.

89 **In spring 1956, Marcella and Victor left the lonely enclave of Forest Hills:** Ibid., 80.

89 **English was all she heard anyone speak for the hours in the office:** Ibid., 83.

90 **The couple's son, Giuliano, was born on the first day of December:** Ibid., 86.

90 **As the years passed, New York started to make both Marcella and Victor miserable:** Ibid., 88.

90 **In June 1962, the family of three boarded a plane to Milan:** Ibid., 89.

90 **She bought red beets the size of oranges:** Ibid., 97.

90 **Her taste memories:** Ibid., 103.

90 **If Victor found a buyer:** Ibid., 113.

90 **Pearl's was the gateway:** Ibid., 123.

90 **named for its proprietor Pearl Wong:** J. Michael Elliott, "Pearl Wong, 86, Restaurant Owner in Mid-Manhattan," *New York Times*, January 21, 1995.

91 **Shanghai-born Grace Zia Chu:** Anne Mendelson, *Chow Chop Suey: Food and the Chinese American Journey* (New York: Columbia University Press, 2016), 199.

91 **Chu abruptly announced she'd soon be taking a sabbatical in China:** Hazan, *Amarcord*, 124.

91 **"American women are crazy":** Linda Wertheimer, "Marcella Hazan Brings Italy to America," National Public Radio, December 28, 2010.

91 **It was October 1969 when Marcella started hosting classes once a week:** Hazan, *Amarcord*, 124.

91 **Neapolitan linguine with clams, Florentine soup of beans and black cabbage:** Ibid., 126.

92 **That August, Victor wrote to the *New York Times* food section:** Ibid., 129.

92 **the list had already gone to the printer:** Victor Hazan, email to author, December 6, 2019.

92 **She prepared upside-down artichokes:** Hazan, *Amarcord*, 132.

92 **"There Was a Time She Couldn't Cook . . .":** Craig Claiborne, "There Was a Time She Couldn't Cook . . .," *New York Times*, October 15, 1970.

92 **Marcella wouldn't have to worry about staying busy from that point forward:** Victor Hazan, email to author, December 6, 2019.

92 **Peter Mollman, an editor at Harper & Row:** Hazan, *Amarcord*, 135.

93 **his English was smoother than hers:** Judith Jones, *The Tenth Muse* (New York: Anchor, 2007), 94.

93 **Back in the 1950s, Ada Boni's cookbooks became bibles for American housewives:** John Mariani, *How Italian Food Conquered the World* (New York: Palgrave Macmillan, 2011), 119.

93 **middle-class ones hoping to sprinkle their dinner parties with global flavor:** Donna R. Gabaccia et al. "Food, Recipes, Cookbooks, and Italian-American Life." *Italian Americana*, vol. 16, no. 1, 1998, pp. 5–23. *JSTOR*, www.jstor.org/stable/29776455.

93 **fish brodetto in the style of Rimini:** Ada Boni, *The Talisman Italian Cook Book* (New York: Crown, 1950), 15.

93 **pork chops in the style of Modena:** Ibid., 116.

93 **cities like New York since the late nineteenth century, though they mostly catered to Bohemian classes:** Paul Freedman, *Ten Restaurants That Changed America* (New York: Liveright, 2016), 178.

93 **"never reeks of garlic":** Joseph Durso, "Joe DiMaggio, Yankee Clipper, Dies at 84," *New York Times*, March 9, 1999. https://www.nytimes.com/1999/03/09/sports/joe-dimaggio-yankee-clipper-dies-at-84.html.

93 **restaurateurs in the twentieth century began serving Italian-inspired preparations:** Mariani, *How Italian Food*, 44.

93 **like manicotti or spaghetti and meatballs:** Hazan, *Amarcord*, 103.

93 **In the realm of the home, meanwhile, Americans clung to convenience foods:** Mariani, *How Italian Food*, 70.

94 **The American edition of English food writer Elizabeth David's *Italian Food*:** Charlotte Turgeon, "Something Fit to Eat," *New York Times*, November 16, 1958.

94 **Nika Hazelton, writing in the *New York Times*, dismissed Root's interpretation of regional Italian cuisines:** Nika Hazelton, "Because All Men Eat," *New York Times*, June 6, 1971.

94   **She bought ball-point pens:** Hazan, *Amarcord*, 137.

94   **in February 1972:** Ibid., 138.

94   **the repeated use of the word** *piquant***:** Ibid., 139.

95   **the talents of an illustrator named George Koizumi:** Ibid., 140.

95   **how to cut pappardelle with a fluted pastry wheel:** Marcella Hazan, *The Classic Italian Cook Book* (New York: Harper & Row, 1973), 122.

95   **how to pare the green off artichoke leaves:** Ibid., 339.

95   **Italians weren't really flag-wavers:** Hazan, *Amarcord*, 141.

95   **With 250 recipes:** Raymond A. Sokolov, "Current Stars: Books on Indian, Italian and Inexpensive Food," *New York Times*, April 19, 1973.

95   **those of Emiglia-Romagna and Tuscany:** "More Classic Italian Cooking," *Kirkus Reviews*, https://www.kirkusreviews.com/book -reviews/marcella-hazan/more-classic-italian-cooking/.

95   **"The first useful thing to know about Italian cooking":** Hazan, *Classic*, 1.

95   **"mountains of orange, cream-colored, and nut-brown wild mushrooms":** Ibid., 12.

95   **"When the** *polenta* **was done":** Hazan, *Classic*, 203.

96   **by no means the "encyclopedic" Italian cookbook:** Sokolov, "Current Stars."

96   **"the best new working cookbooks":** John L. Hess, "Food Lovers, Don't Despair—There Is Life in the Wasteland," *New York Times*, November 29, 1973.

96   **profile the following month:** John L. Hess, "The Best Way to Solve Any Macaroni Crisis: Flour, Eggs and Care," *New York Times*, December 6, 1973.

96   **"will come as a revelation":** Nika Hazelton, "New and Old Angles to Cooking," *New York Times*, December 2, 1973.

96   **Harper & Row didn't seem to be doing much to draw attention to the book:** Hazan, *Amarcord*, 141.

96   **Her husky voice, for example, enchanted Marcella:** Ibid., 271.

96   **Knopf reissued** *The Classic Italian Cook Book* **in February 1976:** Hazan, *Amarcord*, 145.

97   **a more elegant, earth-toned cover:** Ibid., 144.

97   **storefront on Fifty-Ninth Street called Marcella Hazan's Italian Kitchen:** Ibid., 273.

97 *New York* magazine restaurant critic Gael Greene, the actor Joel Grey: Ibid., 159.

97 she established a school for American students in the Italian city of Bologna in 1976: Ibid., 163.

97 She would later say it was the only project she'd worked on in her career that was entirely her idea, not the fulfillment of someone else's wish: Megan O. Steintrager, "A Conversation with Marcella Hazan," Epicurious, September 23, 2008. https://www.epicurious .com/archive/chefsexperts/interviews/marcellahazaninterview.

97 The city's tourism arm even invested: Hazan, *Amarcord*, 178.

98 Swedish meatballs or tuna casserole: Ibid., 158.

98 "the authentic language of the kitchen that is spoken in Italy today": Marcella Hazan, *More Classic Italian Cooking* (New York: Knopf, 1978)

98 spaghetti frittata: Ibid., 349.

98 polenta shortcake: Ibid., 433.

98 black-grape ice cream: Ibid., 453.

98 how to slice veal against the grain: Ibid., 17.

98 grate Parmesan: Ibid., 25.

98 stir the onions as they sautéed: Hazan, *Amarcord*, 274.

98 "further afield in quest of some regional specialties": "More Classic Italian Cooking," *Kirkus Reviews*.

98 "Too often excellent first cookbooks": Mimi Sheraton, "Cook-books," *New York Times*, December 3, 1978.

99 book would win Marcella a prestigious Tastemaker Award in the foreign cookbook category the following year: Melissa Davis, "The Best of the Books," *Washington Post*, May 24, 1979.

99 the Florence-born cooking teacher Giuliano Bugialli's *The Fine Art of Italian Cooking*: Neil Genzlinger, "Giuliano Bugialli, Champion of Italian Cuisine, Dies at 88," *New York Times*, May 3, 2019. https://www.nytimes.com/2019/05/03/obituaries/giuliano-bugialli -dead.html.

99 Edda Servi Machlin's *The Classic Cuisine of the Italian Jews*: Marian Burros, "Distinctive Foods of the Italian Jews," *New York Times*, March 31, 1982.

99 the American Italophile Carol Field's *The Italian Baker*: William Grimes, "Carol Field, Italian Food Expert, Dies at 76," *New York Times*, March 10, 2017. https://www.nytimes.com/2017/03/10/dining/ carol-field-dead-italian-cookbook-author.html.

99 **Knopf published his *Italian Wine* (1982), an acclaimed guide to the country's wines:** Terry Robards, "Two Books on the Best Bottlings of Italy," *New York Times*, January 12, 1983.

99 **Jones was Victor's editor, too:** Victor Hazan, *Italian Wine* (New York: Knopf, 1982), ix.

99 ***Marcella's Italian Kitchen:*** Hazan, *Amarcord*, 275.

99 **disappointed by her puny advance:** Ibid., 278.

99 **it ended up winning the category of Best Italian Cookbook:** Ibid., 279.

100 **a legendarily high $650,000, steeper than any that had been reported for an American cookbook:** Candy Sagon, "Ciao Marcella, One Last Book from the Woman Who Taught Us to Cook Italian," *Washington Post*, October 15, 1997. https://www.washingtonpost.com/archive/lifestyle/food/1997/10/15/ciao-marcella-one-last-book-from-the-woman-who-taught-us-to-cook-italian/fc9ad16e-2be9-456f-9ae4-656bd26f4b94/.

100 **The book won her a James Beard Award in the Mediterranean category:** Joe Crea, "Kamman Scores Top Honors at Beard Awards," *Orlando Sentinel*, May 14, 1998.

100 **In 2000, the foundation gave her its Lifetime Achievement Award and inducted her first cookbook into its Cookbook Hall of Fame:** Florence Fabricant, "New York Chefs Again Gain Top Awards," *New York Times*, May 10, 2000. https://www.nytimes.com/2000/05/10/dining/new-york-chefs-again-gain-top-awards.html.

100 **due to complicatio: from emphysema and arterial blockage:** Bonnie S. Benwick, "Cookbook Author Marcella Hazan Dies at 89," *Washington Post*, September 30, 2013. https://www.washingtonpost.com/lifestyle/food/cookbook-author-marcella-hazan-dies-at-89/2013/09/30/c5ae6bdc-29cb-11e3-8ade-a1f23cda135e_story.html.

100 **ingredients like fennel:** Marcella and Victor Hazan, *Ingredienti: Marcella's Guide to the Market* (New York: Scribner, 2016), 51.

100 **sunchokes:** Ibid., 96.

100 **"Victor does not take me out of the page and put himself in":** Dulcy Brainard, "Marcella Hazan: Educating America's Palate," *Publishers Weekly*, November 3, 1997. https://www.publishersweekly.com/pw/by-topic/authors/interviews/article/26571-pw-marcella-hazan-educating-america-s-palate.html.

101 **the *New York Times* characterized Victor as Marcella's "muse":**

Mark Bittman, "Remembering Marcella," *New York Times Magazine*, November 6, 2013.

101 **"Darling, I never did in my life anything that I was not asked to do it":** Linda Wertheimer, "Marcella Hazan Brings Italy to America," National Public Radio, December 28, 2010.

Her Own Quiet Rebellion: Julie Sahni

102 **Her mother had been planning to call her Deepa:** Julie Sahni, phone interview by author, May 15, 2019.

102 **a few convent-educated aunts of hers:** Julie Sahni, email interview by author, September 4, 2020.

102 **an Arya Samaj, or Hindu reform, school:** Julie Sahni, in-person interview by author, June 26, 2019.

103 **barely tall enough to reach her bicycle:** Julie Sahni, phone interview by author, May 14, 2019.

103 **"Woh ladki phir ayee":** Arthur J. Pais, "A Pinch of This, a Dash of That . . .," *India Abroad*, February 8, 2002.

103 **the whole wheat breads inflate on burners like birthday balloons:** Julie Sahni, *Classic Indian Cooking* (New York: William Morrow, 1980), 397.

103 **Julie's father, Venkataraman Ranganathan Iyer, gave the family's servants a vacation:** Pais, "A Pinch of This."

103 **Using brooms made from twigs:** Julie Sahni, phone interview by author, May 14, 2019.

103 **Julie's parents had wed when Padma was still a teenager:** Pais, "A Pinch of This."

103 **eventually obtaining two graduate degrees:** Ibid.

104 **By the time she was 14, she was performing on her own before audiences of thousands:** Julie Sahni, phone interview by author, May 15, 2019.

104 **her father's job as a botanist who worked with India's Ministry of Defence:** Julie Sahni, in-person interview by author, June 26, 2019.

104 **repeated a ritual:** Julie Sahni, phone interview by author, May 15, 2019.

104 **performing in thirty-two countries:** Julie Sahni, email interview by author, September 4, 2020.

104 **University of Delhi's Ramjas College:** Julie Sahni, in-person interview by author, May 23, 2019.

105 **graced the cover of Delhi's *Times of India* in November 1963:** *Times of India*, November 19, 1963.

105 **Between 1966 and 1967, when she was still in college:** Julie Sahni, email interview by author, September 4, 2020.

105 **Singh's book, which focused on the cuisines of North India:** Nikhita Venugopal, "Why Haven't You Heard of India's Julia Child?" *Taste*, July 19, 2018, https://www.tastecooking.com/why-havent-you -heard-of-indias-julia-child/.

105 **ever since she saw *A Summer Place*:** Julie Sahni, in-person interview by author, May 23, 2019.

105 **America's passing of the Immigration and Nationality Act in 1965:** Vivek Bald, *Bengali Harlem and the Lost Histories of South Asian America* (Cambridge, MA: Harvard University Press, 2013), 5.

106 **Julie's future in-laws insisted upon changing her first name per family tradition:** Julie Sahni, phone interview by author, May 15, 2019.

106 **When Julie arrived in New York in 1968:** Nancy Anderson, "Author Spreads 'Good Word' of Indian Cooking," *Hartford Courant*, November 5, 1980.

106 **their kitchen the size of a coat closet:** Julie Sahni, in-person interview by author, May 23, 2019.

106 **the popularity of the Beatles and their association with the Indian musician Ravi Shankar:** Julie Sahni, in-person interview by author, June 25, 2019.

106 **She was short, she was a woman, she was brown:** Julie Sahni, in-person interview by author, May 23, 2019.

106 **Sure, she got some stares when she wore a sari to class at Columbia:** Jennifer Wolcott, "Ambassador of Indian food Serves Up a Side Dish of Culture," *Christian Science Monitor*, June 1, 2005. https://www.csmonitor.com/2005/0601/p14s02-lifo.html.

107 **she went on to work for the City Planning Commission in 1970:** Patricia Wells, "The Indian Brunch: Fragrant Feast," *New York Times*, February 14, 1979.

107 **recommending improvements to subway infrastructure:** Julie Sahni, in-person interview by author, May 23, 2019.

107 **Viraht wanted anything *but* Indian food:** Bert Greene, "A Pair of Recipes in the Classic Style of India," *Los Angeles Times*, March 5, 1987.

107   **three cookbooks in particular:** Julie Sahni, in-person interview by
         author, May 23, 2019.

107   **night classes in Chinese cooking:** Anderson, "Author Spreads
         'Good Word.'"

107   **how to jelly duck blood:** Julie Sahni, phone interview by author,
         May 14, 2019.

108   **"Indian Actress Is a Star in the Kitchen, Too":** Craig Claiborne,
         "Indian Actress Is a Star in the Kitchen, Too," *New York Times*, July 7,
         1966.

108   **"To me the word 'curry' is as degrading":** Madhur Jaffrey, *An Invi-
         tation to Indian Cooking* (New York: Knopf, 1973), 5.

108   **populated American cookbooks as early as 1824:** Sarah Lohman,
         Eight Flavors: The Untold Story of American Cuisine (New York: Simon
         & Schuster, 2016), 91.

108   **later in the nineteenth century, when an Indian chef named J.
         Ranji Smile:** Colleen Taylor Sen, *Curry: A Global History* (London:
         Reakton, 2009), 55.

108   **"rare Oriental ragout":** Jane Holt, "Old-Fashioned Cookie Jars
         Give Shop Rural Tone That Marks Its Wares," *New York Times*, June
         16, 1941.

108   **"Indian food is not just 'curry'":** Jane Nickerson, "'Spicy' Cook-
         book Sheds Light on Indian Dishes," *New York Times*, October 11,
         1956.

109   **"Western minds":** Santha Rama Rau, *The Cooking of India* (New
         York: Time Inc., 1969), 24.

109   **Jaffrey worked from a template similar to Rau's:** Antoinette Bur-
         ton, *The Postcolonial Careers of Santha Rama Rau* (Durham, NC: Duke
         University Press, 2007), 112.

109   **pullaos of rice with lamb:** Ibid., 199.

109   **shrimp with dill and ginger:** Ibid., 118.

109   **green peppers stuffed with keema:** Ibid., 57-58.

109   **Americans could seemingly understand Indian food only
         through the framework of curry:** Julie Sahni, in-person interview
         by author, June 25, 2019.

109   **she struggled to get crucial spices and herbs for Indian cooking
         in New York:** Julie Sahni, in-person interview by author, May 23,
         2019.

109   **She held six weekly sessions:** Florence Fabricant, "Proper Use of
         Spices Key to Indian Cooking," *New York Times*, November 10, 1974.

110 **food should be soft enough to break with three fingers:** Julie Sahni, phone interview by author, May 14, 2019.

110 **until the fall of 1974, when she got a call from a mysterious woman:** Pais, "A Pinch of This."

110 **a November 1974 profile of Julie:** Fabricant, "Proper Use of Spices."

110 **For Julie, Fabricant's piece marked a turning point:** Julie Sahni, phone interview by author, May 14, 2019.

110 **fully booked for two years:** Julie Sahni, email interview by author, September 4, 2020.

110 **heading a Planning Department task force:** Charles Kaiser, "New York City Sidewalk Cafés May Ignore 9 Agencies at Once," *New York Times*, December 29, 1977.

111 **how to make lamb rogan josh:** Patricia Wells, "Cooking Schools: Other Boroughs," *New York Times*, December 6, 1978.

111 **In 1975, following Fabricant's article:** Julie Sahni, email interview by author, September 4, 2020.

111 **Julie found a kindred spirit in Marcella Hazan:** Julie Sahni, in-person interview by author, May 23, 2019.

111 **"Julie Sahni was raised to be an achiever":** Patricia Wells, "The Indian Brunch: Fragrant Feast," *New York Times*, February 14, 1979.

111 **In fact, she didn't even have an agent:** Julie Sahni, phone interview by author, May 14, 2019.

112 **In early 1979, she found out she was pregnant:** Julie Sahni, phone interview by author, May 15, 2019.

112 **obtain her American citizenship in October 1979:** Julie Sahni, email interview by author, September 4, 2020.

112 **"There is no mystical secret behind Indian cooking":** Sahni, *Classic*, 2.

112 **"It is the crushed cardamom":** Ibid., xiii.

112 **how to butterfly a leg of lamb:** Ibid., 183.

112 **peel broccoli spears:** Ibid., 297.

112 **ruh (flower essence):** Ibid., 57.

112 **vark (silver foil):** Ibid., 58.

112 **how to powder asafetida:** Ibid., 65.

112 **how to brown-fry onion, garlic, and ginger root:** Ibid., 71.

112 **Hindu Brahmins from West Bengal ate fish:** Ibid., xvi.

113 **Mysore rasam:** Ibid., 138.

113 **dahi machi:** Ibid., 253.

113 **"two exceptionally fine and much needed volumes on Oriental cooking":** Mimi Sheraton, "Cookbooks," *New York Times*, November 30, 1980.

113 **"classic cookbook library":** Mimi Sheraton, "Choosing a Basic Cookbook Library," *New York Times*, August 15, 1981.

113 **"The publisher thinks this book":** Walker and Claudine Cowen, "Cookbooks," *Virginia Quarterly Review*, Fall 1981, 138.

113 **While on her book tour:** Julie Sahni, in-person interview by author, May 23, 2019.

114 **Her first published article:** Julie Sahni, "Welcome Fall with a Burmese Buffet," *Cuisine*, October 1982.

114 **The magazine, which folded in 1984, was one of five leading food glossies:** Suzanne Hamlin, "Demise of Cuisine Has Competitors Scrambling," *Chicago Tribune*, January 31, 1985.

114 **Anglo-Indian cuisine for *Food & Wine*:** Julie Sahni, "Enticing, Fragrant and Subtly Spiced," *Food & Wine*, November 1986.

114 **savory and sweet chutneys for *Bon Appétit*:** Julie Sahni, "Chutneys Sweet and Savory," *Bon Appétit*, November 1988.

114 **Julie did the bulk of her writing in the wee hours of the night:** Julie Sahni, email interview by author, September 4, 2020.

115 **the occasional cooking class at Bloomingdale's:** Julie Sahni, phone interview by author, May 14, 2019.

115 **top floor of 30 Central Park South:** Nicolas Gage, "A Nightclub Owner Says He Has Woes—the Mafia," *New York Times*, October 10, 1974.

115 **fresh roses were on each table:** Patricia Murphy, "Atop New York Skyscrapers, Fine Dining Rooms with a View," *Philadelphia Inquirer*, January 17, 1982.

115 **He was an employee of the restaurant, he confessed:** Julie Sahni, phone interview by author, May 14, 2019.

115 **founded Nirvana in 1970:** Gage, "A Nightclub Owner."

115 **a place called Kashmir, and found the quality horrid:** Lizzie Collingham, *Curry: A Tale of Cooks and Conquerors* (New York: Oxford University Press, 2006), 234.

115 **run-ins with the law and the mafia:** "The City," *New York Times*, July 18, 1979.

116 **when she was 37:** Julie Sahni, email interview by author, September 4, 2020.

116 **the first Indian woman to hold the post of executive chef at a**

New York restaurant: Alex Witchel, "On the Spice Route from India, Properly Loaded," *New York Times*, April 28, 2010.

116 **lobster meat cooked in coconut milk, chile, and fresh ginger:** Jay Jacobs, "Nirvana," *Gourmet*, May 1984.

116 **Julie started out at Nirvana as a consultant:** Julie Sahni, phone interview by author, May 14, 2019.

116 **a discotheque to rival Studio 54 and Limelight:** Julie Sahni, in-person interview by author, May 23, 2019.

116 **opened in April 1984:** Marian Burros, "Restaurants," *New York Times*, June 8, 1984.

116 **a menu identical:** Bryan Miller, "Diner's Journal," *New York Times*, April 20, 1984.

116 **"one of the most romantic":** Jay Jacobs, "Nirvana," *Gourmet*, May 1984.

116 **"sitar music shivers and weeps":** Barbara Costikyan, "Great Places to Have a Party," *New York*, June 4, 1984.

117 **"a silky, golden piece of work":** Jacobs, "Nirvana."

117 **lavished praise on Julie's aloo samosa and malai kofta:** Burros, "Restaurants."

117 **Julie had trouble gaining the respect of her chefs:** Julie Sahni, phone interview by author, May 14, 2019.

117 **she would sometimes finish her shifts at 2:30 in the morning:** Julie Sahni, in-person interview by author, May 23, 2019.

117 **Julie didn't have time to visit India:** Julie Sahni, phone interview by author, May 29, 2020.

117 **eggless "scrambled eggs":** Julie Sahni, *Classic Indian Vegetarian and Grain Cooking* (New York: William Morrow, 1985) 131.

117 **pullaos of paneer and sweet peppers:** Ibid., 276.

117 **lassi made from ripe papaya:** Ibid., 473.

117 **her sister Reena's wedding:** Ibid., 18.

117 **"leaves you dizzy, wondering where to start":** Linda Greider, "What Is a Cookbook, Anyway?" *Washington Post*, December 4, 1985.

118 **"Of the two":** Nancy Harmon Jenkins, "Recipes Can Evoke Imaginary Journeys," *New York Times*, May 14, 1986.

118 **Duran Duran:** Julie Sahni, in-person interview by author, May 23, 2019.

118 **the Pointer Sisters, Sean Lennon:** Julie Sahni, phone interview by author, April 25, 2019.

118   **In May 1986, Julie announced she would be severing ties with both venues:** Julie Sahni, in-person interview by author, May 23, 2019.

118   **"famous consulting chefs":** Bryan Miller, "Restaurants," *New York Times*, December 12, 1986.

118   **She resumed teaching:** Julie Sahni, phone interview by author, September 4, 2020.

118   **establishing Julie Sahni's Gourmet Tours in 1994:** Julie Sahni, email interview by author, September 4, 2020.

118   **television shows, like the Food Network's *Chef du Jour* in the late 1990s:** *News Journal*, "TV Listings," May 29, 1998.

119   **too often denigrated as an instrument of a lower class:** Julie Sahni, *Moghul Microwave: Cooking Indian Food the Modern Way* (William Morrow: New York, 1990), xiii.

119   **her only nomination from the foundation to date:** "James Beard Awards Toast Authors of Cookbooks," Associated Press, April 24, 1991.

119   **one of the three best cooking teachers in the world in 1998:** "The AWIB 1999 'Entrepreneurial Achievement Award Winner' Julie Sahni," *Asian Women in Business*. http://awib.org/index.cfm?fuseaction=page.viewPage&pageID=791&nodeID=1.

119   **bestowed its Best International Cookbook Award:** Barbara Albright, "Passage to India," *Associated Press*, September 2, 2002.

119   **in 2020, gave *Classic Indian Cooking* its Culinary Classics Award:** "The IACP 2020 Awards Winners Presented by Cuisinart," the International Association of Culinary Professionals, October 24, 2020, https://www.iacp2020.com/awards-winners.

119   **20 Essential Books to Build Your Culinary Library:** "The James Beard Book Awards Committee Names 20 Essential Books to Build Your Culinary Library," James Beard Foundation, November 12, 2007, https://jbf-media.s3.amazonaws.com/archive/jbf-2013/pressreleases/cookbooks.pdf.

120   **"the first chef to bring the sweep and balance of his native Indian cooking to fine dining in the United States":** Julia Moskin, "Floyd Cardoz, 59; Restaurateur Gave American Fine Dining an Indian Flavor," *New York Times*, March 26, 2020. https://www.nytimes.com/2020/03/25/dining/floyd-cardoz-dead-coronavirus.html.

120   **"Long, long ago I learned it was not only important to excel, but also to be content":** Pais, "A Pinch of This."

A Place for the Stateless: Najmieh Batmanglij

121 **a love letter to her sons:** Beverly Aarons, "Najmieh Batmanglij: Keeping Persian Cooking Traditions Alive in the West," *Iranian*, October 1, 2017, https://iranian.com/2017/10/01/najmieh-batmanglij -persian-cooking/.

121 **By then, she'd settled in a village called Vence with her husband, Mohammad:** Najmieh Batmanglij, in-person interview by author, October 28, 2018.

121 **breakfasts of fig jam and butter on fresh barbari bread:** Aarons, "Najmieh Batmanglij."

122 **the way Zal's teacher at school talked to him:** Najmieh Batmanglij, in-person interview by author, April 21, 2019.

122 **America, where she'd attended college back in the 1960s:** Najmieh Batmanglij, in-person interview by author, October 28, 2018.

123 **regard *Food of Life* as a landmark text:** Bonnie S. Benwick, "Persian Food Guru Updates Master Cookbook," *Washington Post*, March 1, 2011.

123 **whole stuffed lamb:** Najmieh Batmanglij, *Food of Life: A Book of Ancient Persian and Modern Iranian Cooking and Ceremonies* (Washington, DC: Mage, 1986), 70.

123 **large red snapper loaded with tamarind:** Ibid., 80.

123 **pudding startled with saffron water:** Ibid., 206.

123 **"and to all Iranian children living far from the country of their heritage":** Ibid., 3.

123 **stars in their own right:** Margaret Talbot, "Vampire Weekend Mom," *New Yorker*, May 10, 2013. https://www.newyorker.com/ culture/culture-desk/vampire-weekend-mom.

123 **"In exile, you become so much more conscious of your culture":** Jennifer Wilkinson, "Weather or Not: The Persian Spring of Mrs. Batmanglij," *Washington Post*, March 17, 1993.

123 **born in 1947:** Najmieh Batmanglij, in-person interviews by author, October 28, 2018, and April 21, 2019.

123 **Her father, Mohammad, was a religious scholar:** Najmieh Batmanglij, in-person interview by author, October 28, 2018.

124 **In the autumn of 1967:** Najmieh Batmanglij, in-person interview by author, April 21, 2019.

124 **Oklahoma to live with one of her brothers:** Najmieh Batmanglij, in-person interview by author, October 28, 2018.

124 **clueless about international travel:** Najmieh Batmanglij, in-person interview by author, April 21, 2019.

124 **the giving nature of "Okies":** Najmieh Batmanglij, in-person interview by author, October 28, 2018.

124 **a distant cousin:** Najmieh Batmanglij, in-person interview by author, April 21, 2019.

124 **She abstained from drinking and smoking:** Najmieh Batmanglij, in-person interview by author, October 28, 2018.

125 **Architectural Association School of Architecture in London:** Mohammad Batmanglij, in-person interview by author, April 21, 2019.

126 **they would not wed until 1979:** Najmieh Batmanglij, in-person interview by author, October 28, 2018.

126 **a low-key wedding:** Najmieh Batmanglij, in-person interview by author, April 21, 2019.

126 **javaher polow, or jeweled rice:** Batmanglij, *Food of Life*, 112.

126 **One of Najmieh's older sisters once lived in France:** Najmieh Batmanglij, in-person interview by author, April 21, 2019.

127 **walked alone down the Promenade de Anglais:** Najmieh Batmanglij, in-person interview by author, October 28, 2018.

127 **via telex:** Najmieh Batmanglij, in-person interview by author, April 21, 2019.

127 **Though there was a considerable population of Algerians and Moroccans:** Najmieh Batmanglij, in-person interview by author, April 21, 2019.

127 **very few Iranians lived there:** Mohammad Batmanglij, in-person interview by author, April 21, 2019.

127 **It was a neighbor's suggestion that Najmieh write a cookbook:** Najmieh Batmanglij, in-person interview by author, April 21, 2019.

128 **Mohammad wasn't working at the time:** Mohammad Batmanglij, email interview by author, June 10, 2020.

128 **"tah-tchine":** Najmieh Batman, *Ma cuisine d'Iran* (Paris: Jacques Grancher, 1984), 97.

128 **it took her a full two weeks to translate:** Najmieh Batmanglij, in-person interview by author, April 21, 2019.

128 **looked to the chef Roger Vergé's *Ma cuisine du soleil*:** Ibid.

128 **He had worked extensively in Algeria and Morocco:** William Grimes, "Roger Vergé, a Founder of Nouvelle Cuisine, Dies at 85,"

New York Times, June 8, 2015. https://www.nytimes.com/2015/06/09/
world/europe/roger-verge-a-founder-of-nouvelle-cuisine-dies-at-85
.html.

128 **one in France, the other in Switzerland:** Najmieh Batmanglij, in-
person interview by author, April 21, 2019.

130 **She was vaguely familiar with Maideh Mazda's *In a Persian
Kitchen*:** Najmieh Batmanglij, in-person interview by author, October 28, 2018.

130 **baklava with rosewater, chicken with pomegranate syrup, and
beef with fresh peaches:** Maideh Mazda, *In a Persian Kitchen: Favorite Recipes from the Near East* (North Clarendon, VT: Tuttle, 1960), 17.

130 **"quickly accessible to the American housewife":** "In a Persian
Kitchen," *Kirkus Reviews*, accessed December 11, 2019. https://www
.kirkusreviews.com/book-reviews/maideh-mazda/in-a-persian
-kitchen/.

130 **"at once a fascinating collection":** Craig Claiborne, "Pleasures of
Old Persia in Spices and Stories: New Book Flavors its Recipes with
Reminiscence," *New York Times*, August 25, 1960.

130 **referring to herself as "Persian" and to Iran as "Persia" in the
book's introduction:** Mazda, *Persian Kitchen*, 11.

130 **what she termed the "exotic" nature of Persian food:** Ibid., 17.

130 **Mazda's cooking certainly felt closer to the Iran that Najmieh
knew:** Najmieh Batmanglij, in-person interview by author, October
28, 2018.

130 **soy sauce in dishes of eggplant kuku:** Nesta Ramazani, *Persian
Cooking: A Table of Exotic Delights* (Bethesda: Ibex, 2000), 59.

130 **chicken kebabs:** Ibid., 199.

131 **"sheep's eyes and testicles":** Claudia Roden, *The New Book of Middle Eastern Food*, rev. ed. (New York: Knopf, 2000), 8.

131 **she incorporated a variety from Iran:** Claudia Roden, *The Book of
Middle Eastern Food* (New York: Knopf, 1972), 3.

131 **eshkeneh shirazi:** Ibid., 124.

131 **lamb with apples and sour cherries:** Ibid., 248.

131 **Knopf editor Judith Jones published it in the United States:**
Judith Jones, *The Tenth Muse* (New York: Anchor, 2007), 93.

131 **"a landmark in the field of cooking":** Ibid.

131 **images that stoked anti-Iranian sentiment:** Stephen Kinzer,
"Old Animosities Aside, Americans Are Touring Iran," *New York*

Times, June 8, 1997. https://www.nytimes.com/1997/06/08/world/old-animosities-aside-americans-are-touring-iran.html.

131 **"Death to America, Death to Carter"**: Neda Maghbouleh, *The Limits of Whiteness: Iranian Americans and the Everyday Politics of Race* (Stanford: Stanford University Press, 2017), 28.

131 **"Deport All Iranians! Get the hell out of my country!"**: Ibid.

131 **query letters she sent publishers between 1983 and 1984:** Najmieh Batmanglij, in-person interview by author, April 21, 2019.

132 **titling it became a point of stress:** Najmieh Batmanglij, in-person interview by author, October 28, 2018.

132 **opened up the telephone book and found the names of roughly a thousand Iranians:** Najmieh Batmanglij, in-person interview by author, April 21, 2019.

132 **how the scent of onions and garlic:** Batmanglij, *Food of Life*, 1.

133 **rhubarb stewed with meat:** Batmanglij, *Food of Life*, 146.

133 **long-grain rice studded with sour cherries:** Ibid., 104.

133 **rose petal jelly:** Ibid., 177.

133 **the crucial role of soup in Iranian tradition:** Ibid., 23.

133 **Iranian love for fluffy, thick egg kukus:** Ibid., 53.

133 **forty-eight color photographs:** Mohammad Batmanglij, email interview by author, August 19, 2020.

133 **like Hafez:** Batmanglij, *Food of Life*, 4.

133 **Omar Khayyam:** Ibid., 40.

133 **a positive review from *Publishers Weekly* in July 1986:** Penny Kaganoff, "How-To—Food & Drink: Food of Life," *Publishers Weekly*, July 18, 1986.

133 **They would write her letters:** Najmieh Batmanglij, in-person interview by author, April 21, 2019.

134 **The new edition included revised recipes and other tweaks based on suggestions from readers:** Batmanglij, *Food of Life* (Mage: Washington, DC, 1990), 3.

135 **"nostalgically but unsentimentally":** Nancy Harmon Jenkins, "Sometimes a Good Read Is as Flavorful as Good Food," *New York Times*, June 6, 1990.

135 **"Ours is an age of political turmoil":** Grace Kirschenbaum, "Cookbooks: A Fan's Notes," *Los Angeles Times*, November 8, 1990.

135 **Some film critics were rightly unkind about Brian Gilbert's *Not without My Daughter* (1991):** Maghbouleh, *The Limits of Whiteness*, 29.

135 **"manages to balance her traditional roots with modern reality":** Candy Sagon, "The Thoroughly Modern Traditionalist; Keeping Persian Values Alive," *Washington Post*, May 6, 1992.

136 **an array of new recipes and 120 photos:** Mohammad Batmanglij, email interview by author, August 19, 2020.

136 **ushered in another wave of attention for Najmieh from the press:** Florence Fabricant, "For Homebodies, A Cookbook Trail Is High Adventure," *New York Times*, June 16, 1993.

136 **"I love America":** Wilkinson, "Weather or Not."

136 **Najmieh wouldn't return to Iran until 2015:** Najmieh Batmanglij, in-person interview by author, October 28, 2018.

136 **explored the food traditions that sat along that historic trading route:** Denise Landis, "For Full-and Part-Time Vegetarians," *New York Times*, December 8, 2004. https://www.nytimes.com/2004/12/08/dining/for-full-and-parttime-vegetarians.html.

136 **The quirks of language, how to use a telephone, the currency:** Najmieh Batmanglij, in-person interview by author, October 28, 2018.

136 **where she paid a visit to her parents' graves:** Najmieh Batmanglij, *Cooking in Iran: Regional Recipes & Kitchen Secrets* (Washington, DC: Mage, 2018), 17.

137 **the soup of lamb's head, feet, and tripe she ate in Tehran:** Ibid., 44.

137 **jam made from pistachio hulls:** Ibid., 511.

137 **no lucrative deals from larger houses have lured her away from Mage:** Najmieh Batmanglij, in-person interview by author, October 28, 2018.

137 **Deravian describes fleeing Iran for Italy:** Naz Deravian, *Bottom of the Pot: Persian Recipes and Stories* (New York: Flatiron, 2018), 7.

138 **"for young Iranians and the struggle for the soul of Iran":** Batmanglij, *Cooking in Iran*, 7.

The Taste of Papaya: Norma Shirley

139 **"It's my dream to open another restaurant in Jamaica where Blacks would be the majority clientele":** Stephanie Stokes, "Norma Shirley: Bringing the Caribbean to New England," *Essence*, April 1979.

139 **chef and manager:** Kevin Knobloch, "Former Stockbridge RR Station Now a Café," *Berkshire Eagle*, June 10, 1978.

139   **"French cuisine with a Jamaican accent"**: "Dining Out," *Berkshire Eagle*, June 28, 1979.

139   **dishes like suckling pig, pumpkin soup, and rice and peas:** Stokes, "Norma Shirley."

139   **She was born in Jamaica:** *At the Table with . . . Norma Shirley.* Season 2, Episode 16. Directed by Eric Geringas. Written by Eric Geringas. Food Network Canada. November 4, 2008.

139   **living in Scotland, Sweden, England, and eventually America:** Jinx and Jefferson Morgan, "Norma at the Wharfhouse," *Bon Appétit,* March 1995.

139   **moving to the city with her son in 1981:** *At the Table.*

140   **jerk chicken pasta salad:** Mischa Manderson Mills, phone interview by author, October 30, 2019.

140   **chilled cucumber soups, and stuffed snow peas:** *At the Table.*

140   **Cornish hen with slabs of fried breadfruit:** Jessica B. Harris, *Beyond Gumbo: Creole Fusion Food from the Atlantic Rim* (New York: Simon & Schuster, 2003), 111.

140   **red pea bisque with a shock of brandy, and rum and raisin cheesecake:** Morgan, "Norma at the Wharfhouse."

140   **applying the principles of French cooking to Jamaica's fruits, vegetables, and spices:** *At the Table.*

140   **"Our soil is a very rich soil":** Cynthia Killian, "Jamaican Accent: Woman Who's Been Called the 'Julia Child of the Caribbean' Will Soon Be Cooking in the Big Apple," *New York Post*, September 8, 1999. https://nypost.com/1999/09/08/jamaican-accent-woman -whos-been-called-the-julia-child-of-the-caribbean-will-soon-be -cooking-in-the-big-apple/.

141   **nostalgic trappings:** Mischa Manderson Mills, phone interview by author, October 30, 2019.

141   **a dish that affluent Jamaicans may have once turned up their noses at:** Ibid.

141   **Call her style nouvelle Jamaican:** Barry Estabrook, "What's Doing in Jamaica," *New York Times*, October 19, 2003. https:// www.nytimes.com/2003/10/19/travel/what-s-doing-in-jamaica .html.

141   **call it Creole:** Harris, *Beyond Gumbo*, 112.

141   **Norma Elise:** *Jamaica Observer*, "Norma Elise Shirley: Kiwanis Club of New Kingston Woman of Excellence," May 3, 2007. http://www

.jamaicaobserver.com/None/Norma-Elise-Shirley:-Kiwanis-Club
-of-New-Kingston-Woman-of-Excellence.

141 **in 1938:** *At the Table.*

141 **Lucy Gibson and Verley Smith:** Rosemary Parkinson, "Homage to Norma," http://rosemary-parkinson.com/homage-to-norma/.

141 **Norma's maternal grandfather was Scottish:** Morgan, "Norma at the Wharfhouse."

141 **She was just 9:** *At the Table.*

142 **St. Hugh's boarding school in Kingston:** Parkinson, "Homage to Norma."

142 **aspirations to become an architect or an interior designer:** *At the Table.*

142 **surgical nursing:** Harris, *Beyond Gumbo*, 110.

142 **at Scotland's Southern General Hospital:** Parkinson, "Homage to Norma."

142 **pallid meats, soggy peas, and sodden cabbage:** Lloyd Gits, "Making It: Delicious Sales," *Black Enterprise*, June 1991.

142 **carrots and tomatoes and chayotes:** *At the Table.*

142 **what other choice would she have? Starve?:** Milton R. Bass, "The Lively World," *Berkshire Eagle*, November 22, 1977.

142 **University of the West Indies Medical School in Kingston:** Morgan, "Norma at the Wharfhouse."

143 **training as a gynecologist:** Michael Shirley, phone interview by author, June 17, 2020.

143 **The pair wed in 1965:** Parkinson, "Homage to Norma."

143 **Norma developed a particular affinity for French cuisine:** Natasha Were, "Norma Shirley Remembered as a Culinary Giant, Innovator," *Cayman Compass*, November 1, 2011. https://www.caymancompass.com/2011/11/01/norma-shirley-remembered-as-a-culinary-giant-innovator/.

143 **But she couldn't even boil water:** *At the Table.*

143 **Norma bought a pile of Julia Child cookbooks:** Delius Shirley, phone interview by author, October 17, 2019.

143 **Always, Michael pushed her to be a better cook:** Michael Shirley, phone interview by author, June 17, 2020.

143 **lived in Västerås, Sweden:** Delius Shirley, phone interview by author, October 17, 2019.

143 **gave birth to a son:** Parkinson, "Homage to Norma."

143 **decamped for Dulwich:** Delius Shirley, phone interview by author, October 17, 2019.

143 **settling on Manhattan's Upper West Side:** Michael Shirley, phone interview by author, June 17, 2020.

143 **head of nursing at the Eastern Women's Center, an abortion clinic:** Stokes, "Norma Shirley."

143 **She enjoyed hosting dinner parties:** Delius Shirley, phone interview by author, October 17, 2019.

143 **like a burger from McDonald's:** Were, "Norma Shirley Remembered."

143 **even a peanut butter and jelly sandwich:** Delius Shirley, phone interview by author, October 17, 2019.

144 **The pots and pans didn't talk back to her:** *At the Table*.

144 **In June 1976:** Bass, "The Lively World."

144 **Berkshire Medical Center:** Stokes, "Norma Shirley."

144 **three hours north of New York:** Morgan, "Norma at the Wharfhouse."

144 **straddled the neighboring towns of Lenox and Stockbridge:** "Realty Sale," *Berkshire Eagle*, June 19, 1976.

144 **two-hundred-year-old former barn:** Delius Shirley, phone interview by author, October 17, 2019.

144 **the rich ladies around her were content with spending their days at home:** Killian, "Jamaican Accent."

144 **She followed an exhausting routine:** Delius Shirley, phone interview by author, October 17, 2019.

144 **After a year, though, Norma left nursing for good:** Bass, "The Lively World."

144 **wondering if she should switch her drapes:** Killian, "Jamaican Accent."

145 **on a Friday evening in summer 1977:** Bass, "The Lively World."

145 **pinning them to bulletin boards:** Stokes, "Norma Shirley."

145 **She bought peach baskets from the farmers' market:** Amitabh Sharma, "A Walk Down Memory Lane," *Gleaner*, November 11, 2010. http://jamaica-gleaner.com/gleaner/20101111/cook/cook9.html.

145 **chicken breasts stuffed with prosciutto and mushrooms:** Bass, "The Lively World."

146 **by 1965, when the building turned into a discotheque:** Abby Pratt, "New Stockbridge Station Owners Offering More Informal Dining," *Berkshire Eagle*, June 5, 1982.

146 **one of Norma's neighbors:** Morgan, "Norma at the Wharfhouse."

146 **Italian actor named Terence Hill:** "Stockbridge Estate Sold to Film Actor," *Berkshire Eagle*, February 5, 1975.

146 **restaurant's chef and manager:** Knobloch, "Former Stockbridge RR Station."

146 **could fit forty people:** Stokes, "Norma Shirley."

146 **resembled a European café:** Knobloch, "Former Stockbridge RR Station."

146 **open five days a week:** "Berkshire Eagle Dining Guide," October 7, 1978.

146 **one set entrée for dinner:** Knobloch, "Former Stockbridge RR Station."

147 **"New England food with Jamaican flair":** James Beard Foundation newsletter, "Special Event: A Taste of Jamaica," September 1995.

147 **Jamaican Blue Mountain coffee:** "Berkshire Eagle Dining Guide."

147 **"where Norman Rockwell lived and painted his view of America":** Stokes, "Norma Shirley."

147 **an article in *Gentlemen's Quarterly*:** *At the Table.*

147 **"does marvelous things in the kitchen":** Anthony Spinazzola, "On the Right Track," *Boston Globe*, January 31, 1980.

147 **reggae singer she'd never heard of:** Morgan, "Norma at the Wharfhouse."

148 **In 1981, she ceded control of the restaurant back to Hill:** Ibid.

148 **Norma, then 43:** *At the Table.*

148 **helped her friend, a fellow Jamaica native named Yvonne Scherrer:** Delius Shirley, phone interview by author, October 17, 2019.

148 **Devon House Ltd. on the Upper East Side:** Judith Katz, "Security Check," *New York*, January 6, 1986, 14.

148 **filet of beef massaged with Pickapeppa Sauce:** Bryan Miller, "Restaurants," *New York Times*, May 24, 1985.

148 **Brooklyn neighborhoods of Flatbush, East Flatbush, and Crown Heights:** Kenneth T. Jackson, *Encyclopedia of New York City: Second Edition* (New Haven, CT: Yale University Press, 2010), 669.

149 **watching soap operas:** *At the Table.*

149 **light, tropical dishes that wouldn't suffer:** Mischa Manderson Mills, phone interview by author, October 30, 2019.

149 **gazpacho, baguettes soaked in garlic butter, and warm chicken breast salads:** Ibid.

149 **These were visual feasts:** *At the Table.*

149 **She wasn't much of a sleeper:** Mischa Manderson Mills, phone interview by author, October 30, 2019.

149 **assistant named Mischa Manderson Mills:** *At the Table.*

149 **around six in the morning:** Mischa Manderson Mills, phone interview by author, October 30, 2019.

149 **Hiro and Irving Penn:** Rosemary Parkinson, "Stormin' Norma," *MACO Magazine*, August 27, 2009, 142.

149 **Christie Brinkley and Raquel Welch:** *At the Table.*

149 **styling for *Gourmet*:** "Julia Child of the Caribbean," *Gleaner*, September 26, 1993.

150 **boarding school in Massachusetts:** *At the Table.*

150 **"Just a few years ago, anyone with a serious interest":** Nancy Harmon Jenkins, "New York Embraces Food of the Caribbean," *New York Times*, April 9, 1986.

150 **Norma settled in Kingston:** Were, "Norma Shirley Remembered."

150 **a pool of $10,000:** Gits, "Making It."

150 **she termed "nouvelle Jamaican":** Kitty Kingston, "Personal Mention," *Gleaner*, June 17, 1986.

150 **what a jackfruit salad was doing on the menu:** *At the Table.*

151 **employ her friends as waitstaff:** Mischa Manderson Mills, phone interview by author, October 30, 2019.

151 **service workers as subordinates:** Were, "Norma Shirley Remembered."

151 **who had, like her, studied abroad:** Morgan, "Norma at the Wharfhouse."

151 **In early 1992, she opened her second restaurant, Norma at the Wharfhouse:** Ibid.

151 **he left a finance job:** "Delius Shirley," Ortanique Restaurants, https://ortaniquerestaurants.com/delius.html.

151 **housed in a three-hundred-year-old former sugar factory:** Sara Waxman, "Jamaica Serves Up Enchanting Fare," *Financial Post*, February 6, 1993.

151 **"the Julia Child of Jamaica":** Richard Alleman, "Island in Spots," *Vogue*, November 1992, 344.

151 **her mother, who lived in New York:** Delius Shirley, email interview by author, September 7, 2020.

151 **"Isn't she dead?":** *At the Table.*

152 ***Ma Chance's French Caribbean Creole Cooking* (1985), by Saint**

Martin's Jeanne Louise Duzant Chance: Toni Tipton-Martin, *The Jemima Code: Two Centuries of African American Cookbooks* (Austin: University of Texas, 2015), 182.

152 *Island Cooking: Recipes from the Caribbean* (1988), by Jamaica native Dunstan A. Harris: Susan Puckett, "A Book for Every Cook," *Sun Sentinel*, December 7, 1988.

152 "To eat jerk is to feel the influences from which it developed": Helen Willinsky, *Jerk: Barbecue from Jamaica* (Freedom: Crossing Press, 1990), 5.

152 she hinted at one in various interviews: Gits, "Making It."

152 throughout the 1990s: Peter D. Franklin, "Island Chefs Turn Up the Heat for 'Foodies' at International Bash," *Baltimore Sun*, September 1, 1993.

152 "an extraordinary, talented woman": Sheila Lukins, *All Around the World Cookbook* (New York: Workman, 1994), 326.

152 A recipe for Norma's shrimp Jamaica: "Shrimp Jamaica: Dinner Tonight," *Washington Post*, January 3, 1996.

153 "Big Three": Deirdre Carmody, "New Flavors for Readers of Food Magazines," *New York Times*, May 23, 1994.

153 *Food & Wine*: Jennifer Quale, "Jamaica: Lavish Resorts and Quiet Retreats," *Food & Wine*, December 1994, 24.

153 *Bon Appétit*: Jinx and Jefferson Morgan, "The Eastern Insider: Dining in the Caribbean," *Bon Appétit*, November 1992.

153 *Gourmet*: Ian Keown, "Gourmet Holidays: Jamaica's North Coast," *Gourmet*, February 1996.

153 1994, the year she lent her name to Norma's on the Beach: Delius Shirley, email interview by author, September 7, 2020.

153 they rode Norma's coattails in naming the restaurant: Polly Summar, "Chef Hooked on Caribbean Food," *Albuquerque Journal*, August 18, 2004.

153 Norma's actual involvement in the operation was minimal: Jerry Shriver, "Miami: South Beach Cuisine Is Simply Scrumptious," *Gannett News Service*, February 26, 1995.

153 Fried ravioli stuffed with crabmeat, jerk pork loin with rum raisins: Jane Lasky, "Miami Beach Restaurants: Lots of Food Facts to Digest," *Journal News*, March 24, 1996.

153 In September 1995, the James Beard Foundation asked Norma to host: Whitney Walker, "Hey, Mon! Can You Make That to Stay?," *New York Daily News*, December 27, 1995.

153 **she stuck jerked chicken breasts on skewers:** James Beard Foundation newsletter, "Special Event: A Taste of Jamaica," September 1995.

153 **"In the last few years, Jamaican cuisine has overtaken the city":** Walker, "Hey, Mon!"

154 **this absence of visual flair could lead Jamaicans to underestimate their own cuisine:** Nordia Henry, "The Grand Dame of Jamaican Cuisine," *Gleaner*, June 19, 2003.

154 **fold it into an ackee soufflé:** Barbara Ramsay Orr, "Much More to Jamaican Cooking Than Jerk," *Vancouver Sun*, October 25, 2005.

154 **whip up an ackee bisque:** Walker, "Hey, Mon!"

154 **three episodes of the popular cooking show *Great Chefs of the World*:** *Great Chefs of the World*. Season 1, Episode 2. Directed by John Beyer. Discovery Channel, March 14, 1998.; *Great Chefs of the World*, Season 1, Episode 11. Directed by John Beyer. Discovery Channel, March 14, 1998.; *Great Chefs of the World*, Season 2, Episode 2. Directed by John Beyer. Discovery Channel, June 4, 1998.

154 **an episode of its spinoff series, *Great Chefs of the Caribbean*:** *Great Chefs of the Caribbean*, Episode 2. Directed by John Beyer. Discovery Channel. February 1, 2000.

155 **"Jamaica does not leap to mind when I think of great food":** John Mariani, "Best New Restaurants," *Esquire*, December 1, 1999.

155 **"Hot List":** "Hot Tables," *Condé Nast Traveler*, May 2000, 140.

155 **Six years later, Norma authored a dinner party menu:** Norma Shirley, "A Night in Jamaica," *Bon Appétit*, May 2006.

156 **"the Julia Child of Jamaica":** Peter D. Franklin, "Island Chefs Turn Up the Heat."

156 **"the Julia Child of the Caribbean":** Killian, "Jamaican Accent."

156 **"the Julia Child of Italian food":** Karol V. Menzie, "The Italian Way: Once More from the Top, Cookbook Author Marcella Hazan Offers a Personal Lesson in Pasta, Sauces and Other Essentials," *Baltimore Sun*, October 22, 1997.

156 **"the Julia Child of India":** Dirk Smilie, "Stir Crazy," *Forbes*, November 29, 2004. https://www.forbes.com/forbes/2004/1129/245.html.

156 **"Oh, God, no . . .":** Nordia Henry, "The Grand Dame of Jamaican Cuisine," *Gleaner*, June 19, 2003.

156 **"hints at the way of the future":** Harris, *Beyond Gumbo*, 112.

156 **afflicted with diabetes:** *At the Table*.

156 **died of pneumonia at age 72:** Bridget van Dongen, "An Appetite for Travel," *Caribbean Beat*, Issue 108, March/April 2011. https://www .caribbean-beat.com/issue-108/appetite-travel.

156 **a final restaurant, Grog Shoppe:** Ibid.

156 **"Her love for our country kept her here":** Laurel DeMercardo, "Letters to the Editor," *Gleaner*, November 4, 2010.

157 **"The aspect of West Indian food":** Michelle and Suzanne Rousseau, *Provisions: The Roots of Caribbean Cooking* (New York: Da Capo, 2014).

Sources

Interviews (including email, telephone, and in-person):

Batmanglij, Mohammad. April 21, 2019; June 10, 2020; August 19, 2020.

Batmanglij, Najmieh. October 28, 2018; April 21, 2019.

Hazan, Victor. December 6, 2019.

Kamman, Alan Daniel. December 12, 2019.

Kamman, Neil. December 19, 2019.

Mills, Mischa Manderson. October 30, 2019.

Sahni, Julie. April 25, 2019; May 14, 2019; May 15, 2019; May 23, 2019; June 25, 2019; May 29, 2020; September 4, 2020.

Shirley, Delius. October 17, 2019; September 7, 2020.

Shirley, Michael. June 17, 2020.

Williams, Tom. November 26, 2019.

Books, Videos, and Articles

Aarons, Beverly. "Najmieh Batmanglij: Keeping Persian Cooking Traditions Alive in the West." *Iranian*, October 1, 2017, https://iranian.com/2017/10/01/najmieh-batmanglij-persian-cooking/.

Advertisement in *Arizona Republic*, November 8, 1977.

Advertisement in *Chicago Tribune*, April 6, 1947.

Albright, Barbara. "Passage to India." *Associated Press*, September 2, 2002.

Alleman, Richard. "Island in Spots." *Vogue*, November 1992.

Allen, Nina. "Sampling Courses in Cookery." *Boston Globe*, December 30, 1975.

Anderson, Nancy. "Author Spreads 'Good Word' of Indian Cooking." *Hartford Courant*, November 5, 1980.

Andries de Groot, Roy. "In Search of the Greatest Restaurant in the United States." *Diversion*, April 1977.

Arellano, Gustavo. *Taco USA: How Mexican Food Conquered America.* New York: Scribner, 2012.

Arnett, Alison. "Too Good for Boston?" *Boston Globe*, March 23, 1980.

"Autobiography of a Chinese Woman." *Kirkus Reviews*. Accessed December 11, 2019. https://www.kirkusreviews.com/book-reviews/ yan-yuenren-chao-duwei/autobiography-of-a-chinese-woman/.

"The AWIB 1999 'Entrepreneurial Achievement Award Winner' Julie Sahni." Asian Women in Business. Accessed December 11, 2019. http://awib.org/index.cfm?fuseaction=page .viewPage&pageID=791&nodeID=1.

Baker, Jean S. "Mexican Cook Book on the Market Today." *Santa Cruz Sentinel*, May 21, 1969.

Bald, Vivek. *Bengali Harlem and the Lost Histories of South Asian America*. Cambridge, MA: Harvard University Press, 2013.

Balderamma, Francisco E., and Raymond Rodríguez. *Decade of Betrayal: Mexican Repatriation in the 1930s*, rev. ed. Albuquerque: University of New Mexico Press, 2006.

Barbas, Samantha. "'I'll Take Chop Suey': Restaurants as Agents of Culinary and Cultural Change." *Journal of Popular Culture* 36, no. 4 (2003): 669-686.

Barber, Edith M. "Foreign Food Intrigues Palates." *Battle Creek Enquirer*, January 13, 1946.

Barrett, Judith. "Gadgets for Gourmet Gift-Giving." *Boston Globe*, November 28, 1984.

Bass, Milton R. "The Lively World." *Berkshire Eagle*, November 22, 1977.

Batman, Najmieh. *Ma cuisine d'Iran*. Paris: Jacques Grancher, 1984.

Batmanglij, Najmieh. *Food of Life: A Book of Ancient Persian and Modern Iranian Cooking and Ceremonies*. Washington, DC: Mage, 1986.

———. *Food of Life: Ancient Persian and Modern Iranian Cooking and Ceremonies*. Mage: Washington, DC, 1990.

———. *Cooking in Iran: Regional Recipes & Kitchen Secrets*. Washington, DC: Mage, 2018.

Beard, James, with Jose Wilson. "Who's Teaching the Great Chefs?" *Los Angeles Times*, October 12, 1978.

Beck, Simone, Louisette Bertholle, and Julia Child. *Mastering the Art of French Cooking, Volume 1*. New York: Knopf, 1961.

Benwick, Bonnie S. "Persian Food Guru Updates Master Cookbook." *Washington Post*, March 1, 2011. https://www.washingtonpost .com/lifestyle/food/persian_food_guru_updates_master_ cookbook/2011/02/24/AB9PdNL_story.html.

———. "Cookbook Author Marcella Hazan Dies at 89." *Washington Post*,

September 30, 2013. https://www.washingtonpost.com/lifestyle/food/
cookbook-author-marcella-hazan-dies-at-89/2013/09/30/c5ae6bdc
-29cb-11e3-8ade-a1f23cda135e_story.html.

"Berkshire Eagle Dining Guide." *Berkshire Eagle*, October 7, 1978.

Beyer, John. *Great Chefs of the World*. Season 1, Episode 2. Discovery Channel, March 14, 1998.

———. *Great Chefs of the World*, Season 1, Episode 11. Discovery Channel, March 14, 1998.

———. *Great Chefs of the World*, Season 2, Episode 2. Discovery Channel, June 4, 1998.

Bittman, Mark. "Remembering Marcella." *New York Times* magazine, November 6, 2013.

"Blind Cook to Display Her Skill." *Los Angeles Times*, March 6, 1955.

"Blind Cook to Feature Enchiladas." *Los Angeles Times*, April 10, 1945.

"A Blindness." *Oakland Tribune*, December 11, 1960.

Blumenthal, Ralph. "Chinese Restaurants Flower following Diplomatic Thaw." *New York Times*, July 27, 1972.

Boni, Ada. *The Talisman Italian Cook Book*. New York: Crown, 1950.

Brainard, Dulcy. "Marcella Hazan: Educating America's Palate." *Publishers Weekly*, November 3, 1997. https://www.publishersweekly.com/pw/by
-topic/authors/interviews/article/26571-pw-marcella-hazan-educating
-america-s-palate.html.

Burros, Marian. "With the Standard of St. Joan." *Washington Post*, July 15, 1979.

———. "Distinctive Foods of the Italian Jews." *New York Times*, March 31, 1982.

———. "Restaurants." *New York Times*, June 8, 1984.

———. "Cooking." *New York Times*, December 2, 1984.

———. "Now Showing on Nation's VCR'S: Adventures in Videotape Cooking." *New York Times*, November 13, 1985.

———. "Flinty, Revered Teacher of Chefs." *New York Times*, August 4, 1993. https://www.nytimes.com/1993/08/04/garden/flinty-revered
-teacher-of-chefs.html.

Burton, Antoinette. *The Postcolonial Careers of Santha Rama Rau*. Durham, NC: Duke University Press, 2007.

Caen, Herb. "Monday Medley." *San Francisco Examiner*, May 1, 1950.

———. "Bay City Breeze." *San Francisco Examiner*, February 3, 1953.

Carmody, Deirdre. "New Flavors for Readers of Food Magazines." *New York Times*, May 23, 1994.

Cecil, George. "Globe-Trotting in Far-Off Lands." *Catholic World*, May 1927, 171-178.

Chamberlain, Samuel. "The Objective: Teaching One to Cook." *Boston Globe*, December 19, 1971.

Chang, Momo. "Q&A with Cecilia Chiang of the Mandarin Restaurant." PBS. Accessed December 11, 2019. https://www.pbs.org/food/features/qa-cecilia-chiang-mandarin-restaurant/.

Chao, Buwei Yang. *Autobiography of a Chinese Woman*. New York: John Day, 1947.

———. *How to Cook and Eat in Chinese*. 2nd ed. New York: John Day, 1949.

———. *How to Cook and Eat in Chinese*. 3rd ed. New York: Vintage, 1972.

———. *How to Order and Eat in Chinese*. New York: Vintage, 1974.

Chao, Yuen Ren. "Yuen Ren Chao: Chinese Linguist, Phonologist, Composer, and Author." Conducted by Rosemary Levenson, 1974, Regional Oral History Office, Bancroft Library, University of California, Berkeley, 1977.

Child, Julia, with Alex Prud'homme. *My Life in France*. New York: Knopf, 2006.

Chu, Grace Zia. *The Pleasures of Chinese Cooking*. New York: Cornerstone, 1967.

Citara, Bill. "Recipes and More." *San Francisco Examiner*, February 22, 1998.

"The City." *New York Times*, July 18, 1979.

Claiborne, Craig. "Snail's Place." *New York Times*, March 24, 1968.

———. "Blindness No Handicap to Author of New Book." *New York Times*, November 13, 1958.

———. "Blind Cook Is in City to Test and Taste National Fare." *New York Times*, August 15, 1960.

———. "Pleasures of Old Persia in Spices and Stories: New Book Flavors its Recipes with Reminiscence." *New York Times*, August 25, 1960.

———. "Chinese Cook Will Teach Ancient Art." *New York Times*, September 14, 1961.

———. "Indian Actress Is a Star in the Kitchen, Too." *New York Times*, July 7, 1966.

———. "The Enthusiasm of Snail Addict Helps Turn a Meal into a Feast." *New York Times*, May 23, 1968.

———. "There Was a Time She Couldn't Cook . . ." *New York Times*, October 15, 1970.

———. "Paul Bocuse, King of Chefs, Creates in an East Hampton Kitchen." *New York Times*, June 30, 1975.

Coe, Andrew. *Chop Suey: A Cultural History of Chinese Food in the United States*. New York: Oxford University Press, 2009.

Collingham, Lizzie. *Curry: A Tale of Cooks and Conquerors*. New York: Oxford University Press, 2006.

Collins, Kathleen. *Watching What We Eat: The Evolution of Television Cooking Shows*. London: Continuum, 2009.

"Controversial Chef Bids 'Au Revoir' to the U.S." *Nation's Restaurant News*, August 20, 1979.

Costikyan, Barbara. "Great Places to Have a Party." *New York*, June 4, 1984.

Cowen, Claudine and Walker. "Cookbooks." *The Virginia Quarterly Review*, Fall 1981.

———. "Cookbooks." *The Virginia Quarterly Review*. Spring 1986.

Crea, Joe. "Kamman Scores Top Honors at Beard Awards." *The Orlando Sentinel*, May 14, 1998.

Daley, Bill. "Karen Hess: Food Historian, Caustic Critic of American Food." *Chicago Tribune*, December 8, 2014. https://www.chicagotribune.com/dining/recipes/sc-food-1212-giants-hess-20141208-story.html.

Davis, Melissa. "The Best of the Books." *Washington Post*, May 24, 1979.

"Deaths." *San Francisco Examiner*, March 4, 1981.

"Delius Shirley." Ortanique Restaurants. Accessed December 11, 2019. https://ortaniquerestaurants.com/delius.html.

DeMercardo, Laurel. "Letters to the Editor." *Gleaner*, November 4, 2010.

Deravian, Naz. *Bottom of the Pot: Persian Recipes and Stories*. New York: Flatiron, 2018.

Devine, Laurie. "The Best Restaurants in Boston." *Boston Globe*, December 3, 1977.

"Dining Out." *Berkshire Eagle*, June 28, 1979.

Dosti, Rose. "Madeleine Kamman: A Controversial Cooking Teacher Who Says the Next Great Chefs Will Be American Men and Women." *Los Angeles Times*, June 7, 1990.

"Dr. Y. R. Chao, Expert On Oriental Languages." *New York Times*, March 2, 1982.

Dunlap, David W. "135 Years Ago, Another Travel Ban Was in the News." *New York Times*, March 17, 2017. https://www.nytimes.com/2017/03/17/insider/chinese-exclusion-act-travel-ban.html.

Dunne, Sara Lewis. "Julia Child." In *American Icons: An Encyclopedia of the People, Places, and Things That Have Shaped Our Culture: Volume One*, ed. Dennis R. Hall and Susan Grove Hall. Westport, CT: Greenwood, 2006.

Durso, Joseph. "Joe DiMaggio, Yankee Clipper, Dies at 84." *New York Times*, March 9, 1999. https://www.nytimes.com/1999/03/09/sports/joe-dimaggio-yankee-clipper-dies-at-84.html.

"Elena." *Kirkus Reviews*. Accessed December 11, 2019. https://www.kirkusreviews.com/book-reviews/elena-zelayeta/elena-5/.https://www.kirkusreviews.com/book-reviews/julie-sahni-2/classic-indian-cooking/.

"Elena Zelayeta, famed S.F. cook." *Associated Press*, April 1, 1974.

Elliott, J. Michael. "Pearl Wong, 86, Restaurant Owner in Mid-Manhattan." *New York Times*, January 21, 1995.

Ephron, Nora. "Critics in the World of the Rising Souffle (Or Is It the Rising Meringue?)." *New York,* September 30, 1968.

Epstein, Jason. "Chinese Characters." *New York Times Magazine*, June 13, 2004. https://www.nytimes.com/2004/06/13/magazine/food-chinese-characters.html.

Estabrook, Barry. "What's Doing in Jamaica." *New York Times*, October 19, 2003. https://www.nytimes.com/2003/10/19/travel/what-s-doing-in-jamaica.html.

Fabricant, Florence. "Proper Use of Spices Key to Indian Cooking." *New York Times*, November 10, 1974.

———. "Food Notes." *New York Times*, December 26, 1990.

———. "For Homebodies, A Cookbook Trail Is High Adventure." *New York Times*, June 16, 1993.

———. "New York Chefs Again Gain Top Awards." *New York Times*, May 10, 2000. https://www.nytimes.com/2000/05/10/dining/new-york-chefs-again-gain-top-awards.html.

———. "Nixon in China, the Dinner, Is Recreated." *New York Times*, January 25, 2011. https://www.nytimes.com/2011/01/26/dining/26nixon.html.

Fitch, Noel Riley. *Appetite for Life: The Biography of Julia Child*. New York: Anchor, 1997.

Fletcher, Janet. "A Grande Dame Steps Down." *San Francisco Chronicle*, February 16, 2000.

Fliegel, Kathleen. "Dining Out: The Greatest restaurant in, Uh, Boston." *Boston*, August 1976.

"France's Best Cooking School." *Bon Appétit*. February 1982.

Francke, Linda Bird, with Scott Sullivan. "The King of the Kitchen." *Newsweek*, August 11, 1975.

Franklin, Peter D. "Island Chefs Turn Up the Heat for 'Foodies' at International Bash." *Baltimore Sun*, September 1, 1993.

Freedman, Paul. *Ten Restaurants That Changed America*. New York: Liveright, 2016.

"Free Instruction in French Cooking." *Philadelphia Inquirer*. September 26, 1968.

"French Cooking Class Meets in Mrs. Lloyd's Kitchen." *Philadelphia Inquirer*. October 15, 1968

Gabaccia Donna R. et al. "Food, Recipes, Cookbooks, and Italian-American Life." *Italian Americana*, vol. 16, no. 1, 1998, pp. 5–23. *JSTOR*, www.jstor.org/stable/29776455. Accessed 4 June 2020.

Gage, Nicolas. "A Nightclub Owner Says He Has Woes—the Mafia." *New York Times*, October 10, 1974.

Genzlinger, Neil. "Giuliano Bugialli, Champion of Italian Cuisine, Dies at 88." *New York Times*, May 3, 2019. https://www.nytimes.com/2019/05/03/obituaries/giuliano-bugialli-dead.html.

Geringas, Eric. *At the Table with . . . Norma Shirley*." Season 2, Episode 16. Written by Eric Geringas. Food Network Canada. November 4, 2008.

Gianotti, Peter M. "Recipe for Ratings: The Chefs Are All Over the TV Dial." *Newsday*. March 29, 1989.

Gits, Lloyd. "Making It: Delicious Sales." *Black Enterprise*, June 1991.

Giuca, Linda. "She Taught." *Hartford Courant*, March 3, 1982.

Goodbody, Mary. "The Cook's Interview: Madeleine Kamman." *Cook's*, July/August 1984.

Great Chefs of the Caribbean, Season 1, Episode 2. Discovery Channel. February 1, 2000.

Greene, Bert. "A Pair of Recipes in the Classic Style of India." *Los Angeles Times*, March 5, 1987.

Greider, Linda. "A Case of Improving on the Classics." *Washington Post*, October 19, 1983.

———. "What Is a Cookbook, Anyway?" *Washington Post*, December 4, 1985.

Grimes, William. "Grace Zia Chu, 99, Guide to Chinese Cooking." *New York Times*, April 19, 1999. https://www.nytimes.com/1999/04/19/nyregion/grace-zia-chu-99-guide-to-chinese-cooking.html.

———. "Roger Vergé, a Founder of Nouvelle Cuisine, Dies at 85." *New York Times*, June 8, 2015.

———. "Carol Field, Italian Food Expert, Dies at 76." *New York Times*, March 10, 2017. https://www.nytimes.com/2017/03/10/dining/carol-field-dead-italian-cookbook-author.html.

Guenther, Jr., Keith J. "The Development of the Mexican-American Cui-

sine." *National & Regional Styles of Cookery: Proceedings: Oxford Symposium 1981*. London: Prospect, 1981.

Haddix, Carol. "The REAL Way French Women Cook." *Detroit Free Press*,
March 10, 1976.

———. "Kamman has finger in many good pies." *Chicago Tribune*, August
30, 1984.

Haffner-Ginger, Bertha. *California Mexican-Spanish Cookbook*. Bedford:
Applewood, 1914.

Hamlin, Suzanne. "Demise of Cuisine Has Competitors Scrambling." *Chicago Tribune*, January 31, 1985.

———. "Meet Madeleine, and Start Cooking." *Daily News*, January 22,
1986.

Hanes, Phyllis. "Teaching the Techniques: Showing How It's done A
French Way from Cordon Bleu Indian Puree Blueberry Bavarian
Cream." *Christian Science Monitor*, January 14, 1971.

Hansen, Barbara. "Legacy of Elena Zelayeta." *Los Angeles Times*, June 6, 1974.

———. "Renowned Teacher and Restaurateur: French Cook Is Enjoying
Success in Her 'American Phase.'" *Los Angeles Times*, February 28, 1985.

Harris, Jessica B. *Beyond Gumbo: Creole Fusion Food from the Atlantic Rim*.
New York: Simon & Schuster, 2003.

Hart, Mary. "Recipes Are a Visitor's Dish." *Star Tribune*, July 24, 1966.

Haughton, Natalie. "Celebrity Chef Martin Yan Takes You on a Chinese Tour." *Los Angeles Daily News*, February 7, 2008. https://www
.dailynews.com/2008/02/07/celebrity-chef-martin-yan-takes-you-on
-a-chinese-tour/.

Hauser, Nao. "Woman with a Vision." *Cuisine*, September 1981.

Hayford, Charles W. "Open Recipes, Openly Arrived At: *How to Cook and
Eat in Chinese* (1945) and the Translation of Chinese Food." *Journal of
Oriental Studies* 45, no. 1/2 (2012): 67–87.

Hazan, Marcella. *The Classic Italian Cook Book*. New York: Harper & Row,
1973.

———. *More Classic Italian Cooking*. New York: Knopf, 1978.

———. *Amarcord: Marcella Remembers*. New York: Gotham, 2008.

Hazan, Marcella and Victor. *Ingredienti: Marcella's Guide to the Market*. New
York: Scribner, 2016.

Hazan, Victor. *Italian Wine*. New York: Knopf, 1982.

Hazelton, Nika. "Because All Men Eat." *New York Times*, June 6, 1971.

———. "Pleasing to the Palate." *New York Times*, December 12, 1971.

———. "New and Old Angles to Cooking." *New York Times*, December 2, 1973.

Henry, Nordia. "The Grand Dame of Jamaican Cuisine." *Gleaner*, June 19, 2003.

Hess, John L. "Food Lovers, Don't Despair—There Is Life in the Wasteland." *New York Times*, November 29, 1973.

———. "The Best Way to Solve Any Macaroni Crisis: Flour, Eggs and Care." *New York Times*, December 6, 1973

Hess, John L. and Karen. *The Taste of America*. New York: Grossman, 1977.

Holt, Jane. "Old-Fashioned Cookie Jars Give Shop Rural Tone That Marks Its Wares." *New York Times*, June 16, 1941.

———. "News of Food." *New York Times*, May 10, 1945.

Hoover, Bob. "Et Cetera." *Pittsburgh Post-Gazette*, December 11, 1985.

"Hot Tables." *Condé Nast Traveler*, May 2000.

Hsu, Madeleine Y. *The Good Immigrants: How the Yellow Peril Became the Model Minority*. Princeton, NJ: Princeton University Press, 2015.

"The IACP 2020 Awards Winners Presented by Cuisinart." The International Association of Culinary Professionals. October 24, 2020. https://www.iacp2020.com/awards-winners.

"Ida Bailey Allen, Cookbook Author." *New York Times*, July 17, 1973.

"In a Persian Kitchen." *Kirkus Reviews*. Accessed December 11, 2019. https://www.kirkusreviews.com/book-reviews/maideh-mazda/in-a-persian-kitchen/.

Inness, Sherrie A. *Dinner Roles: American Women and Culinary Culture*. Iowa City: University of Iowa Press, 2001.

"It's Fun to Eat with Elena." Bay Area Television Archive. Accessed December 14, 2019. https://diva.sfsu.edu/collections/sfbatv/bundles/189406.

Jackson, Kenneth T. *The Encyclopedia of New York City*: 2nd ed. New Haven, CT: Yale University Press, 2010.

Jacobs, Jay. "Nirvana." *Gourmet*, May 1984.

Jacobs, Laura. "Our Lady of the Kitchen." *Vanity Fair*. July 6, 2009. https://www.vanityfair.com/culture/2009/08/julia-child200908.

Jaffrey, Madhur. *An Invitation to Indian Cooking*. New York: Knopf, 1973.

Jaine, Tom. "Marcella Hazan obituary." *Guardian*, October 6, 2013. https://www.theguardian.com/lifeandstyle/2013/oct/06/marcella-hazan.

"James Beard Awards Toast Authors of Cookbooks." *Associated Press*, April 24, 1991.

"The James Beard Book Awards Committee Names 20 Essential Books to Build Your Culinary Library." James Beard Foundation. November 12, 2007. https://jbf-media.s3.amazonaws.com/archive/jbf-2013/pressreleases/cookbooks.pdf.

Janik, Erika. "The Settlement Cook Book." *Edible Milwaukee*, December 1, 2014. https://ediblemilwaukee.ediblecommunities.com/recipes/settlement-cook-book.

Jen, Gish. "The Lives They Lived: Grace Zia Chu, b. 1900; West Meets East." *New York Times Magazine*, Jan 2, 2000. https://www.nytimes.com/2000/01/02/magazine/food-the-lives-they-lived-grace-zia-chu-b-1900-west-meets-east.html.

Jenkins, Nancy Harmon. "New York Embraces Food of the Caribbean." *New York Times*, April 9, 1986.

———. "Recipes Can Evoke Imaginary Journeys." *New York Times*, May 14, 1986.

———. "Sometimes a Good Read Is as Flavorful as Good Food." *New York Times*, June 6, 1990.

Jones, Evan. *Epicurean Delight: Life and Times of James Beard*. New York: Fireside, 1990.

"Julia Child of the Caribbean." *Gleaner*, September 26, 1993.

Kaganoff, Penny. "How-To-Food & Drink: Food of Life." *Publishers Weekly*, July 18, 1986.

Kaiser, Charles. "New York City Sidewalk Cafés May Ignore 9 Agencies at Once." *New York Times*, December 29, 1977.

Kamman, Madeleine. *The Making of a Cook*. New York: Atheneum, 1971.

———. *Dinner against the Clock*. New York: Atheneum, 1973.

———. *In Madeleine's Kitchen*. New York: Atheneum, 1984.

———. *Madeleine Cooks*. New York: William Morrow, 1986.

———. *Madeleine Kamman's Savoie: The Land, People, and Food of the French Alps*. New York: Atheneum, 1989.

———. *The New Making of a Cook: The Art, Techniques, and Science of Good Cooking*. New York: William Morrow, 1997.

———. *When French Women Cook: A Gastronomic Memoir with Over 250 Recipes*. 2nd ed. New York: Ten Speed, 2002.

Kamp, David. *The United States of Arugula: How We Became a Gourmet Nation*. New York: Broadway, 2006.

Kann, Bob. *A Recipe for Success: Lizzie Kander and Her Cookbook*. Milwaukee: Wisconsin Historical Society Press, 2007.

Katalinich, Peggy. "A Master Teacher In the French Mode." *Newsday*, February 19, 1986.

Katz, Judith. "Security Check." *New York*, January 6, 1986.

Kennedy, Diana. *The Essential Cuisines of Mexico*. New York: Clarkson Potter, 2000.

Kenney, Charles. "The Cast-Iron Lady." *Boston Globe*, June 30, 1985.

Keown, Ian. "Gourmet Holidays: Jamaica's North Coast." *Gourmet*, February 1996.

"The Key to Chinese Cooking." *Kirkus Reviews*. Accessed December 11, 2019. https://www.kirkusreviews.com/book-reviews/irene-kuo/the -key-to-chinese-cooking/.

Killian, Cynthia. "Jamaican Accent: Woman Who's Been Called the 'Julia Child of the Caribbean' Will Soon Be Cooking in the Big Apple." *New York Post*, September 8, 1999. https://nypost.com/1999/09/08/jamaican -accent-woman-whos-been-called-the-julia-child-of-the-caribbean -will-soon-be-cooking-in-the-big-apple/.

Kingston, Kitty. "Personal Mention." *Gleaner*, June 17, 1986.

Kinzer, Stephen. "Old Animosities Aside, Americans Are Touring Iran." *New York Times*, June 8, 1997. https://www.nytimes.com/1997/06/08/ world/old-animosities-aside-americans-are-touring-iran.html.

Kirschenbaum, Grace. "Cookbooks: A Fan's Notes." *Los Angeles Times*, November 8, 1990.

Knobloch, Kevin. "Former Stockbridge RR Station Now a Café." *Berkshire Eagle*, June 10, 1978.

Krebs, Albin. "Pearl Buck Is Dead at 80; Won Nobel Prize in 1938." *New York Times*, March 7, 1973.

Landis, Denise. "For Full-and Part-Time Vegetarians." *New York Times*, December 8, 2004.

Langer, Emily. "Florence Lin, Doyenne of Chinese Cooks in America, Dies at 97." *Washington Post*, January 5, 2018. https://www.washingtonpost .com/local/obituaries/florence-lin-doyenne-of-chinese-cooks -in-america-dies-at-97/2018/01/05/78313500-f010-11e7-b390 -a36dc3fa2842_story.html.

La Riviere, Anne. "Blind Cook Tells Happiness Recipes." *Los Angeles Times*, October 24, 1968.

Lasky, Jane. "Miami Beach Restaurants: Lots of Food Facts to Digest." *Journal News*, March 24, 1996.

Levy, Paul. "Elisabeth Lambert Ortiz." *Independent*, November 25, 2003. https://www.independent.co.uk/news/obituaries/elisabeth-lambert -ortiz-37521.html.

Lew-Williams, Beth. *The Chinese Must Go: Violence, Exclusion, and the Making of the Alien in America*. Cambridge, MA: Harvard University Press, 2018.

Lohman, Sarah. *Eight Flavors: The Untold Story of American Cuisine*. New York: Simon & Schuster, 2016.

Lukins, Sheila. *All Around the World Cookbook*. New York: Workman, 1994.

"Madeleine Kamman at Beringer Vineyards' School for American Chefs." *Wine Country International*. June/July 1990.

Maghbouleh, Neda. *The Limits of Whiteness: Iranian Americans and the Everyday Politics of Race*. Stanford: Stanford University Press, 2017.

Manners, Marian. "Give the Cook a Book." *Los Angeles Times*, December 10, 1967.

"Margaret McConnell, Editor, Food Writer." *New York Times*, July 8, 1976.

Mariani, John. "Best New Restaurants." *Esquire,* December 1, 1999.

———. *How Italian Food Conquered the World*. New York: Palgrave Macmillan, 2011.

Marquard, Brian. "Madeleine Kamman, 87, Renowned Chef and Author Who Ran Sought-After Cooking Schools." *Boston Globe*, July 23, 2018. https://www.bostonglobe.com/metro/obituaries/2018/07/23/madeleine-kamman-renowned-chef-and-author-who-ran-sought-after-cooking-schools/o3sprEL5DlFJyomRA2Ke7N/story.html.

Marter, Marilynn. "A Preparer of Chefs." *The Philadelphia Inquirer*. March 25, 1998.

Mazda, Maideh. *In a Persian Kitchen: Favorite Recipes from the Near East*. North Clarendon, VT: Tuttle, 1960.

McKerrow, Steve. "Rating the TV Gourmets." *The Sun*, October 17, 1987.

McLean, Alice L. *Asian American Food Culture*. Santa Barbara: Greenwood, 2015.

McManus, Otile. "A Full Course of Cooking Schools." *Boston Globe*, September 16, 1970.

———. "Teaching the Why of French Cookery." *Boston Globe*, February 25, 1971.

Mendelson, Anne. *Stand Facing the Stove: The Story of the Women Who Gave America the Joy of Cooking*. New York: Henry Holt, 1996.

———. *Chow Chop Suey: Food and the Chinese American Journey*. New York: Columbia University Press, 2016.

Menzie, Karol V. "The Italian Way: Once More from the Top, Cookbook Author Marcella Hazan Offers a Personal Lesson in Pasta, Sauces and Other Essentials." *The Baltimore Sun*, October 22, 1997.

Miller, Bryan. "Diner's Journal." *New York Times*, April 20, 1984.

———. "Restaurants." *New York Times*, May 24, 1985.

———. "Restaurants." *New York Times*, December 12, 1986.

———. "Craig Claiborne, 79, Times Food Editor and Critic, Is Dead." *New York Times*, January 24, 2000.

Miller, Natalie. "Mrs. Chao Tells How to Order in Chinese." *Ithaca Journal,* July 31, 1974.

"Modern Gourmet." *Where It's At: A Gustatorial Search for Fine Wines.* September 1976.

"More Classic Italian Cooking." *Kirkus Reviews.* Accessed December 11, 2019. https://www.kirkusreviews.com/book-reviews/marcella-hazan/more-classic-italian-cooking/.

Morgan, Jinx and Jefferson. "The Eastern Insider: Dining in the Caribbean." *Bon Appétit,* November 1992.

———. "Norma at the Wharfhouse." *Bon Appétit,* March 1995.

Morphy, Countess. *Recipes of All Nations.* New York: Wm. H. Wise & Company, 1935.

Morton, Paula E. *Tortillas: A Cultural History.* Albuquerque: University of New Mexico Press, 2014.

"Monthly Business and Professional Directory." *San Francisco Examiner,* September 1, 1935.

Moskin, Julia. "Floyd Cardoz, 59; Restaurateur Gave American Fine Dining an Indian Flavor." *New York Times,* March 26, 2020. https://www.nytimes.com/2020/03/25/dining/floyd-cardoz-dead-coronavirus.html.

Murphy, Patricia. "Atop New York Skyscrapers, Fine Dining Rooms with a View." *Philadelphia Inquirer,* January 17, 1982.

"National Obituaries." *United Press International.* March 3, 1981.

Nickerson, Jane. "Thanksgiving Feast with Regional Flavor." *New York Times,* November 20, 1955.

———. "'Spicy' Cookbook Sheds Light on Indian Dishes." *New York Times,* October 11, 1956.

"Norma Elise Shirley: Kiwanis Club of New Kingston Woman of Excellence." *Jamaica Observer,* May 3, 2007. http://www.jamaicaobserver.com/None/Norma-Elise-Shirley:-Kiwanis-Club-of-New-Kingston-Woman-of-Excellence.

"Obituary: Larry Zelayeta." *San Francisco Chronicle,* April 26, 2007.

O'Neill, Molly. "For Madeleine Kamman, A Gentler Simmer." *New York Times,* January 14, 1998. https://www.nytimes.com/1998/01/14/dining/for-madeleine-kamman-a-gentler-simmer.html.

———. "Food Porn." *Columbia Journalism Review,* September 1, 2003.

"One-Time Rebel against Old China Traditions Relenting." *Longview Daily News,* February 17, 1958.

"Official Guide of the Railways and Steam Navigation Lines of the United

States, Porto Rico, Canada, Mexico and Cuba." Compiled and edited under the direction of E. S. Allen and A. J. Burns. June 1921.

Orr, Barbara Ramsay. "Much More to Jamaican Cooking than Jerk." *Vancouver Sun*, October 25, 2005.

Ostmann, Barbara Gibbs. "Cooking with 'La Mere Madeleine.'" *St. Louis Post-Dispatch*, November 2, 1983.

Pais, Arthur J. "A Pinch of This, a Dash of That . . ." *India Abroad*, February 8, 2002.

Parkinson, Rosemary. "Stormin' Norma." *MACO Magazine*, August 27, 2009.

———. "Homage to Norma." Accessed December 11, 2019. http://rosemary -parkinson.com/homage-to-norma/.

Penny, Prudence. "Elena's Famous Mexican Recipes Available." *San Francisco Examiner*, August 31, 1944.

———. "Elena Does a New Book." *San Francisco Examiner*, September 4, 1947.

Perrin, Gail. "Jungle Cats Eat Well." *Boston Globe*, May 15, 1974.

———. "The Microwave Oven: Some Pros and Cons." *Boston Globe*, November 27, 1974.

Peters, Erica J. *San Francisco: A Food Biography*. Lanham, MD: Rowman & Littlefield, 2013.

"Picks and Pans Review: The Video Cooking Series: Madeleine Kamman Cooks." *People*, March 25, 1985. https://people.com/archive/picks-and -pans-review-the-video-cooking-series-madeleine-kamman-cooks -vol-23-no-12/.

Polan, Dana B. *Julia Child's the French Chef*. Durham, NC: Duke University Press, 2011.

———. "It's Fun to Eat: Forgotten Television." In *How to Watch Television*, ed. Ethan Thompson and Jason Mittell. New York: New York University Press, 2013.

———. "Joyce Chen Cooks and the Upscaling of Chinese Food in America in the 1960s." WGBH. Accessed December 11, 2019. http://openvault .wgbh.org/exhibits/art_of_asian_cooking/article

Pollan, Michael. "Out of the Kitchen, onto the Couch." *New York Times Magazine*. July 29, 2009. https://www.nytimes.com/2009/08/02/ magazine/02cooking-t.html.

"Popular Dancers Enroll in 'Times' Cooking School." *Los Angeles Times*, October 29, 1944.

Pratt, Abby. "New Stockbridge Station owners offering more informal dining." *Berkshire Eagle,* June 5, 1982.

"Program Hi-Lites." *San Francisco Examiner,* October 13, 1952.

Prud'homme, Alex. *The French Chef in America: Julia Child's Second Act.* New York: Knopf, 2016.

Puckett, Susan. "A Book for Every Cook." *Sun Sentinel,* December 7, 1988.

Quale, Jennifer. "Jamaica—Lavish Resorts and Quiet Retreats." *Food & Wine,* December 1994 Ramazani, Nesta. *Persian Cooking: A Table of Exotic Delights, Revised and Updated.* Bethesda: Ibex, 2000.

Rau, Santha Rama. *The Cooking of India.* New York: Time Inc., 1969.

"Realty Sale." *Berkshire Eagle,* June 19, 1976.

"Recipe for Chicken Breasts." *Philadelphia Inquirer,* February 27, 1969.

Rice, William. "As the Year 4671 Arrives, a New Wave of Snobbery Tempts Eager Diners." *Washington Post,* February 1, 1973.

———. "An Enduring Entente." *Washington Post,* October 3, 1974.

"Richard Walsh, Publisher, Dead." *New York Times,* May 29, 1960.

Robards, Terry. "Two Books on the Best Bottlings of Italy." *New York Times,* January 12, 1983.

Roden, Claudia. *The Book of Middle Eastern Food.* New York: Knopf, 1972.

———. *The New Book of Middle Eastern Food,* rev. ed. New York: Knopf, 2000.

Ross, Nancy L. "Mastering Julia's French Recipes." *Washington Post,* November 5, 1970.

Rousseau, Michelle and Suzanne. *Provisions: The Roots of Caribbean Cooking.* New York: Da Capo, 2014.

Rubin, Marilyn McDevitt. "French Chef with Class." *Pittsburgh Press,* September 6, 1981.

Sagon, Candy. "The Thoroughly Modern Traditionalist; Keeping Persian Values Alive." *Washington Post,* May 6, 1992.

———. "Ciao Marcella, One Last Book from the Woman Who Taught Us to Cook Italian." *Washington Post,* October 15, 1997. https://www.washingtonpost.com/archive/lifestyle/food/1997/10/15/ciao-marcella-one-last-book-from-the-woman-who-taught-us-to-cook-italian/fc9ad16e-2be9-456f-9ae4-656bd26f4b94/.

Sahni, Julie. *Classic Indian Cooking.* New York: William Morrow, 1980.

———. "Welcome Fall with a Burmese Buffet." *Cuisine,* October 1982.

———. *Classic Indian Vegetarian and Grain Cooking.* New York: William Morrow, 1985.

———. "Enticing, Fragrant and Subtly Spiced." *Food & Wine*, November 1986.

———. "Chutneys Sweet and Savory." *Bon Appétit*, November 1988.

———. *Moghul Microwave: Cooking Indian Food the Modern Way*. William Morrow: New York, 1990.

Sandomir, Richard. "Madeleine Kamman, Chef Who Gave Americans a Taste of France, Dies at 87." *New York Times*, July 22, 2018. https://www.nytimes.com/2018/07/20/obituaries/madeleine-kamman-87-celebrated-french-chef-is-dead.html.

Schlack, Layla. "*The Settlement Cookbook*: 116 Years and 40 Editions Later." Taste, June 21, 2017. https://www.tastecooking.com/the-settlement-cookbook-116-years-and-40-editions-later/.

Schrambling, Regina. "Julia Child, the French Chef for a Jell-O Nation, Dies at 91." *New York Times*, August 13, 2004. https://www.nytimes.com/2004/08/13/dining/julia-child-the-french-chef-for-a-jello-nation-dies-at-91.html.

Sen, Colleen Taylor. *Curry: A Global History*. London: Reakton, 2009.

Severson, Kim. "For Better, for Worse, for Richer, for Pasta." *New York Times*, September 9, 2008. https://www.nytimes.com/2008/09/10/dining/10hazan.html.

———. "Marcella Hazan, Author Who Changed the Way Americans Cook Italian Food, Dies at 89." *New York Times*, September 29, 2013. https://www.nytimes.com/2013/09/30/dining/Marcella-Hazan-dies-changed-the-way-americans-cook-italian-food.html.

Shapiro, Laura. *Something from the Oven: Reinventing Dinner in 1950s America*. New York: Viking, 2004.

Sharma, Amitabh. "A Walk Down Memory Lane." *Gleaner*, November 11, 2010. http://jamaica-gleaner.com/gleaner/20101111/cook/cook9.html.

Sheraton, Mimi. "Cookbooks." *New York Times*, December 3, 1978.

———. "Cookbooks." *New York Times*, November 30, 1980.

———. "Choosing a Basic Cookbook Library." *New York Times*, August 15, 1981.

Sheridan, Margaret. "An Expert Solves All the Mysteries of Indian Cooking." *Chicago Tribune*, May 6, 1982.

Shirley, Norma. "A Night in Jamaica." *Bon Appétit*, May 2006.

"Shrimp Jamaica: Dinner Tonight," *Washington Post*, January 3, 1996.

Shriver, Jerry. "Miami: South Beach Cuisine Is Simply Scrumptious." *Gannett News Service*, February 26, 1995.

Silverman, Jan. "Viva, Elena!" *Oakland Tribune*, December 13, 1967.

Smilie, Dirk. "Stir Crazy." *Forbes*, November 29, 2004. https://www.forbes
.com/forbes/2004/1129/245.html.

Smith, Andrew F. *The Oxford Companion to American Food and Drink*. New
York: Oxford University Press, 2007.

———. *Food and Drink in American History: A "Full Course" Encyclopedia*.
Santa Barbara: ABC-CLIO, 2013.

Sokolov, Raymond A. "Cultures of the World Depicted in Ounces, Cups
and Spoonfuls." *New York Times*, October 5, 1972.

———. "Current Stars: Books on Indian, Italian and Inexpensive Food."
New York Times, April 19, 1973.

"Special Event: A Taste of Jamaica." James Beard Foundation. September
1995.

Spinazzola, Anthony. "Let's Eat Out." *Boston Globe*, July 3, 1975.

———. "On the Right Track." *Boston Globe*, January 31, 1980.

Spitz, Bob. *Dearie: The Remarkable Life of Julia Child*. New York: Knopf,
2012.

Steiman, Harvey. "Madeleine Kamman: Champion of 'Women's Cuisine.'"
San Francisco Examiner, May 13, 1981.

Steintrager, Megan O. "A Conversation with Marcella Hazan." Epicurious, September 23, 2008. https://www.epicurious.com/archive/
chefsexperts/interviews/marcellahazaninterview.

"Stockbridge Estate Sold to Film Actor." *Berkshire Eagle*. February 5, 1975.

Stokes, Stephanie. "Norma Shirley: Bringing the Caribbean to New
England." *Essence*, April 1979.

Strauss, Pat. "America Goes Mexican." *Morning Call*, November 14, 1982.

Strehl, Dan. *Encarnacion's Kitchen: Mexican Recipes from Nineteenth-
Century California, Selections from Encarnación Pinedo's El cocinero
español*. Berkeley: University of California Press, 2003.

Summar, Polly. "Chef Hooked on Caribbean Food." *Albuquerque Journal*,
August 18, 2004.

Talbot, Margaret. "Vampire Weekend Mom." *New Yorker*, May 10, 2013.
https://www.newyorker.com/culture/culture-desk/vampire-weekend
-mom.

Taylor, Howard. "Gay Chinese Cookbook." *The Philadelphia Inquirer*, May
13, 1945.

"Television Schedule." *Los Angeles Times*, April 28, 1950.

Tennison, Patricia. "Madeleine Kamman's Encore for 1984." *Chicago Tribune*, October 4, 1984.

"Tidbits: Cooking School Cut." *Star Tribune*, April 17, 1983.

Times of India, November 19, 1963.

Tipton-Martin, Toni. *The Jemima Code: Two Centuries of African American Cookbooks*. Austin: University of Texas, 2015.

Turgeon, Charlotte. "Something Fit to Eat." *New York Times*, November 16, 1958.

———. "Favorite Dishes of Gertrude Stein and Others." *New York Times*, December 7, 1958.

"TV Listings." *News Journal*, May 29, 1998.

van Dongen, Bridget. "An Appetite for Travel." *Caribbean Beat*, Issue 108, March/April 2011. https://www.caribbean-beat.com/issue-108/appetite -travel.

Van Geider, Lawrence. "Poppy Cannon White, 69, Dead; Writer Was Authority on Food." *New York Times*, April 2, 1975.

Varkonyi, Charlene. "Cookbooks Moving from Kitchen to Coffee Table." *Sun Sentinel*, December 11, 1985.

Venugopal, Nikhita. "Why Haven't You Heard of India's Julia Child?" *Taste*, July 19, 2018. https://www.tastecooking.com/why-havent-you-heard -of-indias-julia-child/.

Video flyer, *Madeleine Kamman Cooks*.

"Virginia Lee, Noted Teacher and Chinese Cooking Expert." *New York Times*, October 19, 1981.

Vitello, Paul. "Robert Lescher, Editor and Literary Agent, Dies at 83." *New York Times*, December 8, 2012.

Voltz, Jeanne. "Cookbooks I'd Like to Give." *Los Angeles Times*, November 21, 1971.

Wagner, Alex. "America's Forgotten History of Illegal Deportations." *Atlantic*, March 6, 2017. https://www.theatlantic.com/politics/ archive/2017/03/americas-brutal-forgotten-history-of-illegal -deportations/517971/.

Walker, Whitney. "Hey, Mon! Can You Make That to Stay?" *New York Daily News*, December 27, 1995.

Wasser, Fred. "The Matzo Ball Matriarch of American Jewish Food." National Public Radio, April, 12, 2009. https://www.npr.org/templates/ story/story.php?storyId=102913413.

Waxman, Sara. "Jamaica Serves Up Enchanting Fare." *Financial Post*, February 6, 1993 "WCVB's Station Timeline." WCVB 5. May 12, 2005. https://www.wcvb.com/article/wcvb-s-station-timeline/8135747.

Wedeck, Harry E. "Buwei Yang Chao's Many-Sided Autobiography." *New York Times*, April 27, 1947.

Weiss, Steve. "Madeleine Kamman 'Is' the Modern Gourmet." *Institutions*, August 15, 1977.

Wells, Patricia. "Cooking Schools: Other Boroughs." *New York Times*, December 6, 1978.

———. "The Indian Brunch: Fragrant Feast." *New York Times*, February 14, 1979.

———. "Chef-Teacher Starts a New Life." *New York Times*, January 7, 1981.

Were, Natasha. "Norma Shirley Remembered as a Culinary Giant, Innovator." *Cayman Compass*, November 1, 2011. https://www.caymancompass.com/2011/11/01/norma-shirley-remembered-as-a-culinary-giant-innovator/.

Wertheimer, Linda. "Marcella Hazan Brings Italy to America." National Public Radio, December 28, 2010.

Wharton, Rachel. "Wok of Ages." *New York Daily News*, January 22, 2006, 32.

Wilkinson, Jennifer. "Weather or Not: The Persian Spring of Mrs. Batmanglij." *Washington Post*, March 17, 1993.

Willinsky, Helen. *Jerk: Barbecue from Jamaica*. Freedom: Crossing Press, 1990.

Willis, Laurie D. "Rulan Pian, 91: Chinese Music Scholar, Harvard Professor." *Boston Globe*, January 1, 2014. https://www.bostonglobe.com/metro/obituaries/2014/01/01/rulan-pian-scholar-chinese-music-and-chinese-language-teacher-harvard/tMj1O7nqzBiahlctPuQubI/story.html.

Wissow, Larry. "Over the Coals." *Bennington Banner*, August 10, 1974.

Witchel, Alex. "On the Spice Route from India, Properly Loaded." *New York Times*, April 28, 2010.

Wolcott, Jennifer. "Ambassador of Indian Food Serves Up a Side Dish of Culture." *Christian Science Monitor*, June 1, 2005. https://www.csmonitor.com/2005/0601/p14s02-lifo.html.

Zelayeta, Elena. *Elena's Famous Mexican And Spanish Recipes*. San Francisco: Dettners, 1944.

———. As told to Lou Richardson. *Elena's Lessons in Living*. San Francisco: Dettners, 1947.

———. *Elena's Fiesta Recipes*. Pasadena: Ward Ritchie, 1952.

———. *Elena*. Englewood Cliffs, NJ: Prentice-Hall, 1960.

———. *Elena's Favorite Foods California Style*. Englewood Cliffs, NJ: Prentice-Hall, 1967.

———. *Elena's Secrets of Mexican Cooking*. Garden City, NY: Dolphin, 1973.

Suggestions for
Further Reading

BELOW IS A LIST of the memoirs and cookbooks authored by the women profiled in this book. Though some are out of print, I encourage you to seek out these books and, where applicable, cook from them. You will notice that Norma Shirley is absent from this list, given the fact that she wrote no cookbooks of her own.

Chao Yang Buwei

How to Cook and Eat in Chinese (1945)
Autobiography of a Chinese Woman (1947)
How to Order and Eat in Chinese to Get the Best Meal in a Chinese Restaurant (1974)

Elena Zelayeta

Elena's Famous Mexican and Spanish Recipes (1944)
Elena's Lessons in Living (1947)
Elena's Fiesta Recipes (1952)
Elena's Secrets of Mexican Cooking (1958)
Elena (1960)
Elena's Favorite Foods California Style (1967)

Madeleine Kamman

The Making of a Cook (1971)
Dinner against the Clock (1973)
When French Women Cook (1976)
In Madeleine's Kitchen (1984)

Madeleine Cooks (1986)

Madeleine Kamman's Savoie: The Land, People, and Food of the French Alps (1989)

The New Making of a Cook (1997)

Marcella Hazan

The Classic Italian Cook Book: The Art of Italian Cooking and the Italian Art of Eating (1973)

More Classic Italian Cooking (1978)

Marcella's Italian Kitchen (1986)

Essentials of Classic Italian Cooking (1992)

Marcella Cucina (1997)

Marcella Says: Italian Cooking Wisdom from the Legendary Teacher's Master Classes, with 120 of Her Irresistible New Recipes (2004)

Amarcord: Marcella Remembers (2008)

Ingredienti: Marcella's Guide to the Market (2016)

Julie Sahni

Classic Indian Cooking (1980)

Classic Indian Vegetarian and Grain Cooking (1985)

Moghul Microwave: Cooking Indian Food the Modern Way (1990)

Savoring Spices and Herbs: Recipe Secrets of Flavor, Aroma, and Color (1996)

Julie Sahni's Introduction to Indian Cooking (1998)

Savoring India: Recipes and Reflections on Indian Cooking (2001)

Indian Regional Classics: Fast, Fresh, and Healthy Home Cooking (2001)

Najmieh Batmanglij

Food of Life: Ancient Persian and Modern Iranian Cooking and Ceremonies (1986)

New Food of Life: Ancient Persian and Modern Iranian Cooking and Ceremonies (1993)

Persian Cooking for a Healthy Kitchen (1994)

A Taste of Persia: An Introduction to Persian Cooking (1999)

Silk Road Cooking: A Vegetarian Journey (2002)

From Persia to Napa: Wine at the Persian Table (2006)

Happy Nowruz: Cooking with Children to Celebrate the Persian New Year (2008)

Joon: Persian Cooking Made Simple (2015)

Cooking in Iran: Regional Recipes and Kitchen Secrets (2018)

Index